JAMES A. MICHENER'S

USA

"The young man waits on the side of the road . . .
The thumb moves in a small arc when a car tears hissing
past. Eyes seek the driver's eyes. A hundred miles
down the road. Head swims, belly tightens, wants
crawl over his skin like ants . . .

". . . waits with swimming head, needs knot the belly;
idle hands numb, beside the speeding traffic.

"A hundred miles down the road."

JOHN DOS PASSOS
U.S.A.

JAMES A. MICHENER'S

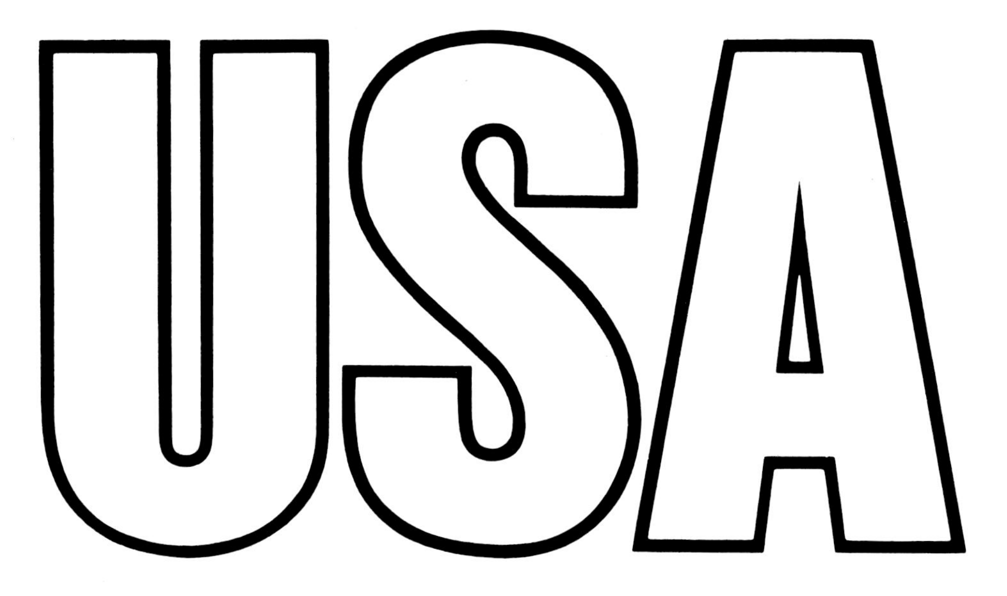

Foreword by

JAMES A. MICHENER

Edited by

PETER CHAITIN

Crown Publishers, Inc. New York

Publisher's Note

The U.S.A. is covered regionally in this book, but there are themes and topics that transcend region and link one part of the country to another. In a particular geographical region, there may be references to persons and matters from other regions. The index is intended to guide the reader both thematically and geographically. Essentially, the text of this book is from the script of the television series "James Michener's USA." In addition, there are some contributions by the editor. Such contributions are indicated by a ❑ at the beginning and the end of these portions of text.

Inquiries should be addressed to Crown Publishers, Inc.,
One Park Avenue, New York, New York 10016
Printed in the United States of America
Published simultaneously in Canada
by General Publishing Company Limited
ISBN 0-517-545276
Book design by Camilla Filancia
10 9 8 7 6 5 4 3 2 1
First Edition

The book is based on the television series entitled "James Michener's USA," © 1981 by Emlen House Productions, Inc. The series was directed and produced by Albert Waller; written by John Mernit, Patty Conroy, Stuart Hersh, and Albert Waller; chief photographer, Gregory Andracke.

All photographs unless otherwise noted were obtained from the television series "James Michener's USA."

Contents

Acknowledgments

James A. Michener's U.S.A. is the result of a close and unique collaboration between the world of book publishing and the world of film. Crown Publishers, Inc., and Emlen House Productions, Inc., acknowledge the efforts and contributions of the following individuals and organizations that have helped to make this publication possible: James A. Michener; Peter Chaitin; Edward J. Piszek; Albert Waller, executive producer and director; Gregory Andracke, Rick Robertson, Alicia Weber, and Joan Churchill, camermen and camerawomen; John Mernit, producer; Leslie Aisner Novak, Valerie Gordon, Stuart Hersh, and Marc Brugnoni, field producers; Karen Irwin Dorsett, associate producer; Patty Conroy, chief researcher; Larry Klein and Patricia Millman, film picture researchers; Victor Kanefsky, supervising film editor; Larry Mischel, negative cutter; Amy Ostrower, production assistant; TVC Laboratories, Inc.; Trans/Audio, Inc.; Ed Klein of Eastman Productions; Amy Hempel, book picture researcher; Camilla Filancia, book designer; the production staff of Crown Publishers, especially Rusty Porter and Ed Otto; Laurie Stark, production editor; and Daphne Abeel, picture editor and supervising editor of the book.

The film scripts were authenticated by the *Reader's Digest*.

Foreword

The Statue of Liberty, a lovely gift from France, has symbolized the fact that, except for the first Americans, the Indians, the rest of us began by belonging somewhere else. America is the melting pot, the land of immigrants. We *are* the huddled masses.

If America has been shaped by any one essential force, it has been that of movement. Speed and transiency and the call of the open road seem always to have been part of America's destiny. From beyond the city limits the land called to us, drawing us ever farther toward new frontiers. As America enters the 1980s, we have many more hundreds of miles to travel down the road Dos Passos described.

I have been asked why I traveled so much as a young boy. At fourteen I would leave home with maybe fifteen, twenty-five, or thirty-five cents in my pocket and hitch to Florida or some other distant place. It never occurred to me I wouldn't make it. Those were easy days for a hitchhiker. I think that before I was fifteen I had been from Canada to Key West. Why did I do it? Life at home was not very pleasant. We were a very poor family. Things on the road were just about as good as at home. I think I traveled because I had an innate love of seeing what was around the bend. I've never lost that sense of curiosity.

The Statue of Liberty.

For me the most natural place to look at the country called the United States of America is my home town, Doylestown, Pennsylvania. I was born here in 1907, and to this day I call it my home. Its streets, its institutions, its joys, its sorrows are familiar to me. But perhaps because I have never known who my parents were, I am also a child not so much of this particular place but of a larger place, a place of language and national identity: the whole United States. The psychology of this country is infused into who I am. Though I have lived and written in many countries of this world, when someone who does not know me asks what I do, my answer is constant—I am an American writer.

I have thought a good deal about our society, but I am not a philosopher. I have written a good deal of history, but I am not a historian. In the past, I've even taught sociology, but I am not a sociologist. And although I love politics, and even ran for Congress from the Doylestown area, I cannot be considered a political theorist.

I have had, however, one set of experiences that partly qualify me for the task of taking a fresh look at our nation: As much as I have worked and written at home, I have also worked extensively abroad. I have had an opportunity to see the United States from a distance; to see it whole; to see it through the eyes of others.

America is a nation with many flaws that only the stupid would deny, but with hopes so vast that only the cowardly would refuse to acknowledge them. We are not much different, therefore, from the great nations of the past: We have enormous opportunities to accomplish good, yet we contain within ourselves the seeds of our own destruction.

I have observed this nation from near and far for three quarters of a century, and I am impressed by one overriding fact: that though we are a relatively young nation we now have the oldest continuing form of government on earth. In the last two centuries every other nation has had to revise its governmental structure—often radically. China, oldest among the nations, has experienced change of the most violent sort. Russia, one of the most powerful states, has undergone total upheaval. Spain, France, Turkey—all of them have tried one form of government after another, in search of the stability that we, miraculously, have attained. Even stolid Britain has changed its strong kingly privileges to weak, and its powerful House of Lords to one that serves only as a cautionary council.

When I look at my country, I take pride in its stable system. I think of the United States as experienced and tested. From this vantage point it is significant and exciting to take stock of the U.S.A.—where we are, and where we are likely to go.

July 1981

James A. Michener

Close-up of the Statue of Liberty in New York City Harbor. Created by the Alsatian sculptor Fréderic Auguste Bartholdi and unveiled in 1886. A gift from France, it has been an inspiring landmark for generations of immigrants. (Colour Library International, Ltd.)

THE NORTHEAST

AMERICA'S PAST AND PRESENT

Ellis Island is a tiny dot off the southern tip of Manhattan. For decades, from the late nineteenth century into the early 1940s, it was a place of tension, excitement, and crowds. Here one heard the babble of a hundred tongues: French, German, Italian, Serbo-Croatian, Yiddish, Polish, Russian, Norwegian—the "refuse" of Europe's teeming shores—clamoring at the gates of a New World, for a chance to succeed and live free. This was the neck of the immigrant hourglass. Through Ellis Island's Victorian buildings came the floodtide of our mothers and fathers. At the turn of the century, some twelve thousand people a day were shepherded into America—the Irish to Boston, Poles to Chicago and Philadelphia, German and Eastern European Jews to New York, Swedes to the Midwest, Italians to the Northeast. On and on they came, a tremendous influx of talent and energy for an America bursting with the Industrial Revolution.

A sense of America's past, and even its present, can be felt in Ellis Island's now empty and silent Great Hall, for the spirit that animated the millions who passed through this building on their way to new lives still animates millions, from all over the world, who dream of someday living in America. I have never worked in any foreign nation without

Ellis Island, in Upper New York Bay, was once an arsenal and fort. It is best known, however, for its role as the nation's primary immigration center from 1892 to 1943. (The Bettmann Archive)

James Michener standing in front of the main building at Ellis Island.

being approached by some of its citizens who want to come to the United States. "In your country," they say, "a man has a chance to get ahead. Children get a free education. With the same amount of work I could live better." And always, voiced in a dozen different ways, there is the hope: "In America I could be free." Among intellectuals there is another reason that has become increasingly important: "In America you're trying to do new things. A man with ideas has laboratories to work in and colleagues who will listen."

The farther the immigrant of old got from Ellis Island, the more assimilated, the more American he became. Freedom was no longer a dream but a reality. And yet there were always millions more clamoring at the gates for whom the dream burned as brightly and enticingly as ever. My experience tells me that this dream, though perhaps a bit faded, is still there.

THE GREAT AGE OF IMMIGRATION

❑ During the first half of the nineteenth century, a great wave of immigration—the first of many—brought thousands of the poor and hungry to America's shores. Fleeing from famine, war, political and religious persecution, millions landed in New York, Baltimore, Charleston, and Boston. Overwhelmingly, this first cohort had emigrated from northern and western Europe. Between 1820 and 1860, some 1.5 million came from Germany alone; another 1.6 million fled Ireland's persistent famine to find New World homes.

The Irish immigration was on a scale unprecedented in the short history of the independent United States. The Irish themselves—landless peasants for the most part—came with little more than the clothes on their backs and an iron determination to carve a place for themselves in America. That place, for almost all of them, was to be in the cities.

One of these early Irish immigrants was Patrick Kennedy. In 1848, this twenty-five-year-old from County Wexford arrived in Boston and took work as a maker of whiskey barrels. Distilling was a thriving trade in Boston, for whiskey was the solace of the poor, and most of the poor were Irish. Fleeced and robbed as soon as they set foot on land, sweated by employers, they were jammed into jerry-built slums slapped up on mud flats. To Boston's staid Puritan citizens, the Roman Catholic Irish seemed a horde of barbarians for whom little could be done, and from whom even less could be expected. The illnesses—typhus, tuberculosis, and cholera—that flourished in the Irish shantytowns were merely unfortunate facts of life, a happenstance to be ignored by polite society. That 60 percent of all children in the city's Irish slums died before their fifth birthdays was hardly the concern of Boston's elite; that Patrick Kennedy died of cholera in 1859, soon after his son Patrick Joseph was born, was undoubtedly of notice only to the barrel-maker's widow.

In his early teens, Patrick Joseph worked as a stevedore and, saving what he could from his wages, eventually bought a saloon in Irish East Boston. Slowly but determinedly, he became a man of substance. Though the financial and social elite of Boston remained a closed society, Irishmen like Kennedy found their way to power through control of local politics. Patrick Joseph was elected to the state legislature. His son Joseph became a banker, a financier, an adviser to President Franklin Roosevelt, the ambassador to Great Britain, and the father of America's thirty-fifth president, John F. Kennedy.

The Kennedys of Boston are, of course, an extraordinary family. But for the descendants of the Irish, and for those of the successive waves of immigrants that followed, the New World experience has resembled—even if it has not been as splendid—that of the Kennedys: arrival at an East Coast port; years of deprivation and hard work; slow but steady acculturation; accumulation of power and modest wealth through politics and business enterprises; education of children and grandchildren; and finally—for many millions—ascent into the solid middle class.

Beginning in the 1880s and lasting until 1914, a new tide of immigration dwarfed even the pre–Civil War experience. Not only were the numbers astounding, but the nature of the immigration had drastically altered. Northern and western Europe was no longer the primary source. Now immigrants poured in from southern and eastern Europe—Italy, Serbia, Greece, Poland, Austria-Hungary, and Russia. Few of the arrivals spoke any English; few had marketable skills.

Notable among the immigrants were the Eastern European Jews. Largely from peasant and petty-merchant stock, these oppressed people had been driven from their native lands by officially inspired pogroms. Faithful to a tradition that placed religious law above all other considerations, this group seemed the least likely candidates for success in America. Yet they possessed qualities that would enable most to leave their big-city ghettos within a generation. Like the Poles and the Italians, they were a family-oriented people—each family member watched out for and felt responsible for the others. And, like the Puritans of Colonial days, the Jews prized intellectual attainment. Once caught up in the American ethos it was not difficult for them to move from the study of religious texts to engineering, physics, medicine, history, and law and to the practice of the arts.

Much of the Jewish experience in America has been duplicated by the Poles, the Slovaks, the Italians, and other ethic groups that came to our shores less then a century ago. Yet, if these people have prospered and become Americanized, they have not been completely homogenized. One need only stroll through any large American city to be struck by the ethnic diversity of our society. Little Italys, Little Polands, Little Austrias, and Chinatowns still abound. And there are newer Little

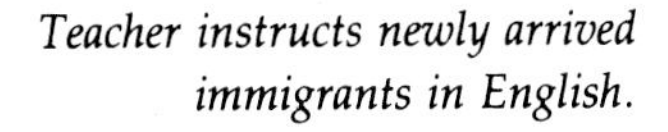
Teacher instructs newly arrived immigrants in English.

Cubas, Little Haitis, Little Vietnams, Little Thailands, and Little Puerto Ricos. It is among America's proudest achievements that we continue to attain unity through diversity. The motto *E Pluribus Unum* is as true today as it was on the eve of the American Revolution two hundred years ago. ❑

Russian-Jewish immigrants greet their families at JFK Airport.

Jet-Age Ellis Island

❑ A day at New York's John F. Kennedy Airport is evidence that the dream still lives. Here is our jet-age Ellis Island, and here hundreds of new immigrants arrive every day to set foot on American soil for the first time. Here families and friends are reunited, new futures begun. Today well over 1.5 million Europeans, Asians, Africans, and Latin Americans every year seek out the United States for work and opportunity. Though we have become a stable society, though the old farming and ranching frontier has long since closed, we remain a nation of immigrants. ❑

Michener Talks with Claudia Lapidus

For today's Russian-Jewish immigrants, the way to America begins with an application to Soviet authorities for an exit visa. Should they be lucky enough to secure this vital document, their road then winds through Vienna or Rome, where some leave for Israel and others wait for permission to enter the United States. While still in Europe, they may receive financial aid from the Hebrew Immigrant Aid Society (HIAS), the worldwide Jewish immigration agency that has helped to bring refugees to America for nearly a century. (In the past few years, HIAS has assisted many thousands of refugees from the Soviet Union and, in addition, thousands of non-Jewish refugees from other troubled nations.) Finally, United States visa in hand, they embark on the flight that will take them to JFK Airport, and America.

Many of the refugees who settle in New York receive help from another agency, the New York Association for New Americans (NYANA). The new immigrants shown here have just arrived in the United States. Through NYANA, they study English, receive financial assistance and medical care, and learn to discover what they can usefully do in their new country.

One of NYANA's students a few years back was a girl in her early teens named Claudia Lapidus. Today Claudia is a student at Yale University, the winner of a $7,500 scholarship for academic achievement. I spoke with Claudia in New Haven, Connecticut, on the Yale University campus.

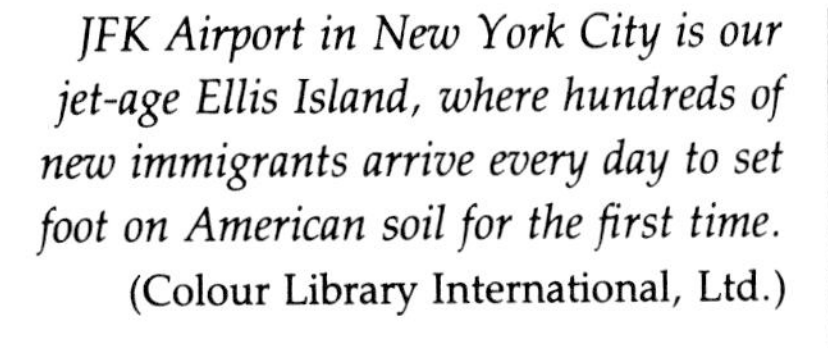

JFK Airport in New York City is our jet-age Ellis Island, where hundreds of new immigrants arrive every day to set foot on American soil for the first time.
(Colour Library International, Ltd.)

James Michener talks with Claudia Lapidus at Yale University.

MICHENER: We in America think of immigrants as little old ladies in babushkas, but you're an attractive young woman. Tell me, did you know any English when you came over?

LAPIDUS: I could say "hello." And on the plane I learned how to say "water."

MICHENER: Yet today you took an advanced calculus examination at Yale University. How did you make the transition from no knowledge of English to advanced college courses at Yale?

LAPIDUS: I guess I didn't want to be looked at as just a poor immigrant who doesn't know the language. I wanted to be on the same level as the people of my age. The first few months in high school were very difficult—I practically lived with a dictionary in my hand. But slowly my classmates started to help me. Without them I would never have succeeded here.

MICHENER: Claudia, where did you enter America?

LAPIDUS: I came from Rome to New York, to the John F. Kennedy Airport.

MICHENER: Why not directly from Russia to New York?

LAPIDUS: People have to have destinations, and it takes time to find where they can go and where their professions can best be used. So HIAS takes care of you when you're in Italy. They handle your visa and help you with money. . . . It would be very hard to survive without HIAS helping you.

MICHENER: You had two years of education in what we call high school in Russia, and two years here. How do they compare?

LAPIDUS: Well, in Russia, the school program is the same no matter where you are or what school you go to. At the same time of the year, everyone studies the same things. But in the United States, you get to choose your courses. And if you don't like something, you don't take it. . . . Then, in Russia, when you go to a lecture you sit down and you just listen. In the United States you can speak to the teacher and ask questions. It's a different atmosphere—you feel freer in a class here.

MICHENER: The education in mathematics in Russia is much better, isn't it?

LAPIDUS: You start earlier. When I was in the eighth grade I finished trigonometry and went on to calculus. But my brother, in a new program in Russia, started algebra in the first grade. You start math much earlier there than in the United States.

MICHENER: How were you received at school here?

LAPIDUS: Well, at first people didn't talk to me, because I couldn't even answer. But there were some people who started to say hello every morning. My math teacher was very good—he taught me how to say pen, pencil. . . . He became my very good friend. And gradually I got to know some people. It took a year. And after that, it didn't matter that I came from Russia, and they had grown up in the United States.

MICHENER: Did you feel when you left high school that you were pretty well prepared for Yale?

LAPIDUS: I was scared. I was afraid that only two years in high school would not be enough.

MICHENER: Could you have gone to Yale if you hadn't gotten the scholarship?

LAPIDUS: Well, it would be much harder. But there are banks to lend money. If you really want to do something, you can do it.

MICHENER: I think anyone who met you, Claudia, would be very happy that you've come to the United States. America is very lucky to get immigrants like you. Do you have anything you'd like to ask me?

LAPIDUS: Yes. In my literature class here we are studying Russian literature of the nineteenth and twentieth centuries, and what I see is that the writer was always directed about what he must write, especially right now in Russia. It's different in the States. But how different?

MICHENER: I'm aware that Russian writers have always been under very heavy social pressure. We are not, in the United States. No writer of a novel that I know has ever been under any pressure from the government. The novelist has a freedom here that he doesn't have in a lot of other places. I've never had censorship of any kind. I write exactly what I want to write, the way I want to write. Sometimes people don't like it, and they tell me so. But I've had great freedom.

On the other hand, I think that the writer has a lower position in America than almost anywhere else. Certainly in almost all the countries I've lived in, writers have a higher intellectual position than they have in the United States. From the point of view of social utility, it might be four or five times better to be a really good writer in Russia than in the United States. I've been in Russia often, and Russian writers live a very good life indeed. They're listened to, they're profoundly important. I think they enjoy a higher position than we do.

We're a frontier country, so America doesn't have too high an opinion of the intellectual life.

The New Wave

As it was a century ago, so it is today. America remains, for millions in foreign lands, "man's last hope." In 1980 alone, more than 800,000 legal immigrants crowded America's shores, a number rivaling the annual totals at the turn of the century. Adding the hundreds of thousands of illegal immigrants—their exact number is unknown—who overstay their visas or filter across the United States–Mexican border, the totals might be higher than at any time in history.

Young Italian-Americans near Christoforo Columbus Park, Worcester, Massachusetts. (Robert Simone)

Employee of the Chicken Box Restaurant in Washington, D.C.
(Robert Simone)

Perhaps no modern immigrant group has more successfully adapted itself to American life than the Cubans who began reaching our shores when Fidel Castro came to power in 1958. During the 1960s almost 300,000 fled the Communist regime. Few arrived with more than a handful of pesos in their pockets, but within six or seven years, most achieved amazing success. Many settled down in Miami, to become a vital element in that city's economic life; others fanned out across the nation. Union City, New Jersey, for example is a major Cuban-American center. But wherever they settled, the Cubans made their mark. By 1967, some 2,500 held teaching posts and nearly 2,000 were physicians.

Equally impressive have been the tens of thousands of South Vietnamese who, in leaky boats, fled their homeland in the wake of the Communist victory there. Like most refugees they came here with nothing. With the help of the government and private sponsors, they have established themselves on farms, in factories, as fishermen and as small entrepreneurs. Their industry and dedication to hard work has already caused some native-born Americans to charge them with unfair competition.

America's continuing economic problems have led to demands for new restrictions on immigration. Perhaps this will be necessary in the short term. But the experience of the recent immigrants testifies to the fact that however hard are the times, this land remains one of opportunity and hope. Yesterday's immigrants have helped make America great; tomorrow's will help make her greater. ❑

TO THE MOON AND BEYOND: OUR NEW MANIFEST DESTINY

It seems to me that the concept with which to describe America is that of Manifest Destiny. In our past Manifest Destiny formed the ideological backdrop for our taming and population of this land from the East Coast to the West. Robert Frost put it aptly when he wrote: "The land was ours before we were the land's." In the name of Manifest Destiny we rolled railroad lines across the plains, planted vast fields

Walking on the moon, astronaut Edwin E. Aldrin, Jr., deploys scientific instruments upon the lunar surface on July 20, 1969. Fellow astronaut Neil A. Armstrong took this photograph. (NASA)

with crops, and then later tore up many of the fields to build cities. The land was ours, and we felt there was never going to be an end to it.

Today America can no longer claim a manifest destiny in the old sense. The frontier as we knew it ended when we ran our cities right up to the Pacific shore. But the key to understanding the American psychology lies in the manifest destiny idea: the idea of the frontier.

In my view, our new frontier lies in the skies, in the vast, uncharted darkness of space, in the world of the astronaut, the space engineer, and the astrophysicist. Already our space program has launched us to the moon. America's communal eye has turned upward.

I am not afraid of technology. Many of my fellow writers see the rise of the machine, the computer, as a killer of the human spirit. I do not share that view. In fact, I am honored to be serving as an adviser with the National Aeronautics and Space Administration (NASA). For me, the exploration of space stands as the central metaphor for our nation's spirit and its willingness to respond to challenge, a new kind of manifest destiny.

On February 1, 1979, I testified before the Senate subcommittee on science, technology, and space, in support of an enlarged space program. The following are excerpts from that testimony.

"It is extremely difficult to keep a human life or the life of a nation

A ground-level view of NASA's space shuttle Columbia *at the Kennedy Space Center, Florida. In Spring 1981,* Columbia *completed its first successful earth orbital mission with astronauts John W. Young and Robert L. Crippen aboard.* (NASA)

Astronaut Edwin E. Aldrin, Jr., pilot of Apollo 11, *the first lunar landing mission, poses on the moon beside the United States flag, July 20, 1969. This photograph was taken by astronaut Neil A. Armstrong.* (NASA)

moving forward with enough energy and commitment to lift it into the next cycle of experience. My own life has been spent chronicling the rise and fall of human systems, and I am convinced that we are all terribly vulnerable.

"I was not overly impressed when men walked upon the moon because I knew it to be out there at a specific distance with specific characteristics, and I supposed that we had enough intelligence to devise the necessary machinery to get us there and back. But when we sent an unmanned object hurtling into distant space and when it began sending back signals—a chain of numbers, to be exact—that could be reassembled here on earth to provide us with a photograph of the surface of Mars, I was struck dumb with wonder. And when computers began adjusting the chain of numbers, augmenting some, diminishing others, so that the photographs became always more clear and defined, I realized that we could accomplish almost anything, there in the farthest reaches of space. My life changed completely on the day I saw those Mars photographs, for I had participated in that miracle. My tax dollars had helped pay for the project. The universities that I supported had provided the brains to arm the cameras. And the government that I helped nourish had organized the expedition. I saw the universe in a new light, and myself and my nation [with] a new set of responsibilities.

". . . The high technical requirements for success in space are so fundamental that spinoff rewards are almost automatic. Radio, television, medical instrumentation, miniaturization, watches, new food processes, communications, health advances, and improvements in clothing are some of the . . . advantages that I myself have gained because of the space program, and I am speaking only of small items that can be comprehended and used by the individual.

"If one considers the larger items, like intercontinental communications satellites, the mapping of weather patterns, the analysis of soils and forests, the exploration for minerals including oil, the management of fisheries and the like, the potential rewards are multiplied many times. . . . I have followed our past space adventures about as carefully as an uninstructed layman could, and I have a rather imaginative mind, but I anticipated almost none of these significant by-products, and I doubt if any of us in this room today could predict where the next contributions will be made.

"Are there military advantages to be gained from a space program? . . . I fear that the potentials of space warfare have even yet not been impressed upon the American public. We do not realize the overwhelming advantage a nation would enjoy if it alone commanded space, if it alone could direct by radio beam when and where an object or its cargo was to be brought down to earth. Any nation that allowed its enemies such a superiority would be doomed. But if all nations have the capacity to utilize space defensively, then the peril is diminished and reasonable arrangements can be worked out. But only through parity can this be done. Therefore, the United States must have a sensible space program whether it wants one or not.

"[Space] is the great unknown ocean of the universe and we . . . are as obligated to probe it and use it and participate in its control as the nations of Europe were obligated to explore their terrestrial oceans [in the fifteenth century]. The future and the safety of those nations depended upon their mastery of the seas; ours depends in shocking measure on our cautious control of space, and if we abandon it to others we condemn ourselves. . . . All the thoughts of men are interlocked, and success in one area produces unforeseen successes in others. It is for this reason that a nation like ours is obligated to pursue its adventure in space. I am not competent to say how much money should be spent. I am not competent to advise on how the program should be administered. But I am convinced that it must be done."

Michener Talks with Astronaut Michael Collins

On July 16, 1969, the spacecraft *Apollo 11* was launched from the Kennedy Space Center in Florida, and four days later its lunar module touched down in the Sea of Tranquillity. Neil Armstrong and Col. Edwin E. Aldrin, Jr., became the first men to walk on the moon, while Lt. Col. Michael Collins orbited in the mother ship. The moon landing was an epochal event for those millions who watched it on television screens around the world, for it was the moment when humanity first touched land that was not the earth's.

Michael Collins is the former director of the National Air and Space Museum in Washington, D.C., where I met with him.

MICHENER: When the astronaut program was begun, the original plan was to use only civilians. And I believe it was Eisenhower who changed that idea by pointing out that our Army, Navy, Marine Corps, and Air

James Michener and former NASA astronaut Michael Collins. Collins flew with the Apollo 11 *mission to the moon in 1969 and has been director of the National Air and Space Museum.*

James Michener and Michael Collins seated at the National Air and Space Museum.

Force produce the best pilots in the world. So all of the first astronaut group were from the military, were they not?

COLLINS: Yes. The original group of seven were all from the military. The second group of nine included two civilians; Neil Armstrong was one of them. And since then the mix has been more toward civilians—I think it's close to fifty-fifty today. Of course in working with each other, we got to the point where we forgot whether a man was military or civilian.

Originally, NASA thought that to operate new and complicated hardware in space required the skills of people accustomed to operating new and complicated hardware in the air: test pilots. So the first and second groups were restricted to test pilots. And the test pilot community in this country is nearly all military. I think most of the early astronauts looked upon their work simply as an extension of the test piloting that they had already been doing.

MICHENER: Mike, you were in one of the *Gemini* earth-orbiting flights before *Apollo*. . . . The space in the *Gemini* was very compact, wasn't it?

COLLINS: Very crowded. It was like two people in the front seat of a tiny subcompact car, with something like a color television console between them. But *Apollo* was roomier. We have the *Apollo 11* command module, *Columbia,* here in the space museum, and people look inside it and say, "Gosh, isn't that tiny!" But really, it's fairly commodious. . . . Walk into a room here on earth, and you find everybody crammed into the lower six feet, and all that overhead space is wasted. It's not that way when you're up in space. In weightless conditions, you use the entire interior volume.

MICHENER: In the great period of exploration with *Gemini* and *Apollo,* did you feel that this was the beginning of a venture that would continue indefinitely?

COLLINS: Oh, yes. I thought that the entire space program was a feeble first step in the direction of the exploration of the whole solar system. And although we're on a sort of quiet plateau right now, I think over the long run we'll probably keep right on going out into space. We'll go to Mars, to Titan. . . . I think eventually we'll even leave the solar system.

MICHENER: Our present exploration of quasars and black holes and the great outer reaches of space—do you think that this new exploration in astronomy will have an effect on the layman?

COLLINS: I don't think knowing about quasars is going to pay off in better computers or different kinds of Teflon frying pans. . . . But basic human knowledge is what feeds us, what keeps us going . . . and to be ignorant of the universe in which we dwell is a terrible thing. So I think the fact that we're learning more, and getting a much clearer picture of where we are, will lead to a clearer picture of who we are, and what we should be, and how we should live.

Benefits to Come

MICHENER: Very soon, as you know, we're going to put a telescope up into space outside the atmosphere. [The space telescope will be placed in orbit by the space shuttle at an altitude of three hundred and twenty miles above the earth. Since its operation will not be obscured by the earth's atmosphere, it will permit astronomers to see perhaps ten times farther into the universe than they can using earth-based telescopes.] That telescope is going to reveal astonishing facts about our universe. It's not a wildly expensive project, but the feedback, intellectually, is going to be staggering. I can hardly wait until we get it up there, to find out what is happening beyond the reaches of our present instruments.

COLLINS: Astronomers today are frustrated people because they scurry around on the surface of the earth with this dense atmosphere over their heads. Of all the information coming in from the stars, I think over ninety percent never reaches a ground-based telescope. So the idea of getting a telescope up above the atmosphere is extremely exciting.

MICHENER: Are you involved at all in aviation these days?

COLLINS: Oh, I get to fly an airplane occasionally. I've been a pilot for a quarter of a century or so, and I like to keep my hand in.

MICHENER: Do you foresee new advances in aviation—in helicopters, short takeoff and landing aircraft, supersonics?

COLLINS: I do indeed. I think the commercial jetliner, the basic Boeing 707, was such a wonderful machine that it's very difficult to improve on it. The airplanes that we're flying now—the Widebodies and the great big planes—are just slight variations of that original Boeing 707. We're not going to see a great change in commercial aviation until another really good idea like that 707 comes along.

MICHENER: Does it worry you that a lot of the developmental work in commercial airplane design is now being done in Europe, and not in the United States?

COLLINS: Yes, it does worry me. Our agricultural products and our aerospace products are the two exports that contribute most favorably to our balance of trade. Our aerospace industry may not be able to keep that position of preeminence in the world market. The Europeans are getting better and tougher and more competitive.

MICHENER: How do you keep preeminence?

COLLINS: You have to have better ideas, and the technology to translate those ideas into metal. European governments subsidize their airlines and their aerospace industries, and perhaps that gives them a bit of a competitive edge, because we don't subsidize ours. I'm not recommending that we should, because once you start the subsidy business, where do you draw the line?

MICHENER: It seems to me that the government ought to subsidize the development of new ideas.

COLLINS: Well, probably basic research is where you begin that process. Basic research is not especially popular on Capitol Hill because the payoffs are not immediately obvious. The guy who discovered penicillin wasn't looking for penicillin—he was looking for something entirely different. But it's difficult to explain to a congressional committee that you need money, but you're not quite certain what's going to be the result of their funding.

MICHENER: We have the capacity now to fly to Mars or to put probes out into the farthest reaches of the solar system. Should the United States continue exploration and technological development in space?

A New Frontier

COLLINS: The United States is a nation of the frontier. I think of exploration as starting on the east coast and moving westward, past the Appalachians and across the United States. I see going out into the solar system as a logical extension of the kind of exploring our country has always done. From the Wright Brothers to going to the moon—and now I think we should go beyond the moon.

MICHENER: The Air and Space Museum is one of the most beautiful

Aerial view of the National Air and Space Museum, part of the Smithsonian Institution in Washington, D.C. (National Air and Space Museum, Smithsonian Institution)

The Spirit of St. Louis *on display at the National Air and Space Museum. On May 21, 1927, Charles A. Lindbergh landed this plane in Paris after making the first solo flight from New York across the Atlantic.* (National Air and Space Museum, Smithsonian Institution)

buildings in Washington, and—as I understand it—it is visited more than any other. More people come in here than to any other museum in the world, isn't that so?

COLLINS: That's true. We see about ten million visitors a year here. It's the most popular building in Washington. . . . Maybe it's the most popular building in the world—I don't know if Guinness keeps records for such things. . . .

MICHENER: You were responsible for setting this up, were you not?

COLLINS: I was, along with a number of other people. I was the director of the Air and Space Museum during the years of its construction [1972–76]. It started with a parking lot and ended up with what you see here today. I think probably the most difficult part was getting the bureaucrats to stop parking in the parking lot, so we could dig the hole in the ground and put the building up.

MICHENER: Well, you've done a marvelous job! These great instruments of flight—many of them are originals, aren't they?

COLLINS: The airplanes are all originals. When we could get an original spacecraft back, we put it on exhibit. But of course so many things—like the probes that went past Venus and Saturn—never returned to earth, so we show only the backup vehicle, or ground-test equipment, or in some cases a replica of the original. . . .

To the Stars—Washington's Air and Space Museum

❑ A replica of an eighteenth-century manned balloon; the original Wright Flyer that carried aviation's inventors aloft from the sand dunes of Kitty Hawk in 1909; a realistic mockup of a World War I air base; the *Spirit of St. Louis*, the very plane that vaulted Lindbergh across the Atlantic in 1927; a DC-9, the workhorse of the skies for three decades; the flight deck of a World War II aircraft carrier: These represent humanity's recent airborne past, and the exhibits are fascinating. But it's the future that creates most of the excitement in this fabulous museum. Each day, thousands of small children course through the 200,000 square feet of exhibit space and make straight for the replica of the *Apollo* space capsule, or stare in open-mouthed wonder at a simulated Martian landscape.

For the children, the old planes, the goggles, the leather pilots' helmets are relics of a primitive age. What rivets their attention are the spaceships, the rockets, the Skylab workshop, and all the other shiny miracles of space exploration—today's working realities. And tomorrow's may be glimpsed in the museum's Spacearium, where visitors take a simulated trip through the universe's vastness.

Child or adult, all those who tour the ingenious exhibits of the Air and Space Museum seem awed by the prodigious possibilities they offer. To spend a day here is to taste the future, when some of us may walk among the stars. ❑

NEW ENGLAND RENAISSANCE

❑ The heart of New England is still, as it has always been, the small town. Built around a village green—itself bordered by churches, a library, the town hall, a few small stores, and perhaps an inn or a school—the New England village has long since entered the American consciousness as everyone's home town. To millions of Americans,

A view through white birches of Lake Winnipesaukee in the Mt. Washington area of New Hampshire. (Colour Library International, Ltd.)

many of whom have never visited a Center Sandwich in New Hampshire or a Newfane in Vermont, the very thought of such places is sustaining. Even to imagine oneself in such a setting seems to bring visions of dappled sunlight filtering through the brilliantly colored foliage of a New England October.

In the not so very distant past, New England was also the workshop and the educational heart of America. Its towns were the market centers for the ocean-borne commerce and the agricultural and manufactured products that once helped to sustain the nation. But the great days of world-traveling merchant ships out of Rhode Island, Massachusetts, and Maine ports have entered the realm of history and legend. The textile and shoe industries, to which New England gave birth, fled decades ago

Galilee Fishing Port at Point Judith, Rhode Island. This is a point of departure for Block Island, one of the loveliest islands in New England. It is also the scene of an annual tuna-fishing tournament. (Colour Library International, Ltd.)

The Touro Synagogue, built in 1763, and located in Newport, Rhode Island, is the oldest synagogue in the United States and was designated a National Historic Site in 1946. The building, a fine example of Colonial architecture, was designed by Peter Harrison. (Newport County Chamber of Commerce, photo by John T. Hopf)

Trinity Church, Newport, Rhode Island, is one of the outstanding Colonial churches in America and one of the best preserved. Built in 1726, its three-tiered, wine-glass pulpit is the only example left in the United States. (Newport Chamber of Commerce, photo by John T. Hopf)

One of Newport's historic mansions. This Rhode Island town is dotted with impressive houses built by wealthy residents. Few are now occupied by private families, and many residences and their grounds are now open to the public. (Colour Library International, Ltd.)

The state Capitol building in Hartford, Connecticut. (Colour Library International, Ltd.)

to regions of cheaper labor. Even today a quick tour of rural Vermont or New Hampshire can turn up hundreds of traces of once well-tended farms now abandoned. And certainly there are few more depressing examples of urban decay than once prosperous mill towns such as Bellows Falls, Vermont, or North Adams, Massachusetts.

But today, one feels a sense of movement, of new wealth, of better times. A visitor to New England is aware of a new optimism at the bustling Faneuil Hall marketplace in Boston or in the workshops of SALT on the Maine coast. It is also evident along Boston's Route 128, an American center for high technology where scores of computer and communications firms work with scientists from such neighboring institutions as Harvard, M.I.T., Boston University, and Brandeis University. Hartford, Connecticut's capital city, has a revitalized downtown that is another testimony to the region's new prosperity. And the ever popular Tanglewood Music Festival in the Massachusetts Berkshire Hills reminds one of the central role New England has always played in the creation and support of a national culture.

With its well-educated citizenry, its port facilities, and bustling recreation areas, with its many top-ranked institutions of higher education, New England seems situated to reclaim its position as the hub of America. ❑

Speaking of SALT: The Past Preserved

I do not for a moment believe that the true spiritual well-being of our nation depends primarily on a successful space program. There are, as William James said, moral equivalents to war, moral substitutes for any charismatic national experience. We must as a nation attain spiritual reassurance from rebuilding our cities, or distributing our farm produce more efficiently. But it is the concept of challenge, of the idea of the frontier in the American imagination, that I believe we cannot do without.

The frontier is not limited to space. America's own inner space is ripe with challenge. Our future resides with our youth.

There is down east, on the coast of Maine, the town of Kennebunkport. And in that town American kids are engaged in a project that strikes me as a good metaphor for the dream our country embodies. It's called SALT—an experiment with teenagers run by high school teacher Pam Wood.

WOOD: *Salt* started back in 1973 with a group of kids who began interviewing their own people: their grandfathers, their aunts, their

Pam Wood, teacher and organizer of the SALT program for high school students, in Kennebunkport, Maine.

Examples of publications written and assembled by students in the SALT program.

neighbors, about what their work was, what their lives were, what was important to them—in an attempt to translate what their own culture was. The whole thing grew and grew, until at the end of a year we had ninety kids involved, both in and out of the high school, putting together a magazine. And after a number of years we had enough material to make a book.

When we wrote the magazine, we had worked in a kind of partnership with the community; we couldn't have written the magazine or taken the photographs without the grandmothers and the uncles and the neighbors. So when the book came out, we had the biggest publication party that I've ever known about. We had a hundred and some odd authors gathered in the Community House. We had almost a hundred people who had been written about. It was a huge celebration of a joint production. And as we began to get royalties from the book, we did some serious thinking about how those royalties could be shared, because they did not belong to any one person. After a lot of thought, the young people who'd been involved, and who make up the majority of the board of trustees of *Salt,* decided that the money had to be plowed back into the community that had made it happen. The partnership between the old people who had been interviewed and the younger people who'd worked on the material had to produce something that went back into the community. That's when they decided to buy this boatyard.

The boatyard was already important to us. We knew its history. We've been in it; we've done interviewing here. We knew it had sent two hundred good boats down the Kennebunk River to the ocean. And we didn't want to see it become just a center for tourists and shops. So

A Kennebunkport fisherman tending to his bait.

with some fear and trepidation, we bought the boatyard in late 1977, and decided to turn it into a center where young people could find themselves and find their footing in the world.

SALT MEMBER: This is an old boatyard. It's been here for many, many years. It's been used as a regular boat building for two or three boat builders in this area. One was my grandfather. It's the SALT boatyard now. We have a youth training program where we teach kids from the ages of sixteen to twenty-one. We teach them boat building, carpentry; layout and design for the magazine; video and photography.

A young SALT student talks about his grandfather's boatyard in Kennebunkport, Maine.

WOOD: When we moved into this boatyard, we discovered that it's not a very large jump from writing a magazine to learning to do some of the things that you write about. Through the years we'd been writing stories about how you build boats and about particular Maine craft, so it was not a large kind of evolution to begin to do some of those things in the boatyard. And the kids began learning how to build boats. They began working intensively in various media, video and radio as well as the magazine. They began to look at other ways in which they could take hold of their environment and be a part of it, actively.

We have a variety of ages in SALT. We have teenagers who are participating in a Department of Labor project to determine how kids can successfully find a place for themselves in the world of work. And we have older people who are becoming boat builders, who are learning skills that they intend to make a part of their lives.

From the very beginning we've been product-oriented, because all of us like to do something we can hold, or see, or point to. So the magazine was a product, and it just earned its way. And in the same way, we're attempting to make boats a product for which money can be earned.

The whole long-range goal is self-sufficiency.

SALT MEMBER: I could never talk to older people. . . . I hadn't really grown up with them, but when I began interviewing I found out that

A SALT student interviews a fisherman about his life and occupation.

they've had exciting lives, and there was a lot I could learn from them. Just about everywhere I go I end up talking to a lot of people and it makes life much more interesting; and that's good for me. There's a lot out there to share.

SALT MEMBER: I learned to respect older people, not 'cause they're old, but because they hang on to things much more than we do. They find something, and they hang on to that. They always do it that way because they know it's right.

SALT MEMBER: The interviews I did were people that I've always known. . . . That interview on my grandfather—I learned things about him that I never knew before, and when I talk to him today, I talk to him in a different sense than just being his grandson. I talk to him as a person. I learn stuff from him every day. . . . I didn't even know where he was born until I did the story. I didn't know he was a New Yorker—I thought he was born in Maine.

From *The Salt Book*:

❏ The people of Kennebunkport have always done for themselves. In the past, they've built their own boats, raised their own food and preserved it, chopped the wood for their stoves, tapped their trees for

A view of the fishing piers in Kennebunkport Harbor.

Students in the SALT project repair the hull of a boat in their boatyard.

maple syrup, and made the snowshoes they needed to reach the sugarbush in February. Now, through SALT, Kennebunkport teenagers are rediscovering the crafts that allowed their grandparents to live useful, independent lives. The kids are finding out about attitudes and practices that were supposed to have died in the machine age; and they've done it by asking the oldsters in their community—by listening, by writing, and by publishing their interviews, and by learning the same skills themselves.

The Salt Book preserves the lore of the Maine coast.❑

"There was this guy lobstering in a fifteen-foot dory. First thing he hauled up a lobster trap, and this great big lobster was hanging on it. Right when he hauled it up, the lobster come up and bit the dory right in two. The guy jumped in the stern and sculled her ashore."

—*Stilly Griffin, Lobsterman*

"It isn't where the lobsters are now—it's where they're gonna be next. . . . The secret of bein' a good lobsterman is gettin' where somebody hasn't been and knowin' where they're gonna be next."

—*Herb Baum, Jr., Lobsterman*

"[The great gale of 1933] happened one day after Christmas 1933. We were trawlin' . . . after codfish, haddock . . . until that big gale of wind come up on us, and blinding snowstorm. . . . We tried to go into York Harbor. . . . But we never made it . . . couldn't find the entrance to the harbor, so we turned around and went back out to sea again, 'cause it was the only chance we had. . . . We put out what you call a sea anchor. You took three of these trawl tubs, wrapped them all together, and put them on the end of your anchor line way out ahead of the boat. You know how hard a bucket draws through the water. Well, these big tubs pull hard so they keep the bow of the boat up into the wind. . . . And by putting the sea anchor out and by tying the small sail we had—we tied it down low . . . it saved our lives."

—*Ben Wakefield, Fisherman*

Recollections of the Old Days in Maine

❑ Edmund S. Muskie is a former governor of Maine, a former senator from that state, and a former United States secretary of state. Though he is the son of Polish immigrants, Muskie is the archetypal New Englander, spare of speech, direct in his approach to the issues, and firm in his convictions. Like many New Englanders, Muskie remembers the past with deep affection: It was a simpler time when, if life was difficult, values were certain. Here Edmund Muskie reminisces about that time and about the joys of being a boy in a small Maine town in the 1920s. ❑

Muskie munching on a Maine apple.

"I think I have more vivid recollections of my childhood than I have of much of my life since that time. The years that I remember are the early 1920s.

"I suppose that by today's standards we'd be considered poor. But we didn't feel poor. We lived in a small town, in what was called a tenement house: three flats, or tenements, on top of each other, and we lived in the middle one. There were porches front and back, not more than two bedrooms, a parlor, a kitchen, a woodshed, a pantry. . . . My mother sewed all our clothes. When she married, she couldn't cook or sew, but my father bought her a sewing machine, one of the old treadle models, and she became one of the best seamstresses I've ever known. She was still using that sewing machine when she died—the day before, she had made some of the Christmas aprons she loved to make to give to people. We still have that sewing machine. . . .

"On Saturday nights we had our only bath of the week in the kitchen washtub, with hot water that my mother boiled on top of the stove. She did her washing out of that washtub, too. In those days, we only heated one or two rooms in the house, the kitchen and the living room. So all the bedrooms were cold. We all dressed warmly—we wore long underwear, even the girls. We never really knew what the girls looked like until spring, when they had taken off their long underwear. My mother used to have to wash this long underwear, wring it out by hand, and hang it out on the clothesline on the back porch. In the wintertime it froze. In the night, you'd see these white things, stiff with ice, waving in the breezes, looking like ghosts dancing outside. And then in the morning we'd bring it in, thaw it out, and iron it to warm it.

"Washing must have been a terrible ordeal in those days. But you'd never know it to look at my mother. She did all the baking. She made all the bread, she made the doughnuts. Almost every morning she'd make doughnuts for a family of six children. Cooking, sewing, washing—she never had any time for herself. Oh, she and some of her neighbors had what they called 'sewing circles.' They'd gather in each other's homes for maybe an afternoon a week, just sewing together. Even their recreation couldn't be separate from their responsibilities to their families.

"Oh, there are so many vignettes from those years—snow, for instance. I come from a part of the country where there's a lot of snow. And there were no snow plows. Plowing the snow would have made the roads impassable for the sleighs, and there were more sleighs in those days than there were automobiles. And so they packed the snow with snow rollers—huge wooden snow rollers."

Edmund S. Muskie preparing to go ice fishing. Muskie was governor of Maine from 1955 to 1959 and then senator from 1959 until he was appointed secretary of state by President Jimmy Carter in 1980.

A Maine Christmas

"At Christmastime my father would climb a mountain on the other side of our street to cut the family Christmas tree himself. I can remember the Christmas tree perfectly. In those days there were no electric lights. So we used candles, maybe a hundred candles. And in the evening, after supper, they were all lighted. Glorious trees. And then after the tree lighting we would sit around the parlor table playing cards. There was always something to win—chocolate-covered cherries or ribbon candy. And the neighbors would come in.

"And of course Christmas dinner was a triumph of my mother's cooking. Even today the husbands and wives of our family prepare Christmas dinner as my mother did forty or fifty years ago. And Christmas Day was a time of joy for the whole family. We didn't have trees with toys stacked under them. The girls would usually get last year's dolls with new clothes that my mother had sewn. The boys would get boxes of raisins—we loved them—and books to read. There weren't a lot of toys . . . just the same thing year after year, really, but the anticipation was wonderful.

"When I think back, I recall memories of happiness—not of poverty, not of want. Memories of happiness."

QUBE: TOWN MEETING IN THE GLOBAL VILLAGE

We are still a nation of regions. The kid from Kennebunkport, the farmer in South Dakota, the rancher in Colorado, the clothing store owner in Oregon all dress, look, and accent the language differently. The region is still a powerful force. But another force has dramatically altered our concept of ourselves. Television speaks to us in a national language, and its impact has transcended our regional differences.

To a significant extent, America today is the product of the communications revolution. There are more than seventy-three million homes with television sets. That adds up to 90 percent of all American homes. The majority of us get most of our news about what's going on in the world today from our TV sets. And we watch! According to the television pollster A. C. Nielsen, the average American home watches TV for six hours and eleven minutes a day. Through television, America has attained the status of a global village.

In Columbus, Ohio, an intriguing television experiment has become a reality. It's called QUBE; it's the first commercial participatory television programming in America. In early 1981, this system was expanded to serve the city of Cincinnati as well.

❑ Using two-way cable television, QUBE subscribers can talk back to their TV sets. The center of the system is the QUBE home console, a small black box equipped with several rows of buttons. Some of the buttons provide QUBE users with the channel choices most TV cable systems give their customers: regular broadcast stations and special

James Michener visits a television station.

A couple in their home in Columbus, Ohio, use electronic equipment to give feedback through QUBE.

Women contestants in an audience participate in the QUBE show "Power Play."

Quiz-show format in a QUBE television studio.

A QUBE television cameraman at work.

QUBE offerings, including educational and cultural programs, pay-television stations, and an adult soft-core movie channel. But the five buttons on the far right of the box make the difference between QUBE and all its competitors. These are the response buttons, and by manipulating them, QUBE users can respond to the questions their television set asks. On matters of opinion, their response possibilities are limited: five choices ranging from "strongly agree" to "strongly disagree." The same buttons can be used to order merchandise featured on a TV program, or to vote for favorites in a talent show, or to choose one out of five statements that most closely represents a viewer's feelings about politics, the weather, the cost of living—anything.

Participants in a multiple-choice game make use of both television and computers.

QUBE would not be possible without the system's computers. One of them monitors QUBE homes around the clock and tracks who is watching what. Another computer keeps tabs on the votes. A third is used for billing and to identify viewers when necessary—when awards are made to game participants, for instance.

Columbus QUBE subscribers seem delighted. They feel more actively involved with television, with events in their town, with national and worldwide issues. Some of them wonder, though: Is their privacy perhaps being violated by computers that constantly record their political opinions, TV viewing habits, and consumption patterns? And what about participation—how much real viewer input can there be when responses are limited to a form of multiple choice, and some anonymous power chooses the questions?

Subscriber couples and the station's manager discussed their experience with QUBE. ❑

HUSBAND: I think we've watched a lot more better-quality TV, and having a push-button just adds to the fun of it. All of a sudden the TV is not just a piece of furniture that spits out programs. We can actually talk to it, and it talks back to us. It's great fun. I love it. . . . They've got a variety of shows. The "Columbus Alive" program is probably the first interactive program that they came out with; it gets into all sorts of areas—politics, sex, religion, marriage.

WIFE: Whatever you could possibly think about, they will come up with some type of question to ask you. They are constantly checking the audience for their response to the program.

HUSBAND: They have game shows like "Power Play" and "Flippo's Screen Test." And they have a channel that broadcasts all the prices of food items throughout the various stores in town, so you can get your best buy. And people call in periodically and suggest things, and then everybody votes on what they want to have priced for the next week—Contac, eye-washing fluid . . .

WIFE: . . . dog food—anything like that. We vote which ones we want, and they go out and check out prices and come back with them . . .

HUSBAND: On questions where we have completely opposite views, we'll be sitting there tugging at each other, trying to get the box to respond and . . .

WIFE: It's a miracle that this cord has managed to stay where it is in its socket. We pull on the cord and—

HUSBAND: We have arguments over the thing. We sit there and call each other "dummy"—"Why didn't you push the one that I wanted to push?" We have a grand time with it.

A smoke inhalator, which, when activated by smoke, gives out a loud noise and electronic signal stimulating a warning system.

MIKLOS KORODI, QUBE GENERAL MANAGER: In conjunction with QUBE, we have developed several ancillary services—burglar alarm, fire alarm, medical emergency, and police duress. The system works simply by having devices installed in your home, such as an emergency push-button that can be activated by the subscriber. Our computers check that subscriber every ten seconds. Depending on what is required, we will dispatch the fire department, the police department, or the ambulance squad. Based on our computer technology, we can also advise the ambulance squad of certain physical requirements that a patient might have—a susceptibility to drugs, a doctor's telephone number, other pertinent information that they should have on hand. In case of a fire alarm, we use traditional sensors such as smoke detectors and heat detectors—within ten seconds from receipt of a signal we will be in touch with the fire department. The burglar alarm systems we install include magnetic contacts, pressure pads, infrared devices, ultrasonic devices that will sense motion in the home, and a push-button to alert the police that you need their services because you are under duress. All of these devices are monitored through a computer, and in case of an alarm, it is transmitted to the police department for their response.

A command console for monitoring buildings for loss-producing hazards, including burglary, fire, and other emergencies. The console includes a display screen, high-speed printer, and annunciator panels. (ADT Security Systems)

A central-alarm system in a local police station records signals indicating break-in or fire. Trained personnel may then alert police or fire departments to take care of an emergency in a matter of minutes. (ADT Security System)

Electronic Town Meeting

A control panel for a home-alarm system. This panel is mounted inside the house near an exterior door and the alarm system is activated by pressing a button before leaving the house and locking the door. The system may be deactivated by entering a personal code on the push-button panel. (ADT Security Systems)

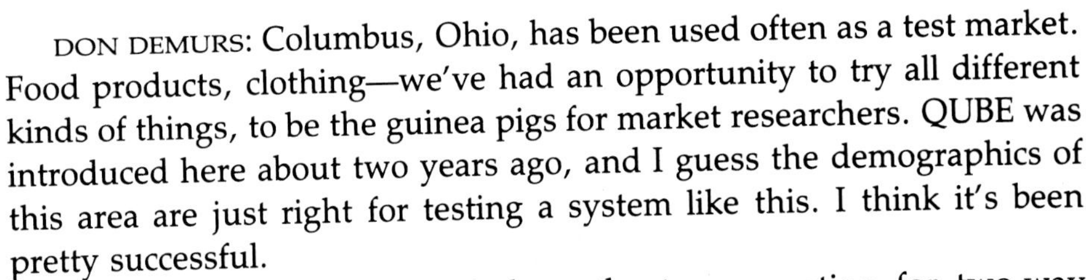

DON DEMURS: Columbus, Ohio, has been used often as a test market. Food products, clothing—we've had an opportunity to try all different kinds of things, to be the guinea pigs for market researchers. QUBE was introduced here about two years ago, and I guess the demographics of this area are just right for testing a system like this. I think it's been pretty successful.

HELEN DEMURS: They opened up the town meeting for two-way communication between the home and the cable system. And we were able to vote on whether we liked or disliked some of the ideas they came up with. We had friends in our home that night, and it gave us a very good chance to discuss what was going on in our town.

DON DEMURS: It's more involvement in the political process of our town than we'd otherwise have had a chance to get. So it was a great experience for us.

They have a series of computers at QUBE, and about every six seconds they communicate with your home and detect whether or not you're connected, what station you're watching, and what response you may have made to a particular question. Sometimes, because of the answers you give, they'll call you and ask you, for instance, what size sweater you'd like to buy. . . . So they know who you are, and that's been very useful for a security system they've put in, and a medical alert kind of thing, so that if you're ill or need an ambulance you can press a button and they'll call the ambulance for you. The security and medical things are optional.

HELEN DEMURS: The people next door have a security system. They have electric-eye-type things on their doors and windows, and should they leave and someone attempt to break in, the system is triggered automatically and the police department is called. Several times when the system has short-circuited, the police department has shown up in force. So it does work—we've seen that.

DON DEMURS: I think the beauty of QUBE is that our interests, our responses, mean something. I don't think that the QUBE audience in general is your average family—the area that they chose to put this system in is a tad above middle class. And this is Republican country. . . . But our responses have made a difference in what kinds of shows we get to watch here locally. There's one show that started out very small, but as people became interested, it grew and grew until it's on now twice a week. And there's a real opportunity here for advertisers and broadcasters to know instantaneously whether or not they're making a hit with the public.

We've learned a lot about the community we didn't know. We've had an opportunity to learn a great deal about the city of Columbus, the kinds of people who live here, the resources of Ohio State University. We've seen researchers and professors, and we've learned things. So it's been an educational process for us as well.

HELEN DEMURS: I watch the program with the market-basket comparison shopping. It's changed my shopping—I go to the stores where the prices are less. And we've seen some food prices come down because of QUBE.

DON DEMURS: I think QUBE is just the beginning of where this kind of technology can go. It sounds a little like *1984*, a little George Orwell. We have a computer in our home that we don't control. Someone else controls it. They can poll us to find out what we're doing, whether we're watching a particular television station, how long we've watched it. They've given us the opportunity to respond to questions they ask and they use those responses in ways that aren't objectionable to us.

QUBE technicians monitor the progress of a television program.

Residents of Reading, Massachusetts, gather for the annual town meeting.

SPEAK-YOUR-MIND DEMOCRACY: THE TOWN MEETING

Underneath the satellites and the telephone lines, we still gather to communicate in a time-honored way. The local town meeting exemplifies our traditional speak-your-mind democracy, where convictions clash head on and the winner is chosen by majority vote.

The town meeting and electronic town polling of the QUBE variety may seem worlds apart, but they really have a great deal in common. Communication is a central need in a democracy, and whether it's accomplished face to face or over the circuits of a television cable system, the essential thing is that it *is* accomplished.

❑ Most New England town meetings convene in March because in earlier days the roads would not be free of snow and passable until then.

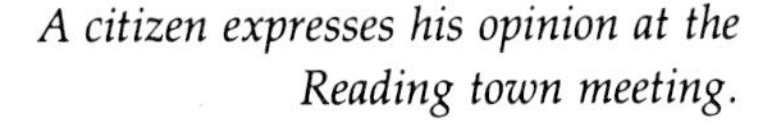

A citizen expresses his opinion at the Reading town meeting.

Many meetings follow the time-honored form: Seven days before the meeting date, a "warrant" is printed and posted in the local grocery store, the library, the town hall. The warrant lists the items to be discussed: the town budget; tax rates; the running of the schools; the purchase of a new fire truck, perhaps, or the repaving of the roads; the election of town officials. The meeting is chaired by an elected moderator. And everyone who wishes can speak up about any issue on the warrant, and can vote on it when the speaking is done. One such meeting took place in North Reading, Massachusetts. ❑

MODERATOR (*Strikes gavel*): This meeting is now called to order.

FELLOW WITH BEARD: Are they proposing a *salary* increase?

OTHER FELLOW: This is not casting aspersions on Mr. Spinny, but he's only been on the job three months and I don't think he deserves an increase.

THE CITIES

History is mainly the account of what happened in the cities. There the power lay; there the wealth was controlled. The city was the center of government, the focus of intellectual and artistic leadership, and although all the food and much of the wealth was created in the country, what happened to it was determined by the cities. In rural areas, there might be large monasteries, but the cardinals who dictated to them lived in the cities. Significantly, the records of history were compiled and kept in cities, so that we see history through city eyes.

Ours is the first generation in which people have had the option to reject the city if they wished. But the consequences of our rejection are now becoming obvious and will color the remaining years of this century.

From a purely technical sense we can dispense with the city. With new concepts in management and new capacity to control our environment, we can run our government and our businesses from any preferred spot, and the city has lost its appeal and its leverage.

Most of the consumer services traditionally provided by the city can now be provided by the suburb. When you add the extra desirability of suburban living, with superior schools and the possibility of lower taxes, the threat to the city becomes formidable; as the surrounding areas increase in attractiveness, the appeal of the city deteriorates.

This historical change, with ramifications we do not even yet appreciate, has come about because a series of factors happened to coincide, all unfavorable to the city. Had we been alert, we could have combated them; we ignored them and must now work overtime to find remedies.

A view of downtown Pittsburgh with the Smithfield Bridge in the foreground. (Colour Library International, Ltd.)

First, at the precise time when the automobile made the suburbs an alternative to the city, large numbers of rural workers found themselves no longer needed in agriculture. As they moved from southern farms into northern cities, they strained the education, housing, and medical resources, creating unavoidable problems in community control and the myriad dislocations that ensue when the median wage of an area has been sharply lowered.

Second, with this exchange of population—for the well-to-do left as the poor came in—the tax base from which the city operates was diminished at the very time when the call for new services was increased.

Third, at a time when the city should have been expanding its horizons, it was forced to contract them. As the tax rolls diminished and expenses increased, we threw around the perimeter a *cordon sanitaire* of self-governing suburbs with restrictive zoning and the power to resist any attempt by the city to bring them within its political or economic boundaries. The city is thus impoverished from within and strangled from without.

Fourth, the freedom of any city to cope with its problems has always been inhibited by state legislatures, which throughout the United States have been dominated by rural representatives.

Fifth, these conditions would of themselves have created problems, but they were aggravated by the race factor. As black workers from the South moved to the big cities, race was becoming a crucial force in American life. Our large northern cities were asked to make decisions for which they were ill prepared, and to adjudicate conflicting claims whose roots they had not even studied. It would have been much better if we could have postponed facing up to questions of education, employment rights, and public welfare for ten or fifteen years, when we might have understood these problems better and avoided mistakes. But making decisions in such areas can never be delayed.

Finally, these historical strands came together in an age when violence was becoming a worldwide way of life.

The city today is a kind of pressure cooker in which steam is generated with inadequate vents for its escape.

"New York, New York . . . It's a Helluva Town"

❑ Despite its fiscal problems and deteriorating services, its graffiti and crime-ridden subways, and its prices, New York City remains the focal point of America's commerce, communications, and

Inner-city children take a catnap on a midtown Manhattan wall. (Christopher Bain)

A view from the Brooklyn piers of lower Manhattan. The twin towers of the World Trade Center dominate this skyline. (Colour Library International, Ltd.)

culture. Within a short walk of the X-rated tawdriness of Times Square are more than sixty major Broadway theaters. A twenty-block stroll up Broadway brings a visitor to Lincoln Center, home of the Metropolitan Opera, the City Opera, the New York Philharmonic, and the incomparable New York City Ballet. To the east and south, small movie houses, one after another, show films from just about every country in the world. If the movie industry is in a state of depression, one would never know it along Third Avenue where, on a Saturday night, film buffs line up by the thousands, heedless of blizzard or burning heat, for the privilege of waiting hours and paying five dollars a head for an evening's viewing.

And everywhere, *everywhere,* there are restaurants. Do you fancy a kabob from Armenia? New York can accommodate you at a score or more eateries. Or how about raw fish from Japan? There's probably a place serving such delicacies within four blocks of any spot in midtown. Or pasta, or haute cuisine, or a corned beef on rye—it's all there for the asking and the paying. If a Szechuan Chinese restaurant opens in Peoria, you can bet New York already has forty such places. The Big

A colorful nighttime display at Mama Leone's Italian restaurant on West 48th Street. (Colour Library International, Ltd.)

A restaurant in Chinatown, located in southern Manhattan. (Colour Library International, Ltd.)

Tourists and residents are drawn to New York's Broadway district, host to many new and long-run theatrical productions, both dramatic and musical. (Colour Library International, Ltd.)

The Russian Tea Room, a popular restaurant, particularly among musicians, on West 57th Street, close to Carnegie Hall. (Colour Library International, Ltd.)

Apple is where the nation's taste is made. Perhaps Hollywood can lay claim to national trend-setter status, but in reality the West Coast Babylon is only a branch office of Manhattan's talent pool of writers, directors, and actors, to say nothing of the television networks and the banks that make the reels go round.

New York is everything to everyman. It is bleak and shabby. It is bright and blooming. It's an impossible place to live and the *only* place to live. It's the human condition spelled out in neon. As the song says, "It's a helluva town!" ❑

Michener Talks with Joseph Papp

❑ A major figure in the New York theatrical world, Joseph Papp also influences theaters across the nation. In 1954, he founded the New York Shakespeare Festival, which gave free performances, first in New York's Lower East Side ghetto, then in Central Park. His Public Theater, which opened in 1967, is a collection of seven small theaters housed within a single building, and has mounted an impressive variety of both experimental and conventional plays. Many of them have been taken to Broadway and were hits; a few have been made into films. Papp was the original producer of the 1967 musical comedy hit *Hair* and the Broadway sellout *A Chorus Line*. ❑

The advanced technological society can use its technology to enhance human relationships and to bring people together. Yet with the kind of technology that QUBE represents, there is the constant danger of human alienation, of cutting people off from one another.

Large cities, it is said, breed alienation. But it seems evident that a truly living city should create the opposite effect, because the city is the locus for the creative arts that can form vital bonds between people.

When I was a boy I came to the city and saw with astonishment its blazing theaters, its live vaudeville, its major-league baseball teams, its splendid museums and, above all, the orchestra hall that hosted musicians from Boston, New York, Philadelphia, and Amsterdam. Later I came to know the libraries and the university. The city for me was an awakening so vast that I would have been cheated of one of the best parts of my life had I missed it.

Able boys and girls since the beginning of time have come to the cities for their imagination and inspiration, to witness things that were larger in scope than they could see at home.

New York serves as that kind of magnet. It is still a great city, where culture, money, and business power exist side by side.

Joseph Papp is one of the most innovative individuals on New York's cultural scene. He runs the New York Shakespeare Festival and the Public Theater. I talked with him in his office.

MICHENER: I follow your career with the closest attention, Mr. Papp. I admire your nerve in doing the great things you've accomplished, and I like your relationship to the culture of the center of the city. Do you work here in the city by choice?

PAPP: I was born and raised in the city, and I know it. I know the people, because I was raised in a multiracial neighborhood, and being a Jew, I was very much aware of the struggle between nationalities.

MICHENER: You've done wonderful work with minorities.

Joseph Papp, founder of the "New York Public Theater" and the "New York Shakespeare Festival" in his Manhattan office.

PAPP: I'm very conscious of the minorities in my life. I have a strong identification with them, and with the poor, because I was poor.

MICHENER: Where did you learn about Shakespeare?

PAPP: In junior high school. I became very interested in just listening to the words, they sounded beautiful. I didn't understand them all, but I liked them, and I memorized large sections of Shakespeare.

MICHENER: Did the movies influence your artistic attitudes?

PAPP: Absolutely. In every sense. In New York, every kid in the neighborhood develops a sense of what's good and what's bad. He'll know a good fighter, a good baseball player, and who's a good movie actor. What was marvelous about being part of that was that you didn't cast judgments. You never said, "That was terrible." There were no critics around. So I could read everything, see everything. I read junk, and it wasn't junk to me. I read it all. I could listen on the same day to jazz and Beethoven. I made no distinction—it was all music.

People develop an elitist idea about art. They think art must be on a particular level, and so they preclude a whole body of art that's enormous and, in a sense, is much more influential and necessary. You need cultural peaks, but you can't live a life of peaks.

Shakespeare for All

MICHENER: How did you get into the business of providing free Shakespeare in the park?

PAPP: It was around 1955. I had begun to do Shakespeare in a small church on the Lower East Side. The Emanuel Presbyterian Church on East Sixth Street. It's no longer there. There was a marvelous Reverend there—Clarence E. Boyer. A fine man. Rather rotund and cheery. He reminded me of an English parson. I said I wanted to start a small Shakespeare Company on East Sixth Street. It was a no-man's-land in that area. Reverend Boyer was very tolerant. He said, "Do you think anybody will come?" I said, "Well, I don't know. But I'd like to try it." He replied, "All right. All you have to do is pay for the heat."

I had no money, and I picked up things wherever I could. I used to beg, borrow, and literally steal. I was working for CBS at the time, and I used my salary to pay for the telephones and the heat. Some of the actors contributed their unemployment insurance. We made our own costumes and sets . . . we used old nails we pulled out of old boards. Nobody got paid.

I had no idea how the public on the Lower East Side would take to Shakespeare. We had no publicity whatever, but forty-five minutes before the show opened, there must have been thousands of people outside waiting to get in. The word spreads in the community very quickly that some strange people are in the church doing something exciting. Now these were people who had never been to the theater, most of them; and I'm sure none of them had ever heard Shakespeare spoken on the stage. It was an entirely new experience for them, but five minutes after we started, they were shouting as if they were at a baseball game. They would shout after each rendition. They loved it.

Then we moved to the East River Park Amphitheater to do two productions—we did *The Taming of the Shrew* with Colleen Dewhurst and J. G. Cannon, and we did *Julius Caesar*. We did a season of two plays. I raised seven hundred fifty dollars to do those two productions. We made our own costumes. All I needed was to rent sound equipment.

Now we have a mobile unit that tours the city. We come to places that are very noisy, because there are a lot of kids on the street at night. Yet it's amazing how poetry catches an audience. We do *A Midsummer Night's Dream:* "I know a bank whereon the wild thyme blows, where oxlips and the nodding violet grows. . . ." Well, you think tough kids are going to say, "What crap is that?" But they listen. You just paint the picture and, boy, people listen. Kids get quiet. They say music hath charms to soothe . . . well, Shakespeare does.

MICHENER: What you accomplished in New York—could it be done in other cities as well?

PAPP: There have been duplications of free Shakespeare in the Park in other cities, but with not as much success. The city of New York has a particular kind of history and ambience that make it a very strong cultural city. We have publishing here . . . we have more newspapers than most cities. We have a mixed population—Hispanics, blacks, people from all over the world. So there's a very rich cultural thing that

Kathleen Widdoes and Sam Waterston in Much Ado About Nothing, *a New York Shakespeare Festival production that later was presented on Broadway and televised on CBS.* (Lawrence Fried)

goes on here. "Culture" doesn't mean just plays and operas; there's culture in the streets. I was very cultured before I ever opened a book. . . . And then, in New York there is still a standard that makes it important for a person in the theater or in publishing to succeed. New York is like playing the Palace—it's the whole tradition of the city. And we have more theaters here than in any other city in the world.

But even in New York, most people don't go to plays. And I've never been able to answer the question, why is the theater so powerful? Because, actually—compared to television and films—its audience is relatively small.

Culture as Commerce

MICHENER: Mr. Papp, is American culture a prisoner of the marketplace?

PAPP: I would say most of it is. Starting with films: The movies are all money, and money affects the output. Publishing is getting more and more into the hands of the marketplace people. There are still a few independent publishers, and they turn out some important books even though they don't make money. But publishing too has become a victim of the huge corporate conglomerates. The commercial theater is still a profit-making venture.

But in New York there are almost two hundred small, noncommercial theaters on Off-Off Broadway. That's larger than any group of theaters anyplace in the world.

In the end, I think it doesn't matter which conglomerate and how much money is taking over—theaters will pop up and writers will write. There'll be generations of young people coming up like grass growing out of a sidewalk. It just takes a few people, two planks, and a passion. You don't need money. You just need a little space and a few people with imagination.

Meryl Streep as Katherine and Raul Julia as Petruchio in The Taming of the Shrew *by William Shakespeare. This production of the New York Shakespeare Festival was staged free to the public at the Delacorte Theater in Central Park.* (George E. Joseph)

I feel the theater is a constant. It will always express itself in some way. It's the most human of all the arts—live people performing before live people and getting and giving an experience: a life experience.

Bostonians Call It "The Hub of the Universe"

It has been said that the Northeast is made up of one big city stretching from Washington, D.C., to Boston, Massachusetts. And it has been given a label: megalopolis. Oliver Wendell Holmes called Boston "the hub of the solar system." Today, Bostonians call their city "the hub of the universe."

I'd like to look at Boston as an example of where our older cities are going. The city proper has almost 700,000 people, but Boston is really a ring of some hundred cities and towns comprising a metropolitan area of more than three million people.

Boston is also the home of one of the most talked about and admired pieces of urban development in America: the rebuilt Faneuil Hall marketplace. Here, amidst jugglers and pushcarts, old brick walls and tree-lined paths, delighted visitors sample a cornucopia of food and drink and shop in a dazzling variety of attractive stores, while their dollars provide jobs for two thousand Bostonians and swell the city and state tax bases. Faneuil Hall redevelopment has managed to build for the future in a way that preserves Boston's colonial architecture and spirit, enhancing rather than destroying the unique character of the city.

The setting sun highlights the newer buildings of downtown Boston behind the residential neighborhood of Back Bay. This view is from across the Charles River. (Colour Library International, Ltd.)

A view of the Quincy marketplace close to Faneuil Hall, Boston. (Colour Library International, Ltd.)

James Michener Talks to Mayor Kevin White

WHITE: This is the famous Quincy Market, part of the Faneuil Hall complex. It's the original marketplace of Boston. The mayor then was Josiah Quincy, and he oversaw the development of this area.

MICHENER: Are we on property belonging to the city?

WHITE: Yes, all of this is Boston property. We did not sell it to the developer, we rented it—put it in a type of trust that will revert to the city many generations from now.

MICHENER: And you rebuilt this with government funds?

WHITE: No. Some of it—what we call "seed money"—started with government funds, but all of this basically is private development . . . and very much a risk that by some miracle caught on.

MICHENER: But all rented?

WHITE: All rented. And two weeks before it opened, they had so few leases that they wrote one-week leases just to attract people. For some reason, from the day the doors opened, it ignited and caught on, and a healthy virus spread right through it. It has been enormously successful.

MICHENER: I've seen a lot of American cities, and Boston seems to be in a rather better posture than a good many of them. You've kept the center of the city viable, you've kept good relations with the suburbs.

WHITE: Boston has a resiliency about it. We've changed the skyline, and—I think more significantly—we've got people to live in the center of the city . . . live in the sense of daily living, night and day, which is unique for most cities. There's a subtle transition going on, and it's embodied in that long word "gentrification." What's happening is that the children of the suburbs are beginning to move back into the city. Those who escaped in the 1950s—their children are beginning to come

The First Church of Christ, Scientist, was established in Boston in 1892. It is the mother church, of which Christian Science churches throughout the world are branches. Boston is also the home of the well-respected newspaper, the Christian Science Monitor, *which has a worldwide circulation.* (Colour Library International, Ltd.)

back in, and they are a generation that delights in the almost psychedelic aspects of the city.

School Desegregation

MICHENER: Have you had a flight of students from your city schools?

WHITE: Because of desegregation and busing? Without a question. And in large numbers. And it has affected the quality of education. Boston schools cannot be integrated unless there are whites present in them—if not in equal numbers, at least in vitality and participation. Even if they are a minority. I think integration is do-able. It takes many strong factors, not the least of which is the will of the community.

MICHENER: Has the racial tension that led to the flight of students been dissipated in any way?

WHITE: Few whites have been converted to the cause of busing. Those who were against busing are still against it. But . . . fatigue sets in, and that starts to move people together. I can see a willingness at least to look at the other side, if not extend a hand of cooperation.

Michener and Mayor White discuss Boston's past and future in the new City Hall that overlooks Faneuil Hall.

MICHENER: Do you see ways to contain racism and diminish it?

WHITE: Bigotry still exists in Boston, as it does in any city. And there have been isolated incidents: There was that stigmatizing Pulitzer Prize picture of a white student lunging with an American flag at a black passerby. . . . A black student was shot in a white section of Boston. . . . But I think the public themselves have slowly come to see violence as a stigma on a city they're proud of living in. This will always be an ethnic city, but there's a fine line between ethnicity and racism.

MICHENER: Mr. Mayor, do you find a lot of property in the city of Boston has been taken off the tax rolls?

WHITE: More than almost any city in the country outside Washington, D.C. It's been taken off by academic institutions, charitable institutions, governmental institutions. The tax base supports the city. Boston derives seventy-five percent of her revenue from property taxes, yet fifty percent of the city is exempt from paying that tax, which puts a staggering burden on the remaining fifty percent.

MICHENER: And a great many of the services that taxes provide are services for the suburbs and for the rest of the state, are they not?

The new Boston City Hall designed by architects Kallman, McKinnell and Knowles. It stands between the new plaza and the older buildings of Faneuil Hall and the harbor front. (Colour Library International, Ltd.)

A replica of the HMS Beaver *at the Boston Tea Party Museum.* (Colour Library International, Ltd.)

The Park Street Church adjacent to the Boston Common at the corner of Park and Tremont streets. (Colour Library International, Ltd.)

The State House, designed by Charles Bullfinch, is the seat of Massachusetts's state government. Located at the top of Beacon Hill, its front facade overlooks Boston Common. (Colour Library International, Ltd.)

WHITE: Yes, they are. And added to that, every single day, commuters swell this city's population. By over five hundred thousand people, to almost double its size. And that puts an enormous pressure on the city.

The Declining Northeast

MICHENER: Mr. Mayor, are you concerned about the relative decline in the importance of the Northeast as an area?

WHITE: The Northeast has traditionally had two resources that have given her a place of prominence, if not dominance. One was academic and intellectual, and Boston has maintained her position in that area. The second has been political: We have always contributed enormously—far in excess of our proportion of the population—to key federal positions in government. Now the rest of the country is beginning to challenge us there.

In addition, we are an area without any natural resources, and we must pay dearly for what we get, in a society whose resources are becoming scarcer and scarcer.

Radcliffe yard in winter. The apple tree, recently planted, is a symbol of the college. The Schlesinger Library, devoted to women's studies, is in the background. (John D. Lach)

The statue of John Harvard presides over Harvard Yard at Harvard College. (Harvard University News Office)

Harry Elkins Widener Memorial Library is the principal building of the university library system. It contains 8.25 million volumes and is the largest university library in the world. Its massive proportions provide a contrast to the slender tower and Doric columns of Memorial Church. These buildings provide the backdrops for the commencement exercises, which take place in the Yard each June. (Harvard University News Office)

An aerial view of Middlebury College, a private college in Middlebury, Vermont. This institution is known especially for its foreign language program and for the Breadloaf Writers' Conference, which is housed on the campus each summer. (News Services, Middlebury College)

Commencement exercises at the Massachusetts Institute of Technology are held in Killian Court. (Calvin Campbell)

Memorial Church in Harvard Yard was built in 1931–1932 and serves as a nondenominational church and center of religious life for Harvard University. It seats about 1,200 people. (Harvard University News Office)

Long view of the Galen Stone Tower at Wellesley College in Wellesley, Massachusetts. (College Information Services, Wellesley College)

MICHENER: I'm told that in the 1980 census our Northeast area has lost a slug of seats in Congress.

WHITE: Yes. There's been a loss in sheer population numbers—and therefore in representation.

MICHENER: I've always been very strong on cities. I love them. I see them as the centers of our operation. Do you think that the nation as a whole has an obligation to keep these centers alive?

WHITE: Not just a moral or a charitable obligation, but a self-centered obligation. Cities are the pulsating points of any civilization. When cities die, so does the civilization. So it's out of self-interest that the American public should be protective, supportive, should nurture American cities. They have not been. There's been a sense that the cities are cancerous areas on the body politic. Immigrants came there, corruption was always there . . . clash and noise and the things Americans didn't like. They turned their backs on the cities. But in fact cities are the pulse, the vitality, the hope of the future for American life.

MICHENER: If one ripped out of American history all the contributions of the men who went to Harvard and M.I.T. and Boston College and Boston University, and women who went to Wellesley and Radcliffe, it would be a pretty impoverished country, wouldn't it?

WHITE: We would be a large Luxembourg. We would be a country that was basically flat, that never engaged in controversy, that never fought forward to break frontiers, that never challenged, that merely sat in the middle of it all. The history of these men and women is the history of America.

Washington Grows into a True Capital

❑ John F. Kennedy once referred to the nation's capital as a "city of northern charm and southern efficiency." Indeed, since long before the Kennedy era, Washington had been notable neither for charm nor efficiency. Tourists found the District of Columbia a splendid, if somewhat mummified, three-dimensional civics lesson. The bureaucrats who labored in thousands of government offices fled every evening to the greener reaches of suburbia. The rich and influential used the city for the contacts they could make and the parties they could attend. And for Washington's increasingly large population of poor blacks, the nation's capital was a decaying hulk, a Potemkin village in which a facade of imposing government buildings imperfectly hid vast stretches of slums.

In that Washington of two decades ago, there was precious little industry and only restricted commerce. Although museums were abundant, a living cultural tradition was sadly lacking: The wealth of

An aerial view of the Pentagon, Washington, D.C. This five-sided building in Arlington, Virginia, across the Potomac from Washington, was completed in 1943 and houses the Department of Defense. It is the largest office building in the world. (U.S. Air Force Photo)

theaters, concert halls, restaurants, and cafes that characterize other great capitals—London, Paris, Moscow—found only a faint echo here. In style and atmosphere, Washington resembled nothing so much as a sleepy southern town writ large.

Well into the middle years of this century, segregation—legally established and rigidly enforced—was commonplace, not only within private and community realms, but within the offices of the federal government itself, making a mockery of American pretensions to equality. Nor was segregation the only problem. In the capital of American democracy, citizens were barred, until recently, from voting in presidential elections. Nor did they have representation in Congress, and for a full century—from 1874 to 1974—they were ruled not by an elected mayor and city council but by a committee of Congress, whose members were far more responsive to their distant constituents than to the 750,000 disenfranchised citizens of the District.

So devoid was Washington of attractive features that for many decades foreign diplomats considered it a "hardship post," and received extra pay to compensate them for cultural deprivation. This disdain for the nation's capital would have come as a distinct shock to the city's founders. None other than George Washington himself selected the exact site for the federal city, and the Paris-born Pierre L'Enfant laid out the capital to be not only the seat of government but a major port and commerical center that would rival New York and Philadelphia. But somehow the design went sadly awry, perhaps because, by the early years of the nineteenth century, these cities already had too great a headstart to be overtaken or even seriously challenged by the upstart on the Potomac.

For Washington, life began to change quite radically in the 1930s. With the Depression and the New Deal, thousands of eager young men and women swarmed into the capital to multiply the responsibilities of government, and, incidentally, to bring an unprecedented liveliness to the District. In search of places to live, many hit upon Georgetown, a once elegant neighborhood gone to seed. Buying up and renovating old buildings there, they restored Georgetown to respectability, an effort that became the model of other neighborhood revivals decades later.

By the late 1940s and early 1950s, however, there was a counter-movement, this one to the suburbs. As whites moved out of the city, blacks—mostly poor, mostly rural, mostly unskilled—moved in. From a city that had been overwhelmingly white and middle class, Washington, in short order, became a town overwhelmingly black and poverty-stricken. Much of this city—intended to be the centerpiece of American democracy—had become a vast ghetto, a tinderbox of social misery

Surrounded by civil rights activists, Dr. Martin Luther King, Jr., delivers his famous "I have a dream" speech to thousands gathered in front of Washington's Lincoln Memorial on August 28, 1963. (Wide World Photos)

The statue of Abraham Lincoln at the Lincoln Memorial, Washington, D.C. (Colour Library International, Ltd.)

A view of the Jefferson Memorial. It is surrounded by Japanese flowering cherry trees planted along the edge of the Tidal Basin. (Colour Library International, Ltd.)

A view of the Capitol dome, Washington, D.C. This beautiful and impressive building, the seat of the United States Congress, houses the Senate and the House of Representatives. It was designed by an amateur architect, William Thornton, and was under construction for 150 years. (Colour Library International, Ltd.)

A front view of the White House, home of the nation's president, in Washington, D.C. (Colour Library International, Ltd.)

A view across the Theodore Roosevelt Bridge of the John F. Kennedy Center for the Performing Arts. (Colour Library International, Ltd.)

needing only a spark to set it off. The explosion came in April 1968, in the aftermath of Martin Luther's King, Jr.'s assassination. For nights on end, great sections of the city burned while police and troops struggled to contain the violence. Washington was left prostrate. In the riot's wake, crime and fear of crime turned the once prosperous downtown into a night-time desert where muggers preyed upon those foolish enough to take an evening stroll.

If someone familiar with the Washington of a decade or two ago were to return to the city today, he would undoubtedly be struck by the extent to which the capital has changed. Each day, as in years past, tourists pour in to gaze at the monuments and visit such magnificent museums such as Air and Space, History and Technology, and the Hirshhorn Gallery. But now, instead of locking themselves into their hotel rooms at night, they join the city's residents and suburbanites for dinner at three-star restaurants or an evening at the theater—perhaps the splendid John F. Kennedy Center for the Performing Arts. On warm evenings, on streets that but a few years ago were deserted after sunset, café patrons sip coffee while they watch the city strolling by. Washington, having known a long night of despair, suddenly pulses with life. Perhaps the change is due, at least in part, to home rule. Perhaps it is the result of an infusion of federal funds that makes life in the District more bearable for the poor, or the establishment of hundreds of new corporate headquarters in the nation's capital. The old, intractable problems—poverty, crime, unemployment—remain. But hope has replaced despair and the possibility exists that this city is on its way to becoming worthy of its title as capital of the world's greatest democracy. ❑

Philadelphia: Racing against Time

The new slogan of the City of Brotherly Love—the one that appears on Chamber of Commerce literature—is "Surprising Philadelphia." It's an oblique way of saying that despite the city's somewhat faded image, there's more here than one might expect. And there is. For perhaps the fourth time in its long history, Philadelphia is showing all the signs of revitalization: new buildings, new bustle, a middle-class influx into renovated neighborhoods (the term "gentrification" was first coined here), new restaurants, and a refurbishing of old historical monuments. And after a decade of confrontation between the city's

IN CONGRESS, JULY 4, 1776.

The unanimous Declaration of the thirteen united States of America,

The Declaration of Independence is probably the most important of all American documents. Although not fully signed until months later, it was adopted on July 4, 1776, by representatives of the thirteen colonies, who met in Philadelphia to announce the separation of those colonies from Great Britain and the formation of the United States. (The National Archives)

Independence Hall is located in Independence Square in Philadelphia. It was built in 1732 to serve as Pennsylvania's Colonial statehouse and was later the scene of the proclamation of the Declaration of Independence and the meeting place of the Continental Congress and the Constitutional Convention. (City of Philadelphia)

The Liberty Bell, housed in the museum of Independence Hall. (City of Philadelphia)

burgeoning black population and its white working class—led by then mayor Frank Rizzo—racial tension is subsiding. For the city's residents, however, the pressing question is whether Philadelphia can outrace the pace of its decay and the pressure of its financial problems and pull itself into prosperity by sheer force of will and hard work.

Philadelphia's heritage is a glorious one. In the eighteenth century it was the American colonies' leading city, the second-largest English-speaking city (after London) in the world. It was here that Quaker founder William Penn hoped to establish a model community where peace, justice, religious liberty, and contentment would reign supreme under the watchful eye of a merciful God. It was Ben Franklin's city, the nursery of American science and art, and the cradle of liberty. Here Franklin and Thomas Jefferson and John Adams met to hammer out the Declaration of Independence in 1776. A decade later, "We the People of the United States" converged upon Philadelphia once more "in order to form a more perfect Union" through the Constitution. From 1790 to 1800 Philadelphia was the nation's capital; and because of the harbor that made it America's principal port, it was the commercial capital as well.

Then Philadelphia began getting short shrift. Washington became the United States capital in 1800. New York took over as the premier port city, commercial center, and finally as cultural fountainhead. Though Philadelphia boomed from time to time—in the great days of the steam engine it was the east coast's primary rail city—it could never come even close to recapturing its preeminence. Philadelphia might compete with New York for the greatest symphony orchestra. It might boast an ancient and exclusive upper class and a string of rich suburban towns. But in almost every other area where a ranking could be made—population, income, number of theaters, restaurants, museums, industrial mix—Philadelphia slipped lower and lower on the comparative scale.

By the mid-1940s, Philadelphia was notable primarily for its slums, its ugly commercial district, the dullness of its social and cultural life, and the rapacity of its corrupt political machine. A decade or so later, however, there was the glimmer of a new day. Under a succession of reform mayors, Philadelphia began to rebuild. The downtown was refurbished; eighteenth-century neighborhoods, gone to seed, blossomed into new elegance; hope and optimism could be felt in the air. Then in the late 1960s came the bust. The city's financial base was proving inadequate to sustain the growth; tensions between blacks and whites were palpable and street crime grew rampant. In fear for the future, the city's electorate turned to the ex-policeman Frank Rizzo to hold down the lid on discontent, and for eight years brotherly love was in very short supply in William Penn's town.

Now Philadelphia booms again. New restaurants, new theaters, new art galleries, new markets, and new commercial buildings all form an exciting backdrop to the quiet of the restored eighteenth- and nineteenth-century neighborhoods. Recently, *New Jersey Magazine*, whose

The Benjamin Franklin Parkway and City Hall Tower, Philadelphia. (Colour Library International, Ltd.)

readers live in the shadows of two great metropolises, compared the amenities of Philadelphia and New York. Surprisingly, "Surprising Philadelphia" held its own. ❑

Levittown Still Offers a Safe Haven from the City's Problems

The desire for a home of one's own, combined with increasingly difficult conditions in our larger cities, sparked a mass migration to the suburbs beginning in the late 1940s. Levittown, Long Island, is one of the largest of the tract developments that sprang up everywhere in those years. As our population grows, and our cities and villages continue to empty into suburbia, we will increasingly be pressed to find the means for communal living in which culture and countryside both may be encouraged and preserved.

❑ Beginning in 1948, developer Abraham Levitt and his sons erected 14,477 houses on 1,200 acres of what had been prime Long Island potato fields. Unlike most postwar housing developments—which were usually nothing more than barren rows of ticky-tacky houses—Levittown was designed with community swimming pools, park-playgrounds, a library, a community center, and small stores set on "village greens." The Levitts used revolutionary building techniques to mass-erect their houses, then put a fireplace, a built-in television set, and a washing machine in each one. To New York City dwellers who were starved for living space and for the mechanical luxuries that had vanished during the war, the Levitt houses were the American dream come true.

Today, the small stores have given way to shopping centers along the highways. And—as they have done since the community's begin-

An aerial view of Levittown, Long Island. This private low-cost housing development was built in 1947 specifically for World War II veterans and their families. (Wide World Photos)

nings—the highways still carry Levittown's working residents to their jobs in the city. ❑

It is now over thirty years since the opening of Levittown. It may be instructive to see what kind of life it has provided for its residents.

EARLY LEVITTOWN RESIDENT: When we were married in 1947, there was a scarcity of apartments. When the Levitt house came on the market, we decided that this would be a great place to live. We could buy a home for fifty-eight dollars a month. We could own a house. We could invest in the future. It was part of the American dream.

I felt very safe here, very protected from all of the things that were happening in the city. Perhaps the one negative thing was that we were too sheltered. The area was too rural and provincial.

There's been a big change in the community in the last thirty years. When we first moved in, most of the men were professional or semiprofessional. Now, the make-up of the community is mostly blue collar: policemen, firemen, construction workers. And there's a new phenomenon now: Young people who were born here are beginning to buy houses from their parents and are moving back in. And there've been a lot of physical changes. The area is very green. It was not green when we moved in.

On our street my husband and our neighbors built our garages and driveways. We'd finish one house, and the women would serve food, and then we'd go on to the next house and build their garage and driveway. A lot of people have done work here together.

RECENT LEVITTOWN ARRIVAL: My likes and dislikes about Levittown are really very basic. In the city, we had drugs, stabbings. . . . Of course, Levittown isn't free from everything, yet it doesn't have a lot of people congested into one place. And it's only about a thirty-five-minute ride into the city where I work.

The first night we were here, at least a dozen families—husbands and wives and children—came over and said "hello," and it really soothed that first night for us and for the kids.

A New Kind of Urban Blight

I do not see how one can logically object to the mushrooming of communities like Levittown, or the services that tend them. We shall soon, probably, be living in one unbroken area reaching from Washington to Boston. We cannot halt this, given the rapid growth of our population, but we can take steps to see that the growth is logical and that it preserves as much natural beauty as possible.

Every year of my life, the land between where I live—Doylestown, Pennsylvania—and Philadelphia has become more jumbled, more abused, and uglier. And along the main highways that take me into New York the deterioration has been appalling, with forty miles of unplanned monstrosities degrading the countryside and cheapening the lives of people who live there or who pass through. Dirt, noise, ugliness, pollution, and lack of care characterize this drift away from natural beauty and into a new kind of urban blight. Our cities reach out to create ever new urban sprawl.

As an example, consider Roosevelt Field on Long Island. Although it hardly looks like it today, this plot of land was the site of one of the most courageous and daring feats of exploration in this century. At 7:52 A.M. on May 20, 1927, a slim young man named Charles Lindbergh sped

Police help guide the Spirit of St. Louis *to the runway at Roosevelt Field on May 20, 1927, just before Charles Lindbergh took off on his historic flight from New York to Paris.* (Wide World Photos)

down the runway here, on his way to making history with the first solo flight across the Atlantic. His flight was a symbol to an entire generation of Americans.

Today, Roosevelt Field has become a more typical symbol of American life: the urban and suburban shopping center. Just as Lindbergh's flight epitomized American values of ingenuity and adventurousness, the shopping center is the symbol of American pragmatism and free-market capitalism.

The shopping center worries me, because it revolves not around culture and community, but around money. Its values are the values of the marketplace. There is either no room or poor lip service for the

Shoppers in the mall at Roosevelt Field.

The Limited, a boutique in Roosevelt Field shopping mall.

library, the theater, the art gallery. A child today could tour a dozen shopping centers throughout the year and not encounter one great idea.

I remember very little of the large stores I visited as a child, but I can recall whole programs at the vaudeville theater, complete baseball games when Babe Ruth or Ty Cobb were playing, and the way pictures hung in the art museums. I wonder what kind of imagination we are going to develop in our children if their big excursion is to the markets of the shopping center.

Although convenient and economical, homogeneous shopping complexes—along with the spread of homogeneous suburbs—are forces that are eroding regionalism in America. We are in danger of losing our sense of place, that blend of culture, tradition, geography, and ethnicity that has made our cities and small towns unique, has made them truly *home*.

A NEW KIND OF CITY

There is an alternative to random suburbanization. Perhaps the prime example of this alternative is Columbia, Maryland, a small city of 52,000 people between Washington, D.C., and Baltimore. Columbia lies near one of the nation's busiest commercial corridors, and not far from some of America's most noxious urban slums. Fifteen years ago, the area was only pasture and swamp; today, there are thousands of homes, some of them representing the most advanced residential architecture in the United States. In fact, Columbia is one of our country's most ambitious urban experiments: a city built from scratch. It's a fascinating idea—the notion of an entire city created at once, with its every detail planned in advance.

Built in the 1960s, Columbia was a response to the deteriorating condition of our urban centers. It is the brainchild of James Rouse, who more recently was one of the major forces behind Boston's Faneuil Hall market. This innovative developer and city planner has had a tremendous impact on the American landscape. In addition to Faneuil Hall market, James Rouse has also been the prime mover behind Harborplace in Baltimore and the projected South Street Seaport in New York City.

❑ Back in the 1960s, Rouse secured the financial backing of the Connecticut General Life Insurance Company, which put up $23 million to buy the land on which Columbia was built. Then, rather than hire a string of builders to put up rows of neat little houses, Rouse formed a committee. "We put together a group of planners," he says, "who knew about people. We started with fourteen drawn from the ranks of architects, doctors, lawyers, ministers, social scientists, psychiatrists . . . and met with them for almost four months." The first question they set themselves to answer was: What had gone wrong in the older cities—why was the quality of life so meager for so many?

Part of the answer, it seemed, was that the traditional city had grown in a haphazard way, with little real planning to meet the basic needs of the city's population. Columbia, the committee decided, would be planned to a human dimension, to meet human needs and provide for human aspirations. In building a city, says Rouse, "You don't have to have the wild scramble of development. You don't have to have houses here, apartments there, schools here, stores there—all developed by accident. It's perfectly reasonable to project growth; and as you project, you can take those pieces and order them in a way that makes sense for people."

What makes sense for people, Columbia's planners determined, is neighborhoods. "We wanted a neighborhood that would focus around an institution that works in the lives of people," says Rouse. "And that institution was the elementary school. So each neighborhood was planned around an elementary school that would take in about twelve hundred people—children and their families. That would be enough population to support a small store, a swimming pool, a park, a playground, and a system of paths. Three of these neighborhoods form a village, with its own center, a middle school, high school, bank, churches, professional offices, and a tennis club." And the villages surround the Columbia city center, with its major services: a symphony hall, a shopping mall, an ice rink, public buildings, theaters, and movie houses. The center fronts on an artificial lake—one of three in the community. There are a symphony orchestra, theater groups, arts and crafts clubs, four institutions of higher learning. In fact, Columbia seems to contain everything needed to maintain an independent community, including jobs. Almost one-third of its working-age citizens make their living within the city's limits, and almost another third work in the immediate vicinity.

Rouse and his committee planned for a mix of housing styles. "It's easy, if you approach it as a matter of plan, to provide for town houses, and apartments, and individual houses—and various kinds of architecture, and various income levels, and various ethnic and racial groups," Rouse says. In Columbia today, well over one-fifth of all residents are nonwhite—although the population remains overwhelmingly upper middle class; the economics of the housing market have made it impossible to build there for the poor. The lack of a true mix of income levels is perhaps Columbia's only failure, and one that was beyond the ability of Rouse and his associates to avoid. But all their other plans have worked very well indeed. It seems abundantly evident that, as Rouse says, "The village system in Columbia has created a mechanism to release the imagination, energy, and gifts of people—and that's the most important result." ❑

Michener Talks to James Rouse

MICHENER: This is a marvelous rural scene, halfway between Washington and Baltimore. You've really got a spot here! How does it feel, Mr. Rouse, to play God—to come here in the middle of an open field and build a city that will ultimately have a hundred thousand people?

ROUSE: Well, I don't think it's so much a matter of playing God as it is a matter of playing rational man. It's rather absurd, really, that we allow our cities to grow by chance—that we assume it's all unmanageable.

MICHENER: I see you have a lot of trees. Did you move them in?

ROUSE: Today there are more trees here, more green leaves, more water surface than there were when we started. We have planted almost half a million trees and bushes as we moved along.

MICHENER: A man who lives here told me that one of the best things

People seated in a shopping mall in Columbia, Maryland.

about Columbia is that you kept the waterways and used them as a kind of highway to divide different districts.

ROUSE: Yes, we did that. During the planning stage we had a group of people going over the land, identifying every gully, every streambed, every significant hill and slope and vista. All this we put on the plan. You could then look at the plan and the land would speak out, telling you what ought to be preserved, what ought to be developed.

MICHENER: When you bought this land, the area right out here was a sort of swampy depression, wasn't it? Why didn't you just bulldoze it over and concrete it in, and have your big buildings there?

ROUSE: Well, normally that's what would have happened. A little stream would have been put in a great concrete vault. That's the American way. But by digging this out instead of filling it in, and by putting the retail center up on the hill, we create a little lake, we get a soft front lawn to downtown, and it costs less money to do it this way than it would have to do it in that gross, bulldozed way that we're accustomed to.

Large-Scale Planning

MICHENER: And on almost any site in America—regardless of where it was—there would be something that would be worth saving, wouldn't there be?

ROUSE: Yes. But the big problem in planning and development in America is that when it's approached on a very small scale, you can't always save what's worth saving. You have to have enough land so that you can afford to "waste" land. Now theoretically, this is wasted land; and if we owned only a hundred acres here, it would be wasted. But owning fourteen thousand acres, it's used to improve the environment, create values, and make a better community for people to live in.

MICHENER: If I wanted to live here, would I come to you to buy a house?

ROUSE: No, you'd go to the exhibit center to find out what it's all about. There you'd learn about Columbia and its diversity of housing. Then you'd go out and visit the developments. There are thirty homebuilders in Columbia who offer every variety of home.

MICHENER: Could you and I, with enough money, duplicate this kind of thing anywhere in America?

ROUSE: Yes, and that's something that isn't adequately understood. But all over America, where cities are growing, there is the choice between rational growth that includes plans for needs twenty years in the future, and our traditional helter-skelter way of doing things. The missing thing in the American city is that no one contemplates what it could be if it worked. The American city can be a far better place than it is if we would only think about it in larger terms, and in terms of people.

MICHENER: It seems to me that Columbia is a happy expression of

James Michener and developer James Rouse in Columbia, Maryland.

capitalist enterprise. A group of thousands of people put their savings in the insurance company, and the insurance company collects all this money and then plows it back into the community. And the thing starts to generate its own energy.

ROUSE: I think you touch on a very important point. Columbia is a very positive expression of the capitalist system. I think that business on the whole, in its preoccupation with the pursuit of profit, fails to understand that it is on the wrong track. Profits should be a residual of a product or a service that people really seek. If business would realize that profit comes second, but serving people well comes first, then profits would grow quite naturally from the service business performs.

THE SOUTH

JEFFERSON AND MONTICELLO

This statue of Thomas Jefferson, architect of Monticello and the University of Virginia, stands in the rotunda of the Jefferson Memorial in Washington, D.C. (Colour Library International, Ltd.)

I think there is no better place to start a trip through the South than at Monticello, the home of the third president of the United States. Many of the early chapters in the story of the American Republic were written here and in the mansions of Thomas Jefferson's neighboring southern contemporaries. From the very beginning, the South has contributed far out of proportion to its size or population to the history of this nation.

I relish the fact that on his tombstone, Jefferson wished to be remembered as—what? The author of the Declaration of Independence, the founder of the University of Virginia, and the author of the early statutes of the Virginia constitution. But nowhere on his own memorial does he mention that he was also president of the United States. I can identify with that ranking of achievements, because in all my own work as a writer, there is nothing I am as proud of as the part I had in revising the Pennsylvania constitution.

Jefferson was a man of contradictions. He was both a philosopher and a pragmatic politician; a scientist and a craftsman; a man who loved liberty, yet kept his slaves when he might have freed them. A gentle, civilized, and moral man, he helped to set in motion one of the most significant revolutions of modern time. Surely his contradictions and his strengths resemble ours today—just as our history, from its beginnings, has deep roots in the same southern soil that nurtured Thomas Jefferson.

Monticello, the "Little Mountain"

❑ Although Jefferson was educated as a lawyer and used his training brilliantly in his political career, he was also an inspired designer, and the first truly American architect. The Virginia state capitol in Richmond was built to his design; many fine old Virginia mansions owe their beauty to Jefferson; and although he designed none of the first buildings that were erected in the new national capital, Washington, he had much to say about the shape and style the city would take. "Architecture is my delight," he wrote, "and putting up and pulling down one of my favorite amusements."

James Michener at Monticello.

No edifice of his is better known to Americans than Monticello, the splendid house set on the summit of a "little mountain" on his Virginia plantation. He began work on Monticello in 1769; the building was not finished for forty years. Using brick made in his own kilns, nails from his forges, and lumber from his forests, and with the labor and craftsmanship of his artisan slaves, Jefferson began his mansion by building a small, one-room cottage "which, like the cobbler's, serves me for parlor, for kitchen and hall . . . for bedchamber and study, too." It was to this "cobbler's cottage" that he brought his bride, in 1772.

The cottage became the South Pavilion of the finished Monticello. In its final form—after a remodeling in which the house was lowered so that it seemed to have only one story, and a dome was added to its central portion—Monticello blended the elegance and proportions of a classical villa with the practical design necessary for the efficient running of a large plantation. It combined, literally under one roof, a central and commodious mansion with storehouses, kitchens, stables, carriage houses, dairies, and barns. The working parts of the building, and the servants' quarters, were positioned in two long wings that stretched behind the central mansion and were connected to it by a series of long porticoes whose roofs served as terraces. From the terraces and from the spacious open lawns, one had a monumental view, a look "down into the workhouse of nature," as Jefferson described it.

The mansion was furnished with pieces brought by Jefferson from France or made on the plantation to his design. The central hall and the parlor behind it housed an impressive collection of paintings and sculpture—the first such collection in America. The floors were of beech and cherry parquet, laid to Jefferson's plan. Clocks, curtains, coffee urns, and candlesticks were all designed by the builder himself. Even the staircases were built to his specifications: They were narrow and steep (Jefferson regarded grand, sweeping stairs as a waste of space), and caused considerable anguish to the ladies of later, hoop-skirted generations.

Monticello was filled with ingenious devices, most of them Jefferson's inventions. A small wooden box unfolded to provide music stands for five musicians. A double-faced clock set in the entrance portico could

A bedroom interior at Thomas Jefferson's Monticello in Charlottesville, Virginia. (Colour Library International, Ltd.)

Interior of Monticello, one of its many sitting rooms. (Colour Library International, Ltd.)

be read from both inside and outside the house. The mansion boasted one of the first water closets in the United States. Various work-savers were built to make the serving of food unobtrusive and efficient: Dumbwaiters connected the dining room with the wine cellars below (Jefferson was an early connoisseur of fine French wines); a shelved, swinging door led to the pantry. And because Jefferson believed that servants were an unnecessary distraction to dinner conversation, he often provided each guest with a small, shelved serving cart on which the entire dinner was laid out at once. The servants kept their distance in the kitchens. ❑

The University of Virginia

❑ Jefferson's final building project, and one he had pondered for many years, was the University of Virginia, built in Charlottesville just a few miles from Monticello. This "hobby of my old age" was to be neither "a barn for a college and log huts for accommodations," nor "one single magnificent building to contain everybody and everything." Instead, Jefferson planned "an academical village . . . [with] a plain small house for the school and lodging of each professor . . . connected by covered ways out of which the rooms of the students should open." The cornerstone of the first house was laid when Jefferson was seventy-three, and the campus was completed only a year before his death in 1826.

The lawn at the University of Virginia, Charlottesville, Thomas Jefferson's original "Academical Village." The beautiful rotunda, designed by Jefferson, dominates the colonnades that house students and faculty.
(University of Virginia)

Jefferson's University of Virginia campus may be ranked, with justification, as the most beautiful in America. It is also the embodiment in brick and stone of many of Jefferson's ideas about education. Professors and students live separately but contiguously; the great rotunda containing the library, the heart of the university, dominates; the parts are woven into unity by colonnades and gardens, hidden walks, and lawns opening out to a view of the mountains.

Among the final additions to the buildings was the clock for the rotunda tower, for which Jefferson drew the specifications in the last year of his life. The clockmaker who built and installed it was greatly impressed. Jefferson's plans, he said, were so accurate that, when he installed the clock in the tower, it fitted precisely—to within one-sixteenth of an inch. ❑

THE CINDERELLA CITY

Atlanta has been called the Cinderella City because of the vast amount of building here in the 1960s. And now, dressed for the ball, Atlanta claims its place as the Southeast's leading urban center. Yet, some ask, is Atlanta really the South at all?

The city's gleaming skyscrapers, busy freeways, and modern rapid-transit system present an urban landscape as futuristic as any in the nation. There seems little evidence of sleepier days of antebellum charm.

From the time that General William Tecumseh Sherman burned Atlanta to the ground in the Civil War, successive generations have rebuilt her. She is a phoenix of the South, rising again and again. Today the city is an international center of industry and commerce. About 440 of the biggest industrial firms among the Fortune 500 have offices here. The world is discovering this city, and through Atlanta the entire American South.

Peachtree Plaza Hotel, part of Atlanta's stunning downtown redevelopment. (Colour Library International, Ltd.)

Just as the railroads once made Atlanta the gateway city for the agricultural South, its newly expanded airport makes it a gateway city for the nation. This airport is already the second busiest in the United States. An old railroad joke has now been adapted for air travel: When a southerner is asked whether he's going to heaven or hell, he answers, "Whichever it is, I know I'll have to change planes in Atlanta."

In the 1980s, Atlanta is known as a model of racial cooperation. The population of the central city is 60 percent black, and its mayor, Maynard Jackson, is considered one of the most prominent elected black officials in the South.

An ironic proof of Atlanta's successful growth is the air pollution that threatens the central city. Most of the air pollution comes from

The burning of the railroad roundhouse in Atlanta, November 14, 1864. Federal soldiers are at work along the track.
(Atlanta Historical Society)

automobile fumes, and new auto registrations have risen twice as fast as the population. The city's hope for dealing with this familiar problem is MARTA—the Metropolitan Atlanta Rapid Transit Authority—a projected fifty-three-mile urban rail line integrated with nearly fifteen hundred miles of bus lines. Experts consider MARTA a model urban transportation system, one that will be copied by many other American cities.

Michener Talks with Two Celebrated Atlantans

Auburn Avenue in Atlanta was for many years the unparalleled center of black social and business activity in the South. Those who lived and worked here called it "Sweet Auburn," for during the bitter years of legal segregation, black enterprise, talent, and wealth were concentrated on this street. Today it is an historic landmark district.

I think that Auburn Avenue's greatest contribution to America is the man who was born here in 1929: Dr. Martin Luther King, Jr. Today, his widow, Coretta Scott King, continues the effort he began.

Andrew Young worked with Dr. King and with many of the great black leaders during the battle for equal civil rights in the 1950s and

1960s. In 1981 he announced his intention to run for mayor of Atlanta. He is a clergyman, a leader in black activism. He's been a congressman and was United States ambassador to the United Nations.

I talked with Coretta Scott King and Andrew Young in Atlanta.

MICHENER: Mrs. King, are conditions better for the blacks in the South now than when you were a girl?

KING: You know, I've seen the change of a whole way of life for two sets of people, one black and one white. These two groups of people have finally learned to sit down at the "table of brotherhood" Martin talked about, and to work out their differences.

YOUNG: Atlanta's changed miraculously. I came here first when I was about twelve years old, and I remember a Ku Klux Klan rally and march right down the center of the black community—a very vicious and public kind of racism. In some ways, that racism brought the black community together, and it also generated a coalition between the community, the banks, and the major businesses back in the middle 1950s.

KING: There's a genuine effort between blacks and whites in the business community to work together. There's no question that there's mutual respect. Even though blacks and whites lived in a segregated system once, they still knew each other very well—much better than

Atlanta, "the Gateway to the South," is known for its busy airport. This view of the city looking north shows part of the lavishly renovated downtown and its network of highways. (Colour Library International, Ltd.)

Memorial to Dr. Martin Luther King, Jr., in Atlanta. (Colour Library International, Ltd.)

blacks and whites in the North. And once the barriers were removed, then they could really be free to be friends.

New Opportunities

MICHENER: How about economic opportunities for southern blacks?

KING: Now, there we have not made enough progress. That's where the battle is to be waged in the 1980s.

YOUNG: The fact that blacks and whites and rich and poor started relating to each other has created a very dynamic social and economic climate. We were way behind, but we're moving rapidly and catching up. On the other hand, labor relations are very bad. Organized labor has never really developed in the South, and wages are still pretty low. I'm hoping, though, that a new style of labor and management relations can emerge in the South—a far more cooperative relationship than the adversary one that exists in the cities in the North.

MICHENER: Are blacks now participating in government here in the South?

YOUNG: In Georgia, we have a sixty percent black turnout for elections. In Alabama, sixty or sixty-five percent. In New York, it's only fifteen, twenty percent. We had to fight for the right to vote. We understood that politics controls the kind of houses we live in, the kind of law enforcement we have, the kind of schooling and hospital care we get. So we *use* the political system.

KING: When I was growing up, there was nobody who voted in my community. We had the grandfather clause in the South: If your grandfather had voted, then you could vote—even if you couldn't read or write. That meant almost every white could vote, but there was no black whose grandfather had ever voted. My father was in his fifties when he voted for the first time. We had to struggle every step of the way. But then, of course, the Voting Rights Act of 1965 moved us forward in terms of black involvement in the political process.

And now you look around the South and you see black mayors in Atlanta, in New Orleans, and in other parts of the country, too—Detroit, Newark. And many black mayors in smaller communities.

MICHENER: Have any of your black acquaintances moved back to the South from the North?

KING: So many blacks who left the South are now coming back!

YOUNG: In my wife's home town, in rural Alabama, many of her classmates went to Detroit to work in the automobile industry, and to escape racism and segregation here. Now they're coming back. They're buying land, running for public office—they're transforming the rural South.

Coretta Scott King, widow of Dr. Martin Luther King, Jr., talks with James Michener in her Atlanta office.

MICHENER: Mr. Young, you were born in Louisiana, I believe.

YOUNG: That's right. We lived in a very poor neighborhood, but it was basically integrated poor. My neighbors were Irish and Italian and Polish as well as black, and the Cajuns from the bayou country. That early integrated upbringing and the tensions that I experienced as a young child being bused from that integrated neighborhood out to a segregated school—that combination of pressures was very helpful in my upbringing.

MICHENER: You were bused as a child?

YOUNG: Well, I couldn't go to the school in the neighborhood because it was segregated. So I had to go by way of public transportation about three or four miles to grammar school.

MICHENER: I live in an area where children have been bused since 1923. It's always been done, and I never heard a single comment about it.

YOUNG: We used to think of busing as progress because, before buses, people had to walk to school. So busing in the early days was really a great blessing to people who had to walk three or four miles to school.

Atlanta citizens on their way to an Elks convention. (Colour Library International, Ltd.)

Andrew Young, former United States ambassador to the United Nations, has announced his intention to run for mayor of Atlanta. Here he chats with James Michener. A mural photograph of Dr. King is in the background.

And even where busing has been used to achieve racial balance in the South, I think we've had far fewer difficulties than you've had in northern cities. In fact, in the state of Georgia now, practically every school has essentially the same population ratio as the black/white ratio in the county. That's particularly true in the small towns in Georgia and in Alabama, Mississippi, and Louisiana. The cities have a little more difficulty.

I think the animosity toward busing comes essentially from second- and third-generation Americans in your northern cities who basically live in their own ghettos. . . . And of course, the people who have just gotten out of the city to the suburbs resent coming back into the city for an education. But they overlook the fact that their children are going to have to operate in a world made up predominantly of colored peoples. And it's almost impossible to get an education, no matter how much you know, if you have not learned to live and work with people who are different.

Maynard Jackson, mayor of Atlanta.

MICHENER: Was segregation a major factor in your life?

YOUNG: Sure. Until I was thirty years old, at least. In fact this city did not desegregate public accommodations until 1964, and so all of my children except the youngest had a taste of it.

Northern Prejudice

MICHENER: How about housing—have you ever experienced segregation in that area?

YOUNG: When I first moved to New York in 1957, even though I was an employee of the National Council of Churches, it took me about four months to get a mortgage. Now, there was nothing in the law that said I couldn't live in such and such a neighborhood. But no bank would lend me money to live in some neighborhoods. They just kept stringing it out, and I kept going back to the bank. . . . Finally a friend who was white—who was my boss and was also a southerner—went down with me and made a big fuss. In fact, he was trying to help me find a home in his neighborhood.

By contrast, when we came back to Georgia a few years later, we got a mortgage in four days.

MICHENER: When I first met you, you were occupying the most expensive suite at the Waldorf Towers, which is the most expensive hotel in New York. You were ambassador to the United Nations then, you had a cadre of ten or fifteen. How did that jump impress you?

YOUNG: I enjoyed it. But in fact, even in the Waldorf as U.S. ambassador to the United Nations, it was not unusual to have somebody give me their claim check to park their car for them. And it reminded me that mine was a special case.

MICHENER: How do you feel about the special-case syndrome: the notion that blacks have no problems because Willie Mays gets a great

Howard University in Washington, D.C., is the most prestigious black institution of higher learning. (Howard University, courtesy of Marvin Jones)

salary or Marian Anderson is a great singer or Bill Russell can be the coach of a great basketball team?

YOUNG: People have to understand that these rare cases don't constitute a really free society, and for every one of these, there are thousands who are just as talented, but are in a sense discriminated against by the social order. I've always felt that it was really an accident of birth, not any particular ability of mine, that made it possible for me to have certain benefits that others didn't have.

MICHENER: You went to Howard, a great black university. Could you have accomplished what you have without that solid education?

YOUNG: I doubt it. But I think I had an education from my parents even before I went to college. One of the best investments my parents made, when I was about five or six years old, was a children's encyclopedia. It rains a lot in New Orleans . . . and even though I was always bored in school, and very very restless, I would read the encyclopedia. I read a lot, but what I wanted to read; if I was interested in something, that's what I wanted to study, and if the curriculum called for something else, I wasn't interested in it then. The only regret I have is that I wasn't ready to learn French when they were ready to teach me. And I really wish I was fluent in French now.

Howard University

MICHENER: Now, when you went to Howard, in Washington, D.C., you must have met a lot of real bright black students from the northern cities, and you were from a southern town. Were you at any disadvantage?

YOUNG: Not really. I think we were at a disadvantage against the African and Jewish students. In a sense, the African students who came were the cream of the crop from their countries. They had much better backgrounds. Some of the Jewish students were exceptional students to start with.

MICHENER: Howard was thought of as a black university, wasn't it?

YOUNG: It was predominantly black, but there was always a variety of Asian, African, and European students, and a few American whites. People who had special interests in special fields came there. There was a very good anthropology department, for instance. Howard Law School was the pioneer in civil rights law.

MICHENER: How did you become a minister?

YOUNG: Well . . . I think Howard is the headquarters of the black middle class in many respects. And in the 1940s and 1950s, it was a part of the black bourgeoisie boom. Its values were superficial and very materialistic, and I rebelled against it—the shallowness of people's goals and aspirations. It just seemed to me that life had to be more than making money and accumulating degrees and public acclaim. And I went into the ministry thinking that I was going to go to Africa as a missionary.

MICHENER: Mr. Young, you've been a clergyman in the South, a southern congressman, one of the South's most distinguished citizens. How do you see your part of the country now?

YOUNG: I'm very proud of the South. I see it as *the* progressive part of the nation, and I think we're probably ten or twenty years ahead of the rest of the country. We are coping with the two problems that the North is still not willing to admit: race and poverty. And we are doing it very well.

MICHENER: You said once that when you were young you were afraid to stop your car in rural Georgia to get gasoline. . . . Could you drive across Georgia now?

YOUNG: Oh, I could *walk* across Georgia! In fact, my oldest daughter, who is now practicing law, drives alone all over Georgia.

MICHENER: Does this mean that racism in the South is dead?

YOUNG: It's almost dead. There's some of the old diehard population still left, but the overwhelming feeling is goodwill.

THE NEW SOUTH—AT LAST!

There is no way to discuss the South—either historically or in terms of contemporary life—without addressing the problem of race. To attempt to do so would be to ignore the single thread that bound a great and gloriously diverse region to a concept more ideological than geographical. The overwhelming impact of race in the South warped all social, economic, and political life from the day slavery was introduced in the seventeenth century until very recent times. The continuing attempt to reach a solution to that race problem, the victory of the forces of equality and democracy, has helped set the region off on a spurt of economic growth and social well-being that observers would have thought impossible a decade or two ago.

Georgia Senator Julian Bond was elected to the Georgia House of Representatives in 1965 but was barred because of his statements on Vietnam. In 1966 the U.S. Supreme Court ruled that his rights had been violated and he was reinstated to his seat in that year. He has served in the Georgia Senate since 1975. Since his student days, Bond has been especially active in the area of civil rights.

Back in the 1880s, a dynamic young Atlanta editor named Henry Grady, speaking to a group of northern businessmen, proclaimed the birth of a New South—a region purged of rebellion and civil war, a land eager to industrialize and put aside old shibboleths that had made it, even in antebellum days, something of an American backwater. This New South, said Grady, looked to her sister regions to help her join the mainstream of American life. Yet even as Grady asserted his belief in a southern renaissance, his words left no doubt that, in one sense at least, the New South would draw inspiration from the Old.

Statue of Henry W. Grady in Atlanta. (Colour Library International, Ltd.)

If the Civil War lifted the burden of slavery from the backs of black men and women, the whites of the South saw to it that the Negro was not really free. Perhaps to salve the consciences of his listeners, Grady, while calling upon them to turn their backs on the problem of race in his region, assured them that the welfare of blacks could safely be left to the "fullest protection of our laws and the friendship of our people." Both Grady and his audience perhaps knew that this was a misrepresentation.

It was, after all, common knowledge that throughout the post-Reconstruction South, blacks were being systematically denied the civil rights that had seemingly been guaranteed them by the thirteenth, fourteenth, and fifteenth amendments to the U.S. Constitution. The right to a decent education, the right to compete freely for employment,

Restored slave house at Boone Hall in Charleston, South Carolina. (Colour Library International, Ltd.)

the right to mingle with whites in public places, the right to equal treatment in the courts, and most significant, the right to vote—these were being taken away from the blacks. From the ashes of slavery, a new social system was taking shape, one that for almost a century would condemn the southern black to peonage and second-class citizenship.

The New South Henry Grady so proudly proclaimed would be stillborn. So too would all of the other New Souths heralded by each succeeding generation of southern whites. Northern capital might flow southward; new industries might be built, old ones expanded. Prosperity might come to this town or that, but as long as this vast section of the nation remained determined to keep blacks in a legally inferior position, there could be no southern renaissance.

"King Cotton," the dominant economic factor in the South for over a century. (Colour Library International, Ltd.)

In the South, racial questions impinged upon every issue involving social change. As recently as the 1950s, and even in the 1960s, the owner of a southern factory—often a northern absentee owner—had only to raise the issue of race mixing in the workplace to prevent the unionization of his factory. Reformers seeking to improve their states' educational or health services could, more often than not, be defeated on the grounds that their proposed changes would benefit blacks as well as whites. Segregationist politicians running for reelection had only to invoke the specter of black equality to maintain their positions in office.

Consider, for example, the case of George Corley Wallace, Jr. In 1958, already an Alabama politician of note, he ran for the governorship for the first time. His platform was basically a progressive one, and on matters of race he showed himself to be a moderate. Wallace lost that year, and remarked to friends that he had been "outsegged." He meant that his opposition had waged a campaign that ignored the real issues, but concentrated on the maintenance of white supremacy. Four years later, when Wallace ran once more, his platform was that of a strict segregationist. As governor, Wallace made himself a symbol of white resistance to integration, but he came a little too late to the cause. In 1963, even as he took his famous stand "in the schoolhouse door" to prevent the integration of the University of Alabama, he knew he was acting out a charade. Though he hurled verbal defiance at a deputy attorney general of the United States, he stepped aside on cue and permitted the registration of two black students.

The time had come when white defiance of the law was no longer effective. By the mid-1960s, the courts, the federal government, and, most important of all, a new generation of black men and women had united on the proposition that in America there was no place for second-class citizenship. There would be political battles, there would be riots, fire bombings, and lynchings, but this time there would be no turning back. A decade later, the forces of segregation were in disarray; by the end of the 1970s, the whole carefully constructed edifice of white supremacy and black inferiority came tumbling down. As civil rights

Alabama State Capitol in Montgomery, Alabama. The office of governor was occupied by George Corley Wallace, Jr., from 1963 to 1967 and 1971 to 1979.
(Colour Library International, Ltd.)

leaders Andrew Young and Coretta Scott King testify, there is a New South at last. More than a hundred years after the Civil War, the South has finally rejoined the Union. ❑

THE SOUTH PRESERVES ITS HERITAGE: JONESBORO, TENNESSEE

How many people in America have the option of returning to the style of an earlier day? In much of America, we erase the past with each rebuilding.

Various experts inform us that by the year 2000 the South will be the fastest-growing region in the country, and that even now the region is experiencing a second Reconstruction, an overturning of economic and racial traditions, a transition from a rural to an urban society. When the change is complete, will we feel a pang for the past?

And yet, as the South moves ever more quickly toward an industrialized future, southerners continue to honor and preserve those traditions that are particularly their own. The great southern writer Eudora Welty describes her country kinsmen as born reciters, great memory retainers, and great talkers—above all, great talkers. Storytelling is an art that has always been much loved in the South. And, as a storyteller myself, I love the southern verbal tradition. The South has a special atmosphere, one where language is as vital an element as air, and where the fine art of conversation comes as naturally as breathing.

❑ In Jonesboro, Tennessee, amid hoe-downs and general good times, storytellers gather from all over the country for an annual three-day festival. Every October since 1972, the small community in the eastern Tennessee mountains becomes a huge theater. On the courthouse steps, on counter stools at the local luncheonette, at the "swapping ground"—a circle of hay bales in the park—storytellers from across the nation come to practice and preserve their craft, and pass it on to eager audiences. The festival is sponsored by a Jonesboro institution, the National Association for the Preservation and Perpetuation of Storytelling (NAPPS). NAPPS works year round, collecting and recording the stories that come its way and maintaining story archives for researchers, writers, teachers, and librarians. But the high point of the year are those three days in the splendid Appalachian fall, when hundreds gather to hear the old stories told anew, and to experience once again the magic that a good storyteller creates between his listeners and himself.

Back in the early 1900s, collectors of folk literature discovered a treasure trapped in the isolated mountain hollows of the southern Appalachians. To their astonishment, they found an indigenous culture that seemed almost identical with that of the early pioneers. Folklorists traveled to the mountains, collecting songs that had long vanished from America and the British Isles but were still sung in the Appalachians by the descendants of the original Scottish-Irish settlers. Linguists discovered that the mountain people spoke an English that seemed virtually untainted by the language changes that had occurred in every other part of the nation. Linguists and folklorists and the occasional writer or photographer made the difficult journey up into the mountains; few others did. For all practical purposes, the region did not exist for most Americans.

The high, rugged ridges of the southern Appalachians begin in northernmost Florida, and rear in an unbroken chain through Tennessee, Kentucky, North and South Carolina, Virginia, and West Virginia. Beginning in the late 1700s, hardy backwoodsmen, hunters, and farmers struggled up into these mountain fastnesses from the populated areas that bordered them. They found a high country that was incredibly rich in game and timber. They cleared garden patches, built log huts, and settled in, maintaining a self-sufficient frontier economy for well over a century. They logged their lands, raised sheep and cattle, fished and hunted, and grew what could most profitably be cultivated in the stony soil—beans and corn. The corn fed their families and their cattle; what was left was distilled into their only cash crop, whiskey.

Few outsiders penetrated into the maze of mountains. And of those who did, most came for a quick profit. By the end of the nineteenth century, timber companies were busy hauling away much of the stupendous Appalachian forest, and coal companies had begun mining the mountains of Kentucky, Virginia, and West Virginia. It was primarily coal that brought work and money into Appalachia and replaced the old self-sufficiency with wages. Appalachian farmers by the thousands sold the rights to the minerals that lay under their fields. Fifty cents an acre was the going price, and the deeds the farmers signed—often with an *X*—granted the coal operators access to the ore by any means necessary. Wherever a mine was hewed out of a mountain, the mountain men put up their battered plows and hunting rifles, and went to work underground.

In the early days of coal mining, there was prosperity of a sort, punctuated though it was by frequent mine disasters and occasional bloody labor conflicts. But eventually oil began to replace coal as America's favorite fuel. And to mine what coal was needed, machines gradually took over from man-labor, and strip mining made many of the underground mines obsolete. Huge veins of coal lay near the surface, and all that was needed to get at them was a bulldozer to tear off the earth layer and a giant auger to pry the coal loose. By the 1960s, southern Appalachia had little but unemployment and, where strip mining was practiced, a devastated countryside.

In 1965, as his first act in the making of the Great Society, President Lyndon Johnson created the Appalachian Regional Commission, a developmental organization that helped to provide the money to build roads; improve schools; and fund hospitals, libraries, nursing homes. The ARC was a small step in the right direction, but most of its programs never reached far enough into the hollows to help the truly isolated and most poverty-stricken. The energy crisis that began in 1973 encouraged the reopening of some of the coal mines—although it also increased the threat of strip mining with its disastrous effect on the land.

Other factors have also combined to allay the region's economic misfortunes: There is more money now, in the form of higher social security benefits, food stamps, and compensation payments to miners with black lung disease. There are more tourists, and the building and staffing of tourist facilities create jobs. There is employment in the textile mills and clothing and furniture factories whose numbers are slowly increasing. Improved economic conditions have brought an end to the

LEFT: *The audience gathers in a tent in Jonesboro, Tennessee, to listen to the storytellers' festival.*
BELOW: *Storytellers at the Jonesboro Festival practice their art all around the town.*

mass migration out of the mountains that began in the 1940s. Hill people have come back from Chicago, Cincinnati, Dayton, and all the other cities—most of them in the Midwest—where thousands of Appalachian folk once lived in "hillbilly ghettos."

Perhaps the isolation of southern Appalachia has at last been ended. Perhaps the popularity of such folk fairs as the Jonesboro storytelling festival, and the many other similar events that occur regularly throughout the mountains, is an indication that the people of southern Appalachia recognize the threat to the culture they created in isolation, and are doing their best to preserve it.

What is certain, however, is that the region will continue to experience conflict. Statistics for an eighty-county region in the heart of southern Appalachia show that over half the total land area is held by absentee owners: 43 percent is in private hands, primarily timber, coal, and oil companies; 8 percent is owned by the federal government. The federal lands produce no tax revenues for the region; the company-held lands yield practically none. Nowhere else in the United States—and in very few other countries in the world—does such a pattern of land ownership exist. And it threatens to return the mountain people to the status they had until very recently: bone poor in a rural paradise, paupers in one of the richest regions of the United States. ❑

RESTORING ITS PAST, SAVANNAH BRINGS NEW LIFE TO THE PRESENT

Statue of James Oglethorpe, 1696–1785, founder of the American colony of Georgia and of the city of Savannah.

❑ To the residents of the oldest Georgian city, Savannah is the real Georgia. Everywhere one sees the genius of the city's founder, James Oglethorpe. His 1733 design for the town—the southern equivalent of a series of New England village greens—shows extraordinary respect for open space. Oglethorpe planned Savannah in units, each unit being a cluster of houses surrounding a large public square. Two and a half centuries later, the squares keep the city a pleasure for walkers. Today the old city is one of the loveliest in the South.

During the 1950s, however, the center of Savannah was in serious decline. Only recently has it been restored to its former beauty. The central area, covering over two square miles, is now the largest urban landmark district in the United States.

The restoration has accomplished far more than a simple rebuilding of some fine old houses. Savannah's restoration has created a new spirit in the town. It has set off a chain of events that has reversed the city's downhill economic progress by attracting new residents and businesses and thousands of appreciative tourists. It has eased the plight of the city's slum dwellers and helped to smooth the path of school desegregation.

James Oglethorpe was a man of exceptional practical wisdom. With great foresight, he laid out the city on the high bank of a river, not far from its mouth on the Atlantic. Savannah thus had easy access to the

sea, and quickly grew into a great port and eventually a commercial and cultural center for the cotton-plantation economy of the South. For decades the city basked in a prosperity based almost exclusively on cotton; but when cotton prices suddenly fell at the end of the nineteenth century, Savannah began a decline that it seemed nothing could arrest.

A stunning fountain in Forsyth Park, one of Savannah's many lovely squares. (Colour Library International, Ltd.)

The abundance of water and of wood pulp from the region's forests attracted a huge paper mill in the 1930s. Later a chemical factory established itself in the city. But Savannah paid a price for the jobs and business these industries provided: the pollution of the Savannah River and the near devastation of the oyster and shrimp beds at its mouth.

For many years wealthy Savannah residents had been leaving the great mansions in the old city center for more modern homes outside the city. But the slow exodus became a flood after World War II. Building after building was left tenantless and empty in the old district, and poor blacks began to supplant middle-class whites in the gingerbread houses of the Victorian District, a region near the old city that had been

A gazebo, tribute to Savannah's sense of beauty and leisure.

LEFT: *The Davenport House.* (Colour Library International, Ltd.)

RIGHT: *The Owen Thomas House, one example of the many beautiful mansions still standing in Savannah.* (Colour Library International, Ltd.)

Savannah's first suburb. The new suburbs thrived, however: Between 1960 and 1970, the city's population shrank by 21 percent (to 118,000), but suburban Chatham County experienced an explosive 78 percent growth.

In one respect, Savannah's history had been a fortunate one. It was spared the devastation the Civil War brought to other southern cities. Later its declining fortunes did not allow it to tear down and rebuild its center. After World War II, the city spurned federal offers of urban renewal. Thus, by the 1960s, old brick and stone buildings that would long have vanished if Savannah had followed the path of other cities still stood. They were ruined hulks, but they were restorable. And when the city realized that it was trading irreplaceable architecture for parking lots and fast-food restaurants, it came to life. First, the Historic Savannah Foundation began to catalog the remaining old buildings in the city's center. Then Savannah Landmarks, another civic group, began restoring the slums in the Victorian District—and doing it without displacing its black residents. Unskilled workers learned valuable trades as apprentices on restoration jobs. The city's schoolchildren studied and began to take pride in their city's architecture. The city's parents, black and white together, began to work to improve their schools.

Certainly, Savannah's restoration movement cannot solve all the city's problems. But it has brought a new spirit and determination to what was, not too many years ago, a southern backwater. Savannah is now a place tourists make sure to visit, a city where many now choose to live. ❑

Two Savannah Restorers Speak

John Hayes, director of the Historic Savannah Foundation, and Lee Adler, chairman of Savannah Landmarks, talked about the city's rebirth:

HAYES: When you look at Savannah today, it's important to realize that, by the 1950s, it had become a gutted, largely abandoned ruin—a slum, by all accounts. Many of the old buildings had derelicts living in them; they were completely open to the weather. Our headquarters building, for instance, had lost its roof and all of its floors, and its basement was full of water.

ADLER: Fifty-eight years ago, when my mother married, she could have bought the Davenport House for two thousand dollars. She didn't—she went out and built a house. People just left downtown Savannah. All people: black, white, everybody wanted to get out. And in those days, government money—FHA money—was only for the suburbs. They wouldn't give money for inner cities. And Savannah's inner city started to die. People did care, though. They refused to let the wonderful squares be cut through for traffic.

My mother and six other women founded the Historic Savannah Foundation in 1955. It's been a tremendous thing for downtown Savannah. It's given the city a real tax base. I reckon that almost two hundred million dollars in private money has been put into downtown. The city government has built things like the beautiful plaza that lines our riverfront. And all that has generated a great pride in Savannah. Our tourist business in 1957 was less than half a million dollars. Today it's eighty million a year, and still growing.

HAYES: There was no consensus, no consciousness of the need for preservation until the tearing down of the old City Market in 1954 to build yet another parking lot. That was the catalyst. . . . The Historic Savannah Foundation . . . has grown over the last twenty-five years. We've saved over a thousand buildings. More than one hundred fifty million dollars in restoration money—most of it from private sources—has been spent in making the downtown community whole again.

How does the Foundation operate? We catalog and identify buildings that have architectural significance. We work with a broad cross section of the community to ensure that the preservation movement serves all the groups in the city. We offer free design consulting services to architects, contractors, property owners, and businessmen to ensure a high standard of restoration. And we have a revolving fund, which has helped to save entire neighborhoods as well as single buildings.

Examples of grillwork on Savannah gates and fences.

LEFT: *Lee Adler, chairman of Savannah Landmarks.*

RIGHT: *John Hayes, director of the Historic Savannah Foundation.*

The revolving fund is used to buy interest in a property that's threatened with demolition or that is neglected. We don't put a large amount of money into a single building, but instead hold the property until we can find a buyer who will move into the building and restore it himself. So instead of using two hundred thousand dollars to buy or restore one building, we use that money to buy an interest in forty buildings. And because of our commitment to an area where we've bought an interest, people move in and restore other houses, and the area is stabilized.

ADLER: The restoration movement was so successful that, after it had worked in the historic district, it began to look at what we call the Victorian District, just on the edge of the old city. The houses there are wooden, built on wonderful tree-shaded streets. The people who live in them are mostly black, and eighty percent of them rent. They pay anywhere from sixty to one hundred twenty dollars a month rent, and they don't get much because it's terrible housing.

Now in the central, historic district, we were working mostly with empty houses, because so many people had moved out. But if the Victorian District was going to be restored and become a desirable place to live, there would be a massive displacement problem—a whole group of poor people would be forced to move. And we weren't going to let that happen.

So Historic Savannah and the NAACP and some other groups formed the Savannah Landmark Rehabilitation Project, a nonprofit housing corporation. Our purpose was first to buy out the slumlords, and then restore about half the houses in the district. We used federal loans for the restorations; they'll be paid back under the federal housing subsidy program. We have private bank financing, too.

Savannah Landmark has a board of thirty who are from all walks of life—they're bankers, ministers, social workers, rich and poor, black and

LEFT: *Work in progress on restoration of residential facades.*

RIGHT: *Restoring an old Savannah house.*

Flag in the doorway of a classic Savannah house.

white, shaven and unshaven. . . . It's the most interesting board in Savannah. And they're dedicated to preventing the displacement of the poor—people who care about where they live, care about their neighborhood, don't want to be uprooted.

Urban Advantages

HAYES: The back-to-the-cities movement in America: It's grown out of the energy crisis, the high cost of new construction, the blandness of suburbia. A city has an extraordinary dynamic—it's a place where a diversity of people work as well as live and find recreation, where they can have a fruitful and wholesome life-style. Because our parents and grandparents escaped the decline of the cities by moving into suburbia, for the last several decades many of us haven't experienced the life-style of a city. But as we get further into the next decade, I feel certain that Savannah will mark the way for other urban centers. The programs that have begun here are test cases—models for other communities. We know of scores of cities who've adapted what we've done here for their own communities.

ADLER: I live in downtown Savannah. I walk to work, I don't have to have a car to get around. I'm getting to know our city, our squares, our architecture. I think the centers of cities all over this country are going to be reused and redeveloped in the way we've done it in Savannah. It's not tearing down. It's using a resource, a valuable resource. It's renewing that resource in the cheapest way possible.

HAYES: It's very important to recognize that architectural quality matters. Living and growing up with buildings of architectural interest raises the quality of perception, lifts the human potential. And urban centers throughout this country share this architectural wealth.

ARKANSAS: IN MANY WAYS, IT'S THE SOUTH IN MICROCOSM

Remember the Arkansas Traveler? Lost in a hilly wilderness, he asked a "pore squatter," "Sir, will you tell me where this road goes to?" And the squatter replied (as he always did), "It's never gone nowhar since I've lived here." In Arkansas, roads never went "nowhar." Until recently, people didn't go nowhar, neither, except—for those who managed the escape—out of the state. Arkansas seemed to exist in suspended animation; if there was movement at all, it was slowly downhill.

Today, although the state still ranks near the bottom by most economic measurements, Arkansas has experienced economic and social improvement on a scale that would have seemed impossible twenty years ago. Industry is moving in. Cities like the capital, Little Rock, gleam with newness and polish. Agriculture is flourishing, and many Arkansas products are exported far beyond continental limits. Tourists visit by the thousands. Roads that until recently went nowhere are now paved, and carry the commerce of a thriving region. Like its sister states in the South, Arkansas is prospering as it never has before.

The state of Arkansas, directly north of Louisiana and bordered on the east by the Mississippi River, can be divided roughly into two distinct regions. To the east, rising up from the river, is the Arkansas prairie, mile after mile of open fields. This is the old plantation country, and even today, farms of ten thousand acres and more exist. In the

University Hall, known to students and faculty as "Old Main," at the University of Arkansas, Fayetteville. The university was founded in 1872 as a result of the Morrill or Land-Grant Act. (Carl P. Hitt)

The Mullins Library, named for David W. Mullins, a former University of Arkansas president. Between 1970 and 1980, the physical plant of the university has doubled in size. (University of Arkansas News Service)

nineteenth century, cotton was grown here, and slave labor was the norm. During the Civil War, eastern Arkansas was passionately secessionist. To the west and north lies the hill country: the Oachita mountains and the rugged Ozark plateau. It was probably in this region that the hapless Arkansas traveler met his squatter. Here the hills are too steep and the soil too rocky for large-scale farming, and the hardscrabble population lived for decades in an isolation that was as profound as that of Appalachia to the east. There were few slaves here, and during the Civil War the sympathies of the region lay largely with the Union.

Despite the Unionist convictions of half the state, all of Arkansas felt the bitter aftermath of the Civil War. The big cotton plantations that had been the source of most of the state's prosperity were broken up. Thousands of poor farmers became sharecroppers, and grew even poorer. In the hill country, although the coming of the railroads opened the way for timbering and mining, poverty remained the common condition of life.

The Great Depression laid economically weak Arkansas flat. The 1930s saw the beginnings of the great migration out of Arkansas, as thousands of "Arkies," in wired-together jalopies, joined their brothers-in-flight, the equally hard-pressed "Okies," on the highway to the golden groves of California. The outmigration continued through the 1940s and 1950s. Between 1950 and 1960 alone, Arkansas lost almost one-quarter of its population. By now, thousands of those leaving the state were blacks, journeying to what had to be a better life in the ghettos of the big northern cities.

The Governor's Mansion, Little Rock, Arkansas.

For most Americans, Arkansas was hillbilly country. In 1957 the hillbilly image took on a darker dimension. In that year, Arkansas's governor, Orval Faubus, grabbed national news coverage when he blocked the integration of Little Rock's Central High School. Federal troops were sent into the city to escort black children into the school through screaming mobs of whites. Faubus profited by the fracas: Despite a long tradition that limited Arkansas governors to only two two-year terms, Faubus was reelected four times. He served until 1966.

In light of Arkansas's history and its image as a hard core in the unyielding Democratic politics of the Solid South, what happened in 1966 can only be described as unprecedented. In 1966, Arkansas voters elected as governor a man who was not only a Republican but who possessed vast wealth and came from the alien East (New York City). His name was Winthrop Rockefeller, grandson of John D. Rockefeller.

Rockefeller came to Arkansas in 1953, bought an immense spread of acreage not far from Little Rock, and began to develop a flourishing ranching and farming enterprise. He lavished money on the estate and on various Arkansas philanthropies: health clinics, schools and scholarships, museums. To help raise money for a new art center in Little Rock, he stumped the state. After a while, Arkansans began to warm up to the stranger in their midst.

Governor Faubus asked Rockefeller to help recruit industry into the state, and the expatriate New Yorker was hugely successful. By 1964, largely through Rockefeller's efforts, over six hundred new factories had located themselves in Arkansas, spinning off thousands of new jobs and pushing per capita income up by over 50 percent. This was a remarkable rise, although not quite as stupendous as it seems: Arkansas had long competed with Mississippi for honors as the poorest state in the nation. In 1950, Mississippi had a per capita income that was just about half of the national figure, and it has never subsequently ceded to Arkansas which, in 1979, ranked forty-ninth.

The Faubus-induced Little Rock school incident had weakened business enthusiasm for the state. Industrialists hesitated about locating plants in an area that was liable to riot and mass unrest. Rockefeller, committed to Arkansas, decided to modernize the state's politics just as he had succeeded in beginning the modernization of its economy. Using massive infusions of money and the power of his by now well-trusted name, he resuscitated the Republican party, which had been moribund for decades. In 1964, he ran against Faubus for the governorship, and lost. In 1966, he ran again, and won.

During his four years as governor, Rockefeller wrought wonders in the state. He continued his push for industry, persuading small plants to locate in rural areas where the need for jobs was greatest. Committed to civil rights, he appointed numbers of blacks to responsible and visible positions in the state government, on local draft boards, and even as state troopers—positions where their presence would once have been unthinkable. Arkansas's governmental machinery was in dire need of overhauling, and Rockefeller tended to it, opening the process for a rewriting of the state's antiquated constitution. Under his leadership Arkansas passed its first effective minimum wage law and its first freedom of information law, which required that the public have free access to the meetings of government bodies. Teachers' salaries were raised; desperately needed prison reforms were undertaken. A climate of change replaced the old somnolent atmosphere. Gradually the number of Arkansans fleeing the state diminished, and, at a certain point, the population figures reversed: Now, not only were the native-born staying but non-Arkansans were moving in, attracted by the climate, the undeniable beauty of the state, and the conviction that Arkansas might be a good place in which to spend the future.

In 1968 Rockefeller was reelected for a second term, defeating a Faubus protégé who ran as an outright segregationist. In 1970, however, he lost a try at a third term to Dale Bumpers, a young Democratic unknown who was quite open about his views on race: Like Rockefeller he thought segregation was "immoral."

In 1974 Bumpers defeated the venerable Senator J. William Fulbright and went to Washington, where he still serves. The governorship was won by Democratic Congressman David Pryor, who in 1978 himself won the Senate seat long held by John McClellan. ❑

Michener Talks with Bill Clinton

❑ The gubernatorial election of 1978 swept into office the youngest governor in the nation, thirty-two-year-old Bill Clinton. A Rhodes Scholar and a graduate of Yale Law School, Clinton was a law professor at the University of Arkansas when he won his first public position, as state attorney general, in 1976. In that office, he achieved high marks as a liberal: He fought to prevent utility rate increases, allowed competitive advertising by liquor stores and opticians, prevented the institution of the twenty-five-cent phone call. In 1978, he won almost two-thirds of

Bill Clinton, former governor of Arkansas. Clinton was elected in 1976 at the age of thirty-two to become the youngest governor in the United States. He lost to a Republican in 1980.

the vote. In his 1980 bid for reelection, however, he was a victim of the great Reagan landslide, losing to Republican Frank White. ❑

To find out more about the South in transition, I spoke with the former governor of Arkansas, Bill Clinton. In his inaugural address, Clinton had said that he hoped to make Arkansas one of the best places in America to live. I wanted to find out how well he had succeeded. And I hoped to discover the answers to such essential questions as how the New South, with its new-found prosperity based on an unprecedented industrial influx, hopes to preserve its southern values; whether the labor force, lacking a union tradition, can be protected from exploitation and can be made wage-competitive with the rest of the country; whether a still heavily agricultural state can protect its environment and its land from some of the negative effects of rapid industrialization; how Arkansas's efforts to attract multinational corporations have affected the state's economy.

I wanted to know more about the race issue in Arkansas: whether the school system is successfully integrated; and how the state's cities fare, with disproportionate black populations in their centers and disproportionate white populations in their suburbs.

I hoped to find out what kind of place the New South is to live in—for the rich and the poor, for both black and white.

My interview with Bill Clinton was conducted before he left the governor's office.

MICHENER: Governor Clinton, I have always thought of Arkansas as a very conservative, backward state, and yet you sent J. William Fulbright, one of the great liberal senators of recent times, back to the Senate for thirty years. How do you account for that anomaly?

CLINTON: Well, first, I think that the image many people had of our state was always just wrong. And second, politics has always been a high calling in Arkansas. There's a strong tradition of electing independent people with excellent credentials and ability. And the people have always wished to have officials in high office who could represent the best of our state to the rest of the country.

MICHENER: Arkansas loomed very large on the national horizon during the Central High School integration conflict a quarter century ago. How has integration worked out in your state?

CLINTON: I wouldn't say that we have no problems with school integration. But I gave the baccalaureate address at Little Rock Central High School a couple of months ago, and I wish the whole country could have seen it. The student body is divided about equally between blacks and whites. There was a black student president, a white class president, . . . a black choir director, a white band leader, a black principal, a white assistant principal. The school is immaculately clean and obviously a place in which both teachers and students take a great deal of pride.

We've made dramatic progress. We went through a painful, traumatic period, which unfortunately still colors the image of our state around the country, but for us it was the beginning of a process that had to be undertaken.

MICHENER: Do you have blacks in your administration?

CLINTON: Yes, I have two black cabinet members, and about eighteen percent of my staff is black. Some of them are leaving government to take their own management positions, but there are still many blacks in my administration.

Race Relations

MICHENER: Is race still a big issue here?

CLINTON: It's still an issue everywhere in this country. I think dramatic progress has been made, especially for minorities who are well educated and who work themselves into employment positions that are protected by legal sanctions. There's still a lot of racial prejudice around—not just in Arkansas, but everywhere. But we are making real progress.

I went to Forrest City, where ten or twelve years ago there were big segregation marches. I spoke to a crowd of about three hundred fifty at a Chamber of Commerce dinner, and there were maybe forty blacks in that crowd. That's pretty good in Arkansas, in the Delta region [the plantation area and heart of white-supremacy feeling].

MICHENER: Have white students left the public schools?

CLINTON: There's been some white flight in heavily integrated areas of the state—the Arkansas Delta, Little Rock, and some of the other large cities. But it hasn't been too pronounced. A lot of our finest teachers are black, and the integration among teachers has gone very well. But it disturbs me that we have had some white flight from our public school system.

MICHENER: Is this still primarily an agricultural state?

CLINTON: In terms of income, we're about fifty-fifty between agriculture and industry. But in agriculture we're first in the nation in the production of rice and of poultry; we're third in eggs; fourth in soybeans; and about forty-five thousand of our people work in the timber industry.

MICHENER: You must do a lot of exporting to Asia.

CLINTON: We do. I took a trade mission to Taiwan, Japan, and Hong Kong not long ago, and some of our people went into China. We sell a lot of agricultural products abroad, especially rice and soybeans. I think Arkansas is beginning to integrate itself better not only with the country but also with the world. We have an office in Brussels and my department of economic development spends a lot of time there trying to export nonagricultural Arkansas products. We're selling running shoes in Belgium—things of that kind. We're beginning to pull ourselves into the world economy.

MICHENER: We hear a great deal about the sun belt as the recipient of most of the favors of the federal government. How does Arkansas fit into the sun belt?

CLINTON: We're a part of the sun belt in the sense that we've had rapid economic growth—more industry, companies moving in or expanding, new businesses springing up. A large number of retirees are coming here to live because it is a warm climate and a beautiful environment. But it isn't true that Arkansas is the recipient of a disproportionate amount of federal largess. When you extract military expenditures and veterans' benefits, you find that many states in the South are not even getting their fair share of federal aid. I know Arkansas isn't.

A Booming State

MICHENER: Is Arkansas getting a fair share of the growth that's come to the South?

CLINTON: Our state has grown about fifteen percent since 1970, second only to Florida's astronomical twenty-eight percent and a bit ahead of other southern states. The problem for Arkansas—and for many other states that were once extremely poor—is trying to diversify the economy enough to make the economic development even. Within every southern state you'll find a Little Rock that is booming and prosperous, but you'll also find real pockets of rural poverty where jobs have not moved in, where there is no trained work force, where there is no money for venture capital. This is a long-term problem that's shared throughout the South, and we must solve it if the South is going to rise to the national average and go beyond it in per capita income.

The industrial base of the South is diversifying, and that is putting some strain on our ability to handle growth safely. Most of the southern states are doing a pretty good job with air and water, but our problems with toxic wastes and other waste products are increasing. Still, if we're really skillful and very well disciplined, we may be able to skip over that stage of economic development that has caused so much environmental destruction in other areas of the country.

MICHENER: I've lived in the Northeast for many years, and I sometimes have the feeling that all of the growth and prosperity that you southerners are now enjoying comes at our expense.

CLINTON: I don't think that's true. There was a study done recently that charted the movement, over the last decade, of five point eight million firms employing about eighty-two percent of all workers in this country. And the conclusion the study drew was that in any given region, including the South, over two-thirds of the new jobs come from the expansion of already existing enterprises or the opening of new businesses. Yes, there is some movement of business out of the North and East to the South. But I don't see that as the bedrock of our future economic growth. And I think most progressive southern governors are more interested in building on the strengths of our region than in robbing other regions of business.

Of course, if I know a company's interested in moving, I'll get on the phone to invite its president down, and do everything I can to persuade the firm to come to Arkansas.

MICHENER: What advantages would a business gain by coming here?

CLINTON: I think the quality of life would be better here. We have a more pleasing environment than in some of the bigger cities of the South. And we're centrally located with excellent river transportation because now the Arkansas River is navigable to the Mississippi. Then, there seems to be a very constructive relationship between management and labor here. I've had several plant managers of industries with national affiliations tell me that their Arkansas plants were the most productive of all their factories in the United States—that the working people worked harder and smarter and better than in the other places where they're located.

MICHENER: Suppose I'm a New York manufacturer, and I get fed up with union problems. Can I escape unionism in Arkansas?

CLINTON: We have a right-to-work law. This means that if a plant votes to go union, those who do not wish to pay union dues don't have to do so. We have many factories here where virtually everyone belongs to the union. We have factories where there's no union, and it's up to the workers themselves to decide whether they need one or not.

Frankly, I'm not interested in having a manufacturer come to this state just so he can get away with paying meager wages because he thinks the unions aren't strong.

MICHENER: How about tourism in Arkansas?

CLINTON: It's our third biggest source of income—it's a billion-dollar business.

Oil refinery in the Mississippi Valley, an example of the South's growing industry. (Colour Library International, Ltd.)

MICHENER: You know, there are two reasons why I think of Arkansas with pleasure. Some years ago I spent a marvelous two weeks at a great gambling center here. It was at Hot Springs. When I was there, I fell into the hands of four or five old-time gamblers, and they gave me a college education in shooting craps. That was a fabulous place. What happened to it?

CLINTON: Time took care of it. Hot Springs was the largest illegal gambling center in America. Because it was illegal, it was controlled by local people rather than by the national crime syndicates. The Justice Department got interested in it and shut down a lot of the more overt gambling, and then Rockefeller closed it down completely. He wasn't against gambling, but he thought that it ought to be legal. I was against legalizing it because among other things, it would certainly have brought the criminal syndicates in. The people of Arkansas—for religious and moral and other more practical reasons—were also against legalizing gambling. And that killed it.

MICHENER: The other contact I've had with your state was when I was writing my first book, *Tales of the South Pacific.* I wanted to create a heroine who represented middle America and I had my navy nurse come from Little Rock. So I've always felt a special affection for your city. In the play Mary Martin used to refer to Little Rock as her beloved home town, from which she was damn glad to be absent at the moment.

I've always loved this part of the country—the mountains you have up north and the way of life you have. Suppose I were living in Massachusetts and got tired of the cold winters. Why would I choose to come to Arkansas?

CLINTON: It's warmer, but with four distinct seasons. There are remarkably beautiful places and fascinating differences within the state. And the people are very warm and friendly. A mood prevails here that's generally more upbeat, more optimistic, more aggressive about the future than you can find, I think, in the country as a whole.

Entrance to the Sanyo Manufacturing Corporation, Forrest City, Arkansas.

The Japanese Like Arkansas

Several Japanese corporations have established factories in Arkansas. In the small town of Forrest City, Japan's Sanyo Corporation produces television sets and microwave ovens for distribution in the United States. The plant also serves as a meeting ground for peoples of very different cultures.

Tanimichi Soma is vice-president and administrator of the plant. Harifumi Uatta is one of some thirty engineers brought over from Japan to help start up operations. Engineer Dennis Wilson has had an unusual

LEFT: *An assembly line inside the Sanyo plant.*

RIGHT: *Arkansas workers add parts to Sanyo microwave ovens on the assembly line.*

opportunity to learn about the Japanese way of doing things. The three men, each with a different perspective on the industry, offered comments on transplantation into the New South.

SOMA: One of the reasons Sanyo came here was to establish business in the United States. And it just so happened that an existing plant was available for us to purchase here. There are several advantages in having Japanese industry in the South. We are located in the center of the United States, so that once our product is produced, we can distribute it very fast to the East or West or Midwest. Then, we have enough labor in the South, and they are very wonderful people. We are the largest employer in this vicinity. Our payroll here is a little over two million dollars a month. After three and a half years' operation, we employ twenty-three hundred people.

Wherever we go, people smile at us and talk about how Sanyo is doing a great job. Our payroll creates lots of buying power. We don't feel any difficulty in doing business. People are very proud to work for Sanyo in this town.

And our Japanese engineers have been accepted by the community very nicely. The Arkansas people want to find out from us about our culture and our customs.

UATTA: I could have refused to come here. . . . But I was interested to visit a foreign country, so I was glad to come. I don't have many problems because I have a job with the company, I can meet many people at work. But my wife cannot speak English well—now she can speak a little bit, but she still has a big communications problem.

I have many friends because I like many sports—golf, bowling. So at the golf course or bowling alley, I made many friends. Also, I like the guitar. So with the guitar also I think I made some friends. But my wife does not do these things. . . . For close to one year, she felt lonely, but

Sanyo employees, American and Japanese, discuss their mutual goals on the job.

after that—I think she's enjoying her life here. And my son, Jiko, goes to the kindergarten. . . . He likes to go to school.

I think the biggest advantage to being here is I can understand more people, any kind of people. . . .

WILSON: I took a trip to Japan in the middle of April 1979, and it was basically to learn what the product was, how they produced it, and to get all the engineering and production data that I could, so we could start producing that product here. There's really a big difference in the philosophies of running a company, and it helps here when you run into problems to know how they would deal with it in Japan.

The way they work over there is quite different than in the United States. Most Japanese marry a company. Very few switch jobs. Most of them join after they get out of college there and stay with the company for the rest of their life.

. . . I'm from Wisconsin, and I looked for a job up there, I looked in Indiana, New York. . . . Then I came down here to be interviewed, and it looked very promising, it was a good promotion for me, and I accepted the job. I was surprised it was Arkansas—I never thought I'd be down here.

INDUSTRY LOOKS SOUTH

Henry Grady, the same newspaper editor who had confidently predicted the birth of a New South in the 1880s, once wrote about the funeral of a fellow southerner. His description of the affair summed up the economic plight of his region: "They buried him in the midst of a marble quarry. . . . Yet a tombstone they put above him was from Vermont. They buried him in the heart of a pine forest, and the pine coffin was imported from Cincinnati. They buried him within touch of an iron mine, and yet the nails in his coffin were . . . from Pittsburgh. . . . The South didn't furnish a thing on earth for that funeral but the corpse and the hole in the ground."

When Grady wrote these words, and for a good half-century thereafter, the South was essentially a colonial area for the rest of the nation. It fulfilled a colony's role, producing certain cash crops such as cotton, rice, and tobacco with which it paid for finished goods from the industrial North and Midwest. Its citizens were constantly in debt to northern bankers, railroadmen, and manufacturers. Except in rare instances, the South could offer its citizens few jobs in manufacturing or commerce, and the poverty-stricken state of southern education—from kindergarten through college—helped keep the region a backwater. Even when some industries in the 1920s and 1930s began moving South, they did so primarily to take advantage of a cheap, docile labor force in states where the authorities used all the force at their command to bar labor unions. As late as 1938 a federal report called the South "the nation's number-one economic problem." Yet that same report maintained that the region was one of enormous economic potential.

Actually, that potential had already begun to be realized, and the agent of change was the federal government itself. In 1933 Congress authorized the creation of the Tennessee Valley Authority (TVA), charged with coordinating and extending flood control, navigation, and hydroelectrical services along the Tennessee River and its tributaries. In the intervening decades the dams, the reservoirs, and the power plants that TVA has built and operated have changed the very face of some forty thousand square miles of land in seven states. By eliminating annual floods, the TVA has brought tens of thousands of areas into productive agricultural use. By providing relatively inexpensive electrical power to a vast area, it created not only the means of improving farming but also offered a great pool of energy for industry. Finally, by deepening channels along the Tennessee River system and encouraging the building of port facilities, it made the river a major artery of commerce.

The TVA helped begin an industrial revolution in the South; World War II speeded its course. Again, the catalyst was the federal government. Army training camps opened throughout the region, the services and facilities they required pumping tens of millions of dollars into local

A giant chemical works in the Mississippi Valley, Louisiana, is one of many petroleum-related industries in the region. (Colour Library International, Ltd.)

economies. More important, for the long run, were permanent facilities for building ships, planes, and armaments. Add to this new chemical plants, vast petroleum and petrochemical facilities in Louisiana, the world's biggest shipyard at Norfolk, Virginia—to mention but a few of the projects. The region had laid the foundations for a great economic advance and as industrial facilities grew, so did wages. By 1950 the average wage in the South for industrial workers had risen 55 percent over 1940—and that was after inflation had been factored in.

Nor did the boom stop in the immediate postwar era. The federal government's largess seemed almost endless. It continued to pour billions into the South, particularly into armaments, defense, and space exploration facilities. Meanwhile, private industry, attracted by a salubrious climate, ample energy and transport facilities, a large pool of nonunion labor, and state governments willing to offer tax abatements, increasingly looked toward Dixie for new plant sites. In six of the seven Deep South states—Georgia, Alabama, Mississippi, Arkansas, South Carolina, and Florida—per capita income rose by more than 100 percent between 1961 and 1971. Only Louisiana showed a smaller but still impressive gain. Such figures are a happy indication of how far the South has come. Yet there are other figures that reveal how far the South has yet to go. Well over two-thirds of the poorest 250 counties in the United States are in the South. In the Deep South almost six million people live below the poverty line, while in the Upper South—Virginia,

Downtown Shreveport, Louisiana. The Red River in the foreground is presently unnavigable, awaiting funds for a port project. (Shreveport Journal)

Baton Rouge, Louisiana, on the Mississippi River is a center of petrochemical industrial development in the South. It is also the capital of Louisiana.

West Virginia, North Carolina, Kentucky, and Tennessee—the figures are almost as appalling. There is, however, no doubt that the region is on the move, that prosperity is reaching greater numbers of southerners—both black and white—year in and year out. The aspirations expressed by former Governor Clinton of Arkansas echo the hopes of all southerners. These hopes are more than dreams; they are realistic projections for tomorrow's South. ❏

THE SOUTH PRESERVES ITS HERITAGE: THE CAJUNS

❏ The bayou country is a few hours' drive from downtown New Orleans, in the heart of southern Louisiana, but it is a world unto itself. It has been created by the infinite meanderings of the hundreds of waterways that trail off the Mississippi River, and by the annual deposit and shifting of millions of tons of sediment that the river carries in its downward plunge to the Gulf of Mexico. The land here is marsh and swamp, ponds, lagoons, and bayous—the slow-moving creeks and streams that snake their way everywhere, and give their name to the region.

Deer, muskrat, nutria, otter, wild turkey live in the bayou country. Shrimp, crayfish, oysters, and alligator populate its waters. Today oil derricks loom over the landscape and prove the presence of the modern world. Yet it's still possible to go up into the bayous and never come out. If you know how to find it, everything you need is here.

The French colonists of that part of Canada called Acadia (primarily in what is now Nova Scotia) were expelled by their British governor in 1755 because they refused to swear allegiance to the Crown. Over the next decade, they wandered in an epic exile that ended in death for some, in slavery for others. A group of Acadians eventually found a haven in French Louisiana, on the rich lands near the Mississippi River. After the purchase of the Louisiana Territory by the United States, their lands were consolidated into huge sugar plantations, and the Acadians were once again forced to move. Some wandered even farther south into the bayous. Others settled on the Louisiana prairie, a flat, open region that, like the bayou country, is intersected by hundreds of creeks and streams. Those who moved into the bayous became primarily trappers and fishermen. The prairie dwellers continued the old Acadian farming tradition: They raised sugarcane, bountiful vegetable crops, rice. (Today, one-quarter of the nation's rice crop comes from the Louisiana prairie.) They bred and raised cattle—in fact, the American cattle industry began in earnest in the 1760s, with the arrival of the Acadian immigrants to the prairie.

When the Acadians came to Louisiana, there was already a sizable French population centered around New Orleans, along with Spaniards, blacks, and Indians. The Indians were rumored to be particularly fierce; one tribe, the Attakapas, were supposedly cannibals. The Acadians were welcomed because it was thought that they could settle into the areas where the Indians lived and pacify them, kill them, or go into native cooking pots themselves. What happened instead was the kind of cultural blending the Acadians had already achieved in Canada, where they had formed a genuine friendship with the local tribes. In Louisiana, they learned Indian ways of fishing, trapping, and building in the watery climates of the bayous and the prairie.

What resulted, then, from the Acadian arrival in Louisiana was a culture that was distinct and unlike any other on the continent. Basically French, and in the beginning trimmed to the rigors of the Canadian landscape, it was a mixture of French and Spanish colonial, with a heavy addition of African (via the French and Spanish West Indian Islands, from where many of Louisiana's slaves had been imported) and a strong dose of Indian. The Acadians became "Cajuns"—a southern slurring of

LEFT: *Cajun children learn the French language in a school in Lafayette, Louisiana.*

RIGHT: *A student in a Lafayette classroom points on the map to the French-speaking province of Quebec in Canada.*

their old name. Their language remained French as it was spoken in eighteenth-century Canada; but it was soon interlarded with words and phrases from English, the local Indian tongues, Spanish, and the black dialects.

Whether they lived isolated in the bayou country or prospered on prairie farms, or (as it happened to a few) flourished and grew rich on the oil that was found on their lands, most of them continued stubbornly to be Cajun—to maintain the language, the attitudes, the customs, and the festivals of their forefathers. They still do, despite the decades of disdain exhibited toward them by the dominant Anglo culture. A proud, energetic people who have done much to shape present-day Louisiana, the Cajuns might be taken as exemplars of ethnic continuity: They live fruitfully within the larger culture and contribute to it, while still maintaining their own. ❑

The Language

Only a few years ago, none of the elementary-school students in the Louisiana public schools studied French—in fact, it was an offense to speak French in school. Although most of the Cajuns spoke French among themselves, few could read or write it. Today, due to the efforts of the Council for Development of French in Louisiana, things are changing. There are now over three hundred instructors teaching French to both Cajun and Creole children. I consider it lucky that this Cajun population, with its special heritage and language, is taking care to preserve them. For me, this sort of pride in one's past is the foundation on which progress in America is built. I feel that there is a lesson in their pride for all of us.

La Boucherie

❑ "Before we had electricity out in the country, you know, people didn't have no refrigerator or nothing, so they had to have what they

Cajun musicians play traditional tunes at the "La Boucherie" festivities.

called 'boucherie companie.' There was no other way you could have fresh meat. It still goes on. A man that has cattle, or sheep, hogs, sometimes goats—he makes a 'boucherie' and invites the neighbors. It's a party." ❑

Music

❑ "Cajun music is born and raised in this area, and there's no way that you can get rid of it. We just learn it by ear from the family, you know. . . . If you get an accordion player and a fiddle player, like the olden times you make a little house party, with a little bit of moonshine—you've got to have that—then you're going to have a good time like you never believed. This is a short life. You're here today, you're gone tomorrow. But the Cajuns—they live forever." ❑

Preparations for a "boucherie" feast. Here a pig has just been slaughtered.

"Boucherie" sausage is made the old way—by hand.

The culmination of the "boucherie"—a buffet feast.

In a local race in Cajun country, the jockey brings his horse into the starting gate.

Horse Racing

❑ "Every Cajun town has its horsetrack. The love of animals and the love of fun bring the Cajuns out for the races every weekend." ❑

A Small Cajun Vocabulary

❑ *Bousillage:* The mixture of mud and Spanish moss used until recently for building house walls, which were then covered with cedar shingles to protect them from the weather. *Bousillage* walls kept houses cool in the hot, humid Louisiana summer and warm in the often bone-chilling winter. Cajun houses are still occasionally built using *bousillage,* and to other typical Cajun specifications: They are on stilts, to keep the wet out, and have an open, cedar-columned *galerie* running across the front.

Couvrage: A festival party convened to shingle a house. Cajun people still manage to transform hard work into the occasion for a community feast. The *boucherie* is such an occasion. And before mechanized farming equipment came into common use, there was the *piocherie,* a hoeing party.

Fais dodo: To go to sleep. Also, a dance. A *fais dodo* hall is a dance hall with a room in the back where the children sleep, while their parents and relatives play music and dance into the night.

Riding to the finish in a Cajun horse race.

Gumbo: A characteristic Louisiana stew, highly prized among the Cajuns. The word may be derived from the African *quin-gumbo,* meaning "okra," a vegetable that's always used to season and thicken the stew; or it may come from the Indian word *kombo,* which means "sassafras." The Indians used ground sassafras leaves as a seasoning and the Cajuns also season with sassafras; they call it *filé.* Cajun *gumbos* are made from every available variety of fish and shellfish, meat and game—but never, for some reason, from beef.

Laissez les bons temps rouler: "Let the good times roll," slogan for—among other events—the Cajun celebration of Mardi Gras. The celebration begins on Shrove Tuesday morning with the ritual donation of a chicken from every household. The day ends with the consumption of an enormous communal gumbo and a *fais dodo. Laisser les bon temps rouler* is also applied to the roll of the dice.

Pirogue: A shallow, flat-bottomed boat that is propelled with a long forked pole through the waters of the bayou.

Traiteur: "Treater," a Cajun folk-medicine practitioner, usually a woman.

Vacher: A Cajun cowboy. ❑

Cajun cooking meets with approval.

CIVIL RIGHTS IN THE SOUTH

Some might date the beginning of the southern renaissance to May 17, 1954, when the United States Supreme Court, by unanimous vote, declared racial segregation in the public schools to be unconstitutional. Perhaps a more authentic date is December 1, 1955. It was then that a black seamstress named Rosa Parks, returning to her Montgomery, Alabama, home from a hard day's work, refused to give up her seat on a segregated bus to a white man. Rosa Parks certainly never thought of herself as the cutting edge of a revolution. But that simple act of defiance, that simple affirmation of her individual human dignity, set in motion a chain of events that was to transform the South, and the nation. The immediate result of Rosa Park's refusal to move to the back of the bus was her arrest. Within days, however, her act had mobilized the entire black community of the city. Under the leadership of a young black preacher named Martin Luther King, Jr., the oppressed blacks announced forthrightly that they had had enough. They declared a boycott of city buses, and they held out for 381 days, forcing the white power structure of the city to its knees and ending segregation on Montgomery's buses.

For the first time in decades, the Solid South of segregation and Jim Crow laws had been breached. More important, perhaps, was the fact that the primary agents of change were not the federal courts or the national Congress, but the black people themselves, who risked prison and even death to achieve their own liberation. Their tactic would be nonviolence. They would put their bodies on the line, submit to the clubs of policemen and the fire bombs of white terrorists. They would mourn their dead, weep for their imprisoned, bind their wounded—and organize their numbers into cadres for reform. For fifteen years and more, they would extend their activities into every realm where the power of whites was employed to degrade and impoverish them. Their ranks would include the prosperous and the poor, professionals and near-illiterates, children and the elderly. But above all it was the young, men and women in their late teens and twenties, who stood out most prominently on the firing line of civil rights. In the early 1960s, black college students began their sit-in campaigns, hunkering down in southern restaurants and lunch counters where law and custom denied them entry. Demanding service of stony-faced waiters and waitresses, they sat patiently for meals that never came. Instead, the police came, billy clubs in hand, to wrestle them to the floor and drag them bodily to paddy wagons. Yet the next day, and the next, there would be new recruits to sit and wait and offer their bodies to the clubs of white power.

And then there were the Freedom Riders, blacks and whites together riding through the South on long-distance buses and defying the ordinances requiring their segregation. Often the buses were ambushed and fire-bombed; often the riders were savagely beaten. Yet they endured. Wherever blacks met to protest and demand relief, they raised their voices in a song that became the anthem of the civil rights movement: "We Shall Overcome. . . . Deep in my heart, I do believe, we shall overcome someday."

Although the blacks of the South were the shock troops of this nonviolent revolution, they were not without allies. The events at lunch counters, at voter registration offices, along bus routes, and at schoolhouse doors became front-page articles throughout the nation, and were featured almost daily on the network television news. Police dogs snarling at and then attacking peaceful demonstrators, bombings of black churches and the homes of prominent black leaders, the murders of two northern white youths and a black companion during a Mississippi voter registration drive—all these outrages created a nationwide wave of revulsion against the forces of white supremacy. Responding to a new national mood, first the federal courts, then the administrations of John F. Kennedy and Lyndon Johnson, and finally the United States Congress took action. New laws were passed forbidding segregation in public accommodations, outlawing discrimination in the workplace and finally—and most important of all—guaranteeing the right of blacks to vote in all elections.

Many struggles remained, but when it became obvious that at last the power of the federal government was ranged beside the forces demanding equality in the South, the tide of white supremacy began to retreat. Soon the retreat turned into a rout. By the late 1970s, the legal barriers that had long maintained the inferior status of blacks throughout the South had crumbled to dust. A new age was dawning.

In 1963 Martin Luther King spoke at a rally of more than 200,000 Americans gathered in front of Washington's Lincoln Memorial. In one of those rare moments of transcendence, King made his fervent "I have a dream" plea for an America purged of bigotry. It was a dream that King, assassinated in 1968, would not live to see realized. It is a dream that even today remains unfulfilled. But in the South, at least, thanks to the courage and determination of hundreds of thousands of black men and women, it is a dream that has partially come true. The civil rights movement that began with a tired lady refusing to give up her seat on a segregated bus has transformed the South. Where only yesterday blacks could not vote, today they cast ballots without hindrance. Where only yesterday blacks could not find decent lodgings, today public accommodations are open to all. Where school integration was once but a hope, today it is a reality. Where the very idea of a black mayor, councilman, or congressman was considered unthinkable, today there are hundreds of elected black officials.

Much remains to be done to improve educational and occupational opportunities, to help minorities achieve an economic security matching that of their white neighbors. But nowhere in the country are these tasks being undertaken with a greater will than in the South. The region that was once a bastion of racial oppression now points the way for the entire nation toward the realization of that American goal: "liberty and justice for all." ❑

CENTRAL FLORIDA'S BOOM MIRRORS THE SOUTH'S RESURGENCE

❑ Old-time Floridians must occasionally contemplate the numbers and wonder: In 1950, the state's population was 2.7 million; in 1980, 8.8 million. In just thirty years, Florida has gained over 6 million people, and ranks as the fastest-growing area in the nation after Texas and California. Florida's cities have tripled and quadrupled in size. Vast regions that once were swamps and coastal tidelands have been filled in to make the foundations for high-priced housing tracts. Tourists pour in by the millions, over intricate networks of new highways, each car

The Seaquarium in Miami is a popular Florida tourist attraction. (Colour Library International, Ltd.)

adding its increment to the accumulation of pollution in the air and water.

A typical truck farm south of Miami.
(Colour Library International, Ltd.)

Although almost every area of Florida has felt the effects of encroaching populations, central Florida has been particularly hard hit. Not too long ago central Florida was where tourist cars tanked up before making the final dash south to the glittering Gold Coast—Miami Beach and its satellites. The cars flashed by immense groves of citrus fruit, cattle ranches, thriving vegetable-raising enterprises, small fishing villages. The region's largest city, Orlando, was a quiet business center for the agricultural enterprises that surrounded it. Daytona Beach, on the Atlantic Coast, was a family vacation spot except in the spring, when the town overflowed with automobile racing enthusiasts and vacation-happy college students.

The orange groves and the cattle ranches still exist, although their number has shrunk visibly. Orlando has experienced explosive growth, with all the problems attending it. Daytona Beach has not yet attained the tourist status of Miami Beach, but the once pristine coast that stretches south from the city is now erupting with small resorts, hotels, motels, and neon-limned fast-food parlors.

On the beach at Fort Lauderdale thousands of college students gather every spring vacation to relax and enjoy.
(Colour Library International, Ltd.)

What happened? First the federal government decided to transform Cape Canaveral—about sixty-five miles east of Orlando—into a major aerospace research and development facility. By the 1950s the population spillover from the Cape was reaching out as far as Orlando, and new highways were built to ease the movement of the thousands of Florida newcomers: workers at Cape Canaveral and at the new factories built to support the Cape's activities by firms like Boeing, RCA, IBM, TWA.

Cape Canaveral's influence, though, was only a modest prelude to the effect of the opening of Disney World in 1971. Walt Disney began his monumental project in 1964 when his agents quietly began buying up land in central Florida. Eventually they amassed 27,400 acres—a fair-sized spread, even to some of central Florida's prosperous cattlemen. Disney's plans for his new Florida dominion were even more ambitious than his earlier (and far smaller) Disneyland in California. Disney World was to be a living encyclopedia of everybody's favorite fantasies (already shaped by Disney through his artful movies) and notions of great historical moments and places. It was to be a kind of perfect contemporary dreamland, where every prospect would please and not even a chewing-gum wrapper would be allowed to litter long enough to disturb the scene. Natural vistas were preserved, and new natural wonders constructed. State-of-the-art technology was employed everywhere—in the marvelous monorail that carries visitors throughout the World, in the forests of underground pneumatic tubes that transport the World's wastes to a highly efficient incinerator, in the design and erection of the fabulous thrill-rides, in the computer-controlled movements and speech of the life-size puppets that duplicate famous Disney-created film figures. When it was finished, Disney World was in many respects a literal paradise of lush lagoons, waving palms, fairy castles. And with its three plush hotels, its variegated restaurants and old-time squares, parades of huge-headed cartoon characters, rococo ferryboats, calliopes, brass bands—it worked, beautifully. In its first year alone, some ten million people came to see it. Today, the average annual attendance is about fourteen million, and many visitors are repeaters who come back again and again because there is nothing else in the world quite like it. ❑

Donald Duck and Mickey Mouse, two very familiar characters at Disney World. (Courtesy of Disney Productions)

Disney World Spinoffs

❑ Other amusement parks soon sprang up in the area, hoping to cash in on Disney World's pulling power. In the immediate vicinity, there are Sea World and Circus World, Reptile World and Alligatorland Safari and Gatorland Zoo; slightly farther away, Silver Springs, Cypress Gardens, and The Dark Continent beckon. When tourists tire of amusement parks, there are the beaches. And just an hour or so from Orlando by car or tourist bus, one can visit Cape Canaveral and the Kennedy Space Center.

Orlando is only eighteen miles from Disney World, connected to it by an efficient interstate highway. And although the city expected a massive influx of tourist dollars from visitors on their way to the Magic Kingdom, it never anticipated other, less attractive spinoffs: huge traffic jams, increased crime rates, a monumental waste-disposal problem, and a housing crisis. Municipal taxes had to be increased to pay for new roads, for the additional policemen needed to control the increased traffic and to arrest the visiting criminals, for new schools to house the increased number of children whose parents had come to Orlando to work in the new tourist attractions. New suburbs were built, and old suburbs enlarged to house the thousands of retired people who came to

The castle at Disney World in Orlando.
(Courtesy of Disney Productions)

visit and, delighted by the climate and scenery, decided to live out their lives here. For miles around Orlando, urban sprawl spread out its grimy tentacles.

While Orlando was suffering its Disney-induced explosion, there were many who were coining money because of the new amusement park. Landowners and land speculators between them have pushed acreage prices up well over five hundred times what they were in 1971. The temptation to sell the old family farm and put a million dollars in the bank was too strong for many people. As a result, Orange County, which includes Orlando, now has only about one-third the number of cattle it raised in the pre–Disney World era, and far fewer orange groves. On the other hand, the land-intensive plant nursery business has grown and now supplies a good proportion of America's houseplants.

The city of Orlando has come to grips with the changes that Disney World wrought. But it may have the whole thing to do over again in a few years, when Disney's last legacy, EPCOT, opens. As envisioned by Disney and his "imagineers," the Environmental Prototype Community of Tomorrow—which is being built now not far from Orlando—will be a concatenation of wonders: a new, planned city whose inhabitants will travel exclusively by monorail; a world's fair that will permanently showcase the arts, goods, and services of all the world's nations; a future world extravaganza, focusing on the newest in science and technology. Development costs for EPCOT are probably by now near the billion-dollar mark; but when it opens, the Disney people expect millions of additional visitors—those who are not enthralled by Disney's fantasies but may well appreciate the real world, presented as only Disney can. In addition, there is the anticipation of a more solid commerce than tourism offers: the new businesses that will establish themselves here, attracted by the potential for international trade.

Whatever else EPCOT brings to central Florida, it will certainly bring more people, straining still further the already tense relations between a population and its earth, air, and water. ❑

Cape Canaveral: The Challenge of Space

❑ Midway down the eastern coast of Florida—where once there were only sand dunes, beach, low-growing piney woods, and a lighthouse—lies Cape Canaveral. In 1948 the Air Force built launch pads here for the new long-range missiles then being developed. Ten years later, under the guidance of the newly created National Aeronautics and Space Administration (NASA), the first American earth satellite, *Explorer I*, was rocket-boosted into orbit from the Cape. Manned space flight, the moon landings, Skylab, and most recently the spectacular space shuttle triumphs were all launched here, at what is now the Kennedy Space Center.

Visitors' Center at the Kennedy Space Center in Cape Canaveral. (Colour Library International, Ltd.)

Space exploration transformed the Cape and all its surrounding region as far away as Orlando. In addition to the workers brought in by NASA, there were scores of aerospace firms that hastened to the area and imported thousands of their own technicians. Even after NASA opened its Manned Spacecraft Center in Houston, Texas—assigning it research and development responsibilities—the Cape continued to burgeon. Brevard County experienced all the trauma associated with an "impacted area"—a region that suffers a population explosion brought on, usually, by some action of the government. Within twenty years, the number of housing units in the county increased from fewer than ten thousand to almost eighty thousand, and population grew 1,000 percent.

Somehow, during the early 1970s, the nation lost its enthusiasm for manned space exploration, although we continued to be enthralled by the awesome accomplishments of the unmanned space probes, the Pioneers and Voyagers that visited and photographed Jupiter and Saturn. Throughout the past decade, NASA has seen its budget shrink and its plans for new projects either canceled or deferred. Lessened activity at Cape Canaveral has had its effects on the region as well: The Space Center payroll was almost halved between 1970 and 1980. In other states the withdrawal of federal activity and monies created ghost towns. But Florida, blessed with beaches, a tropical climate, and a realistic sense of what it is best suited for, turned a potential disaster into another bonanza. Housing developments that had been filled by NASA workers were resold as retirement villages. New businesses emerged to serve the new residents. And hundreds of thousands of tourists made the pilgrimage to Cape Canaveral to see where our space adventure began and to enjoy the by now well developed central Florida seashore.

Florida's good fortune, however, does not affect the uncertain status of NASA. There are many who see America's space exploration efforts as far too costly—especially in view of other pressing needs. Others view the space program as vital if we are to maintain the technological thrust that has brought us to that moment of pure perfection, the flight of the space shuttle *Columbia*. ❑

THE VANISHING LAND

Harris Neck is a small village on the Georgia coast, just outside the boundaries of a national wildlife refuge. A generation ago that refuge was the site of a thriving black community. During World War II, the federal government confiscated the land to build an airstrip,

Harris Neck Wildlife Refuge.

Shrimp boats nestle at the dock awaiting the right tide for a catch. (Colour Library International, Ltd.)

but it was never used. Today residents of Harris Neck live on twenty-six acres nearby, as they continue their long struggle to regain control over what was once their home.

❑ In 1942 the federal government exercised its right of eminent domain to remove the people of Harris Neck from their homes. Washington merely dispatched a group of surveyors who announced to the black farmers and fishermen of the community that they would have to leave. The residents were paid as little as $2.42 per acre in compensation for their holdings. Encouraged by a promise that the land would be returned to them at the war's end, most of the Harris Neck people stayed nearby, in a shantytown of trailers and shacks. They continued to work as oystermen and crabbers. Yet their homes were gone; their land was gone; and their docks were gone. Without docking facilities, they were at the mercy of the processors to whom they sold their catch.

The projected air base was never built, but instead of returning the land to its former owners, the government made it into a wildlife preserve. Today the sons and daughters of the Harris Neck people, and those original residents still alive, continue to hope and fight for their land. They have staged demonstrations. They have camped out on the property, only to be forcibly evicted. They have enlisted the help of the National Association for the Advancement of Colored People and an organization known as the Emergency Land Fund; they have begun court action. And there is a bill pending in Congress to restore their land to them.

After almost four decades, the cause of the people of Harris Neck has aroused sympathy and support. If the dispossessed of this tiny, once prosperous, and self-reliant community have their land returned to them, it will be further evidence of a new day in the South; a confirmation of the fact that black rights can no longer be trampled upon with impunity—not even by the federal government. ❑

Two fishermen talk over the problem of making a living.

The People of Harris Neck Speak

RESIDENT: Our home, Harris Neck, was one of the places on this coast that was a self-sufficient and independent community. We didn't ask for nothing, and we needed nothing from the outside. We planted, we worked the river, we took care of our families, we built our homes. But the government came and changed our lives completely. We went from a state of freedom into slavery.

RESIDENT (Preacher): When my grandmother and grandfather looked across the earth that the Lord had given to them, and the way that God blessed it to feed their families—and the government come in and take it and give it to the birds. There is no justice here. Thirty-seven years ago, our home was taken. Harris Neck is ours. And as long as there is breath in our bodies we will continue this fight.

RESIDENT: After they took the land from us, it was never used. It was never used. And after years of mismanagement, the federal government took it back to the forest, and gave it to the State Game and Wildlife

A Harris Neck fisherman brings in his catch.

Crabbers at a church meeting.

people, in 1961. But we were never given the opportunity to say yes or no.

RESIDENT: This thing that hurts me very much is that when it was my time to do for my country, I did. And we're not asking our country to do for us. We are saying to them, "Give us back that which is ours, so that we can do for ourselves." That's our bottom line. We're not asking the government to *give* us anything. We are saying, "Return what belongs to us."

RESIDENT: I was the first child born after my parents and the others here were forced to leave Harris Neck proper. I was raised partly by my grandfather. He taught me a lot of the things he knew, and which was the way of life of the people here, which was trapping for minks, raccoons, otter, and crabbing and shrimping.

RESIDENT: The federal government don't have to train us, or send any people down here to give us *x* amount of dollars. We already have skills. We are very good crabbers, shrimpers, and oystermen. What hurts me is we have yet to accomplish what our grandfathers have done. And we can do the job, we just need the opportunity. You've taken the land from us, but why is it that we do not at least have a place to put our boats? Although we know how to catch crabs and shrimps and we probably are some of the best seafarers around, we are only allowed to *catch* the seafood, which is the hardest part of the job. Without docking facilities or processing plants we can't venture out into other areas of the seafood business where the money really is. Without access to the outside market, a crabber will never be successful. He'll always have to go season to season. And if he should have one bad season, he will never have another season.

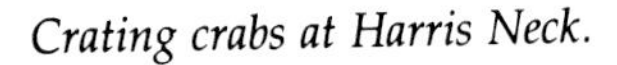

Crating crabs at Harris Neck.

Edgar Timmons, Jr., preaches at his church. The women below are two members of his congregation.

RESIDENT: The crabber, he has to buy all his material from the processor except for his boat and motor. But anytime the crabber starts making money, the processor feel, "Oh, oh, it's time to start taking a little bit more money from the crabber, because he's getting a little bit too high. We can't let this fellow from Harris Neck make too much money. So we've got to keep him down a little bit. If he make four hundred dollars, let's take two hundred. And when winter come, then he's barely making it and he has to borrow more money from me." It's just like sharecropping. They're just taking the money. We just don't have the opportunity.

RESIDENT: What I am concerned about is, what's going to happen to our kids? They're not going to want to leave home. If we had our land, we'd have something for them to do. But when they grow up, what's going to happen to them? Our spirit was not, is not—and I pray will not be broken.

Docking the fishing boats at Harris Neck.

RESIDENT (Edgar Timmons, Jr.): The land was granted to my family by General Sherman in 1864. We have always lived on that land. It's all we know. We were seventy families that held the land. The government took it. They promised it back. We still don't have it. I was a pilot in Vietnam, where I was wounded. I lost eighty percent of my sight. I know these waters well enough that I can run my boat on the twenty percent I have left. I know this land as if I could feel it. All I want is to get back the land that belongs to us.

Wilson Moran, a Harris Neck crabber.

The Disappearing Small Farmer

❑ The story of Harris Neck, though unique in its details, has parallels throughout the South. If there is one group of blacks who are not sharing in the general prosperity that has come to the region, it is the thousands of small landholders, black farmers who scratch a living from the soil. Their lives are hard, their pleasures are few, but like all other Americans they love the land on which they live and take pride in its ownership. Increasingly that land is being lost to them. Just at the moment when southern real estate is becoming valuable, much of it is falling into the hands of speculators. The original owners or their heirs often get little—sometimes nothing—in return. Not long ago, in the mid-1950s, there were 175,000 black landowners in the South. Their holdings amounted to 10 million acres. Today there are a mere 40,000 blacks who own farm property in the region and their total holdings are down to 5 million acres. Land is moving out of black hands at the rate of 300,000 acres per year.

One way that blacks lose land is through tax sales. Often these come about because the owners have died without leaving a will. The property is then technically held for the benefit of the heirs—and there may be dozens of them scattered about the country. Little effort is made to find these heirs, and after a time, county authorities put the land up for sale to pay back taxes. Speculators move in and buy up the acreage at a fraction of its real value, then resell it—often at immense profits—to developers, paper mills, lumber companies, or wealthy farmers. Another tactic is to find just one of the heirs and talk him into selling. The entire property can then be put on the market regardless of the sentiments—or even without the knowledge—of the other heirs. As Edgar Timmons, Jr., one of the Harris Neck people, puts it: "Thousands of acres of black-owned land in the South is lost every week. A lot of blacks are coming back to the South. Isn't no place for them to go. The lumber, pulp, and paper companies own thirty-three million acres, and they're buying more of it every day. The federal government owns more. There isn't enough land anymore." ❑

A stunning row of resort hotels lines the shore at Miami Beach, Florida. (Colour Library International, Ltd.)

MIAMI: CITY IN TRANSITION

❑ Why would a mayor of New York City travel a thousand miles to Miami, Florida, just to "press the flesh"? The answer is simple enough. New York's Mayor Edward Koch was greeting his constituents. At any one moment, thousands of New York residents are to be found in the Miami area, and tens of thousands of retired folks from New York now live there permanently. True, members of this last group no longer vote in Gotham, but they maintain strong family ties with the city. Many of their sons, daughters, cousins, nephews, and nieces still cast their ballots in the Big Apple. According to some wags, Miami and its metropolitan area is, in reality, nothing more than New York City's sixth borough.

Of course, Miami is a great deal more than that. It is a major port for Latin American trade. It remains, in spite of competition from the

Aerial view of Miami. (Colour Library International, Ltd.)

nearby Bahamas and the Caribbean Islands, America's vacation paradise. Miami Beach alone boasts almost four hundred hotels with some thirty thousand rooms. In recent years Miami has become a center of light industry, with thousands of small manufacturing plants, and has achieved a reputation as a scientific center, particularly in the field of oceanography. On the debit side is Miami's role as a nesting ground for organized crime. The illicit drug trade, prostitution, and illegal gambling all thrive here. And race relations in this city lag behind other major southern metropolises. Miami is home to thousands of impoverished blacks, most of whom are jammed together in noxious slums like Liberty City, which exploded in 1980 with the worst riots the nation has seen in more than a decade.

Miami Beach. (Colour Library International, Ltd.)

One sense a visitor gets when touring the Miami area is that of impermanence, of shifting populations and poorly focused energy. In large measure this odd quality, this lack of definition, stems from the area's role as a tourist center, not only in the winter months but in summer as well. The tasteless, ornate lobbies of dozens of hotels, the gargantuan displays of food in their dining rooms, the virtually naked bodies splayed out at scores of poolsides bespeak a culture of bland gluttony. There is, however, another tide of impermanence that cuts to the quick of the Miami region's life. Here, hundreds of thousands of old people—many of them with little to occupy their time, more of them with few financial resources beyond their monthly social security checks—wait in the sun. They wait for their government pension payments, for a phone call from the children up north, for a flying visit from a younger relative, for a sale at the supermarket. Perhaps it is better for them down here in the warmth of the Florida air than it would be at home in the biting chill of Manhattan or Minneapolis. There is, however, no more poignant illustration of the alienation of the old from the young, of America's failure to offer its elderly a meaningful place in society, than these phalanxes of bent bodies and bored minds, waiting in the sun.

Physically close to the geriatric communities and lush tourist hotels of Miami Beach—but light years away in spirit—is another Miami: the world of Cuban refugees, escapees from the Castro dictatorship, who have established on the Florida shore a vital, prosperous Latin enclave. These are new Americans. Their success repeats—and in many cases far surpasses—that of earlier immigrant groups. They came here in the 1960s and 1970s, and again in 1980 in a sudden outpouring from Cuba known as the Freedom Flotilla. Most arrived with little more than a few dollars in their pockets, their brains, and their willingness to work. They did have one advantage over earlier immigrant groups. These were not the "refuse of . . . teeming shores" but, to a great extent, the professional elite of pre-Castro Cuban society—scientists, lawyers, physicians, merchants, bankers, and technicians.

What they have accomplished is truly remarkable. They have

revitalized whole sections of the city, made neighborhoods once falling into decay into healthy communities once more. They have lent a sense of solidity to a city that otherwise seems almost always in the throes of change. And they have endowed Miami with true charm, a grace that becomes quite obvious when compared with the gaudy pleasures and expensive honky-tonk of the resort strips nearby. ❑

Carlos Arboleya in his Miami office.

Michener Talks with Carlos Arboleya

Miami proper is now almost 50 percent Cuban; the city is officially bilingual. It would be nearly impossible to overstate the beneficial effect the Cuban community has had on Miami. Not at all atypical is the story of Carlos Arboleya, whose success in America echoes that of thousands of his countrymen. In 1960 Mr. Arboleya arrived in Florida from Cuba with a wife, an infant son, and all of forty-two dollars. Eight years later he became an American citizen. Today he is president of the Barnett Bank in Miami. I had the pleasure of sharing Thanksgiving dinner with him.

MICHENER: Mr. Arboleya, how did you achieve success so quickly?

ARBOLEYA: It happened because this is America. This is the land of opportunity. I think I have to add that I arrived with something more than forty-two dollars. I had my wife, who I knew would help me. I had

Carlos Arboleya and James Michener at dinner with the Arboleya family.

my two-year-old son. I had the tremendous conviction that this was the land where I could rebuild my life. And I had a lot of faith in God and confidence in myself.

MICHENER: When you landed, did you get a job in a bank?

ARBOLEYA: No. I couldn't find a bank job. I wound up in a shoe factory as a forty-five-dollar-a-week inventory clerk.

MICHENER: How did you get into the banking business here?

ARBOLEYA: Though I went to work in the shoe factory, I never lost my desire to get back into banking. It was my field. During my year and a half at the shoe factory, I was promoted several times. When they made me vice-president and comptroller, I was sent to the Boulevard National Bank to register my signature. As I was talking to the president of the bank, I told him of my sixteen years of banking experience in Cuba. He asked me if I would like to come to work for him. I didn't ask how much he was going to pay me. I didn't ask what I was going to do at the bank. I just told him I'd be there in two weeks. I went back to the factory and resigned.

MICHENER: Do you foresee Miami becoming a kind of gateway city for our contacts with Latin America?

ARBOLEYA: It already has become the gateway to the Americas. New Orleans used to hold that position, but it is falling into second place. The traffic at the port of Miami, the air cargo, the ship cargo, the passenger traffic, the influx of South and Central Americans to Miami, has made this city the primary point of contact.

MICHENER: What classes of people fled Cuba to come to Miami?

ARBOLEYA: All classes. There was, however, a very large influx of middle-class Cubans. I consider myself one of them. About thirty percent of the Cuban immigrants had college educations. Most of the rest had high school diplomas.

MICHENER: In recent years I have been thrown into contact with three Hispanic communities: the Cubans, the Puerto Ricans, and the Chicanos. Do you see any chance of these three groups uniting politically?

ARBOLEYA: I'll be honest with you. I know that what I'm going to say is very controversial. But I am a very proud American. I don't think we have to unite as Hispanics. I think we have to unite as Americans.

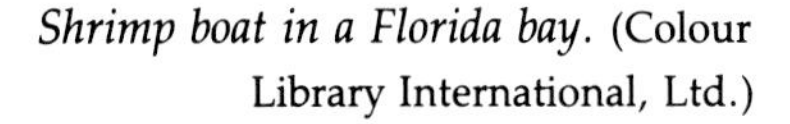

Shrimp boat in a Florida bay. (Colour Library International, Ltd.)

New Orleans streetcar. (Colour Library International, Ltd.)

NEW ORLEANS: QUEEN CITY OF THE DELTA

❑ It is a city of senses and sensuality. The very air is heavy with the fragrance of subtropical blooms, mixed with the aroma of a coffee-chicory blend and the bouquet of gumbo wafting from the entryways of scores of restaurants. It is a city of sounds, preeminently of the jazzman's trumpet and the tinkle of a Dixieland piano. Here, in a hundred bawdyhouses, jazz itself was born at the turn of the century, and here jazz remains enthroned. Indeed, seventy or eighty years ago,

Artists in Jackson Square, French Quarter, New Orleans. (Colour Library International, Ltd.)

Grillwork porches and balustrades in New Orleans. (Colour Library International, Ltd.)

the very word *jazz* had a connotation as much sexual as musical, reflecting its early close association with the demimonde of New Orleans. The city is also one to bedazzle the eye with cascades of flowers, set off against the filigreed railings that lend an extra measure of grace to the architecture of the *Vieux Carré* (the French Quarter). And New Orleans is a city of touch; its soft, hot, humid air, enveloping and caressing, evokes a languor almost impossible to shuck. Finally, it is a city of taste. Nowhere else in America, not even in New York, does food—its preparation and above all its consumption—have quite the obsessional status that it has here. At Carnival time in February, all of these sensual qualities come together in one vast street fair. Then, natives and tens of thousands of visitors go wild. Elaborate floats, marching jazz bands, costumed revelers join in a moment of frenzy—of uninhibited merriment. Meanwhile, in private clubs the city's social and financial elite attend sumptuous balls in praise of the god Bacchus. Writer William Faulkner perhaps put it most succinctly when he described New Orleans as a courtesan, "not old and yet no longer young, who shuns the sunlight that the illusion of her former glory be preserved."

From the time the United States took possession of the city from France in 1803 until this very day, New Orleans has been both quintessentially southern and somehow a little bit apart from Dixie. Nowhere was the Confederacy more revered and the "lost cause" more deeply mourned than in this city rising from the swamps of the Mississippi Delta. Nowhere was the plantation economy—built on cotton, sugar, and slavery—more important, and nowhere, in our own time, was integration of the public schools more fiercely resisted. In 1960 the face of hatred was clearly revealed, as television cameras recorded mobs of white mothers spitting obscenities at two little black girls as they entered a previously all-white school. Few who saw this scene will ever forget it.

Yet even in the "bad old days" New Orleans was different. Where the South was provincial, this city was cosmopolitan—its Franco-Spanish heritage providing a Latin counterpoint to the dominant Anglo-Scottish-Irish ambience of Dixie. Even today, New Orleans marches—or perhaps ambles—to a different drummer. Though New Orleans boasts one of the busiest ports in the nation, though petrochemical plants make the metropolitan region one of the world's great oil centers, though the newly built and massive Superdome proclaims the ascendancy of big-time sports, it all seems quite alien. Houston to the west and Atlanta to the east, these are the real money-making centers of the region, and New Orleanians look upon them with both envy and disdain. Here in the Delta, there is a softer message carried on each breeze. It says, "Don't hurry, don't rush. Come, sit on a café terrace. Breathe deep. Relax. Have an aperitif. Watch the world go by." ❑

NASHVILLE: CAPITAL OF COUNTRY MUSIC

❑ They call it, with the hyperbole typical of the region, the Athens of the South, and not only because it boasts a built-to-scale replica of the Parthenon. (It was erected in 1897 to commemorate Tennessee's statehood and the elevation of Nashville itself to the state's capital city.) Nashville also can claim a number of fine old Greek-Revival buildings, and some fourteen universities and colleges, including the top-ranked Vanderbilt and Fisk. They call it, too, the Wall Street of the South, because it is a booming banking, insurance, and investment center. The town's boosters have not yet found a lofty title to crown Nashville's

The Parthenon in Nashville, Tennessee, is an exact replica of the original building in Athens, Greece. (Nashville Chamber of Commerce)

position as a Jerusalem of American Protestantism: Some of the largest and most powerful churches have their headquarters and their publishing companies here. Nashville is also a major manufacturing center. Over six hundred industrial firms produce chemicals, machinery, textiles, apparel, tires, and food products here. They're loaded on barges at the city's Cumberland River port to be shipped throughout the central United States, or trucked out over the three interstate routes that intersect in Nashville. This city is manifestly one of the most prosperous and progressive in the South, yet it has, it seems, only a single claim to fame for nonresidents: It is the country music capital of the United States.

The figures are breathtaking: nearly sixty recording studios that operate day and night, seven record-pressing companies, 250 music publishers, thirty-four talent agencies, 2,400 on-site musicians, a recording industry that generates billions of dollars—not to mention the Grand Ole Opry House, or Opryland U.S.A.—the huge theme park—or the Opryland Hotel, Tennessee's largest. For many of the more than seven million tourists who come here every year, Nashville is as exciting a place to visit as Hollywood is for movie fans. You can see Roy Acuff and

The Ryman Auditorium was the home of the Grand Ole Opry from 1941 until 1974. It was built in the 1890s as a religious tabernacle. (Nashville Chamber of Commerce)

Minnie Pearl trades jokes with the King of Country Music, Roy Acuff, on the stage of the Grand Ole Opry. (Nashville Chamber of Commerce)

Loretta Lynn in the flesh, catch a glimpse of Dolly Parton emerging from her limousine, or pick out from the throng of would-be country music stars—who come by the thousands to this Mecca of the electric guitar—the next Elvis Presley.

In the days when country music was just a fiddle and a banjo whooping it up together on the front porch of a hill-country house, only southern mountain people knew it. The Grand Ole Opry changed all that. On November 28, 1925, radio station WSN, Nashville, broadcast the first Opry show, using local amateur talent. One of the amateurs, banjoist and singer Uncle Dave Macon, became famous far beyond the Tennessee hills; and by the early 1940s, with singer Roy Acuff leading an increasingly polished and professional cast, the show was being broadcast nationally. In 1974, now a supershow and a national institution, the Opry left its original headquarters in the heart of honky-tonk Nashville for a new $12 million Grand Ole Opry House that boasts a huge auditorium and some of the most advanced radio and television equipment in the world.

Surrounding the new Opry House is Opryland U.S.A., "The Home of American Music," 217 acres of thrill-rides, old-time steam engines, and music, music, music—everything from New Orleans jazz to cowboy to rock-and-roll. Like Disneyland, Opryland is a scrubbed-and-polished, technicolor version of the parts of America it purports to represent. There's not a trace of the black-and-white tones of real country music—the lovers' laments, the hard times, the straight-on realism, and the hard humor of the hill country folk. But for that you can buy a record—probably made in Nashville—by Hank Williams, Charley Pride, Merle Haggard, Johnny Cash, Loretta Lynn. . . . ❑

The Hermitage, a house in the Greek Revival style, is the restored home of Andrew Jackson, the seventh president of the United States. (Nashville Chamber of Commerce)

THE MIDWEST

FOOTBALL IS THE METAPHOR

The poet Keats called autumn "the season of mists and mellow fruitfulness." Here, in the middle portion of our great United States, it is all of that. And it is also the time when young men don armor, divide up into teams of eleven, and do battle against each other on a grid-marked field. In the fall, if you ever want to be sure of gathering fifty thousand or more people together in one place, just get two teams of the caliber of Indiana University and Ohio State, and hold a football game.

It seems to me that football has become a metaphor for the American spirit. A microcosm of American endeavor: competition, favorites, underdogs, pushing toward a goal. Fierce community pride is involved, and yes, even violence is applauded.

Action at the game.

The marching band can often be as spectacular as the football game.

Ours is a country which was born of a revolution, and which achieved greatness by facing up to confrontation without backing down. Our young people are taught that every American has to be Number One.

Vince Lombardi, the late great coach of the Green Bay Packers, phrased it this way: "Winning isn't everything. It's the only thing!" Winning, like football, is as American as apple pie, and nowhere is this ethic more apparent than it is in America's Midwest.

❑ If the twelve states that comprise the American Midwest—Ohio, Indiana, Michigan, Wisconsin, Illinois, Missouri, Minnesota, Iowa,

James Michener at a football game between Indiana University and Ohio State.

Kansas, North Dakota, South Dakota, and Nebraska—were an independent country, it would be a colossus among nations. Taken together, these states are home to sixty million Americans—one-quarter of the population of the United States—and cover 763,500 square miles, an area larger than continental Western Europe minus Scandinavia. But it is not just size and population that makes the region a giant: It is the fact that here, in the American heartland, is America's muscle. These states, with their prairie and plains farms, form not only America's breadbasket but the food reservoir for the entire world. From the Great Lakes states alone—Michigan, Illinois, Indiana, Wisconsin, and Ohio—a subsection more industrial than agricultural—come 42 percent of America's corn, 11 percent each of cattle and wheat, and 26 percent of the nation's hogs. Add to this the millions of bushels of corn, wheat, and soybeans that the great farms of the Dakotas, Minnesota, Nebraska, Kansas, and Iowa disgorge each summer and fall, and the picture of an agricultural cornucopia becomes clear. Is there an earthquake in Guatemala? Midwest commodities will feed the victims. Has drought turned the once lush fields of East Africa into desert? The grain storage silos of America's midsection open wide to ease the resulting famine.

Growing to majestic heights, corn flourishes in a midwestern field.

For all its agricultural diversity and abundance, the Midwest is preeminently industrial. Detroit and its surrounding metropolitan area may be seen as the linchpin of America's entire manufacturing complex. When the automobile industry thrives, America booms; when it falters, America staggers. So many basic industries—steel, rubber, mining, glass, to mention a few—depend upon the health of the auto industry that the ripple effect of a downturn in car and truck production and sales is felt throughout the nation, but most disastrously in the Midwest where millions upon millions of workers are directly or indirectly dependent upon this one industry. The recent depression in the

Soo Locks at Sault Sainte Marie, Michigan, connect Lake Superior and Lake Huron and form a major link in the Great Lake Waterway. (Michigan Travel Commission)

The Blue Water Bridge to Canada, Port Huron, Michigan. (Colour Library International, Ltd.)

automotive industry—made acute by competition from Japanese and German car makers—bids fair to alter drastically the very nature of American manufacturing and quite possibly to depopulate the midwestern industrial centers of their most productive and highly skilled workers. Many workers in the Midwest are moving south in the 1980s to look for better jobs, or any jobs at all.

Troubled though it may be, the Midwest continues to exert a tremendous pull on the American consciousness. To travel the small towns of Ohio, or Kansas, or Minnesota is to be transported to an earlier era. Here there is a feeling for roots, customs, and steady relationships

Great Lakes freighter unloading bulk cargo near Hancock in upper Michigan. (Colour Library International, Ltd.)

Home turf for this racing car is the famous Indianapolis 500 Speedway. (Indianapolis Motor Speedway Corporation)

that mocks the pretensions of a mobile society. Former Senator George McGovern once summed up that feeling in an interview with *Life* magazine, when he spoke of his hometown, Mitchell, South Dakota. "I still love to go back . . . and wander up and down those streets. It just kind of reassures me . . . that there is a place I know thoroughly, where the roots are deep. . . . There are not lots of high schools; there's one. There aren't a lot of libraries; there's the Carnegie Library. Everything had a place, a specific definition. . . . When people talk about the small-town sense of community, the role of the family, relationship with neighbors, fellowship of the church, school spirit—I had all those things, and they meant a great deal to me in providing guidelines, a foundation, a personal security."

In the midwestern small town, there is no question about the nation's values, about the importance of family or patriotism. Here men,

Michigan's largest city, Detroit, boasts a rebuilt downtown set off by the waters of the Detroit River. (City of Detroit)

Boy showing his prize sheep at a typical agricultural fair in the Midwest.

women, and children still stand during a parade when the flag is carried by, and bare their heads without a trace of embarrassment. In America's heartland, for better or worse, the old ideals endure. ❑

SETTLING THE LAND

❑ In 1818 an English immigrant named Morris Birkbeck living in the forest deeps of Illinois sent a letter to his homeland advising his compatriots "to transplant, into these boundless regions of freedom the millions grovelling in ignorance and want." By then, tens of thousands had already reached the same conclusion—Englishmen, Frenchmen, Germans, and most numerous of all, Americans from the Atlantic seaboard states. There were southern backwoodsmen, originally from Virginia and North Carolina, later from Kentucky and Tennessee, who

Electricity power lines at Niagara Falls on the New York State side. The falls are situated on the Niagara River, which connects Lake Ontario with Lake Erie. Hydroelectric power from this source is divided between the United States and Canada and supplies vast amounts of energy for the construction of parks, roads, bridges, and many other projects and uses. (Colour Library International, Ltd.)

forded the Ohio River to hunt the forests of southern Ohio, Indiana, and Illinois. From the mid-Atlantic states came merchants, eager to build new cities in the wilderness—farm centers that would wax rich upon the trade in produce. And there were farmers from the rocky reaches of Vermont, New Hampshire, and Massachusetts who trudged west in search of better soil than that offered by their native heaths. This was fresh land, virgin land, government-owned land that could be bought for a most reasonable sum. And from the old settlements hugging the ocean shore, citizens flocked to the interior in pursuit of a new life and a new chance to succeed. After all, the right to settle the forests and prairies of the West was one of the reasons Americans fought the Revolution.

Iron ore plant at Presque Isle on Lake Superior, near Marquette on the Michigan upper peninsula. (Colour Library International, Ltd.)

At the time the first skirmishes of the Revolutionary War were taking place in 1775, the region bounded by the Appalachians in the east and the Mississippi in the west was wilderness. Here and there English forts and fur trading posts were set down among Indian tribal settlements. British policy had been to prohibit colonization of the trans-Appalachian region, to maintain the area as a preserve of the Indians then being employed in England's highly profitable fur trade. Perhaps as much as the Stamp Act and the Navigation Acts, this policy of exclusion was responsible for colonial discontent. Certainly patriot leaders such as George Washington and Benjamin Franklin looked longingly to the west as an area ripe for land speculation if only the British could be ousted. So, led by George Rogers Clark, rebel columns swooped down upon British forts in the western wilds during the Revolution and secured American claims to the vast area.

Immediately after the British recognized American independence in 1783, a tide of migration surged into the region dubbed the Northwest

The port city of Cleveland, Ohio, on Lake Erie. Ohio's largest city, Cleveland is a great ore port, a large Great Lakes shipping point, and one of the nation's leading iron and steel centers. (Cleveland Chamber of Commerce)

Night skyline of Detroit, Michigan. Michigan's largest city, located between lakes Erie and St. Clair, is a major shipping and rail center. Henry Ford and others made Detroit "the automobile capital of the world." In the late 1970s and early 1980s, Detroit suffered a decline due to intense foreign auto competition and rising energy costs. (Colour Library International, Ltd.)

Territory. By 1803 Ohio had a sufficient population to enter the Union as a state; Indiana and Illinois were not far behind. When, in 1825, the Erie Canal connecting Lakes Ontario and Erie with the Hudson River opened, the tide became a floodtide. The canal meant easy access to the fertile soil surrounding the Great Lakes and an inexpensive means for shipping produce to market. The effect of the canal was galvanizing. Cities seemed to spring up from the soil almost overnight. In 1833, Massachusetts Senator Daniel Webster visited the Lake Erie port city of Cleveland and was stunned by its rapid growth. "Eight years ago," he said, "I enjoyed a brief visit to this place. There was then one steamboat on Lake Erie. . . . There are now eighteen steamboats plying the lake, all finding full employment." No less impressed was the English traveler Harriet Martineau, who wrote of Detroit in 1836: "Thousands of settlers are pouring in every year. . . . Many are Irish, German or Dutch, working their way into the back country, and glad to be employed for awhile."

By the time the Civil War began in 1861, all of the trans-Appalachian west, up to the Mississippi, had been settled. Cities like Chicago, Cleveland, and Detroit were well on their way to greatness. Hundreds of smaller towns had risen where but a few decades before there had been only trees and prairie grass. And everywhere there were farms. Indeed the trail of settlement had actually vaulted the Mississippi itself. Missouri, originally settled by southerners, entered the Union early, in 1821; Iowa and Minnesota became states some years later. And the cutting edge of settlement was pushing toward the 100th meridian in Kansas and Nebraska, where the well-watered prairie yields to the far drier plains. ❑

The Great American Desert

❑ Once the forest and prairie regions of the Midwest were settled, during the first half of the nineteenth century, migration west slowed

Lush farm fields and silo in Iowa.

for a while. Popular lore—backed by the reports of some explorers—had it that the wide plains beyond the 100th meridian were virtually uninhabitable, a "Great American Desert," in the phrase of the day. The short-grass country of western Kansas, Nebraska, and the Dakotas was seen primarily as Indian land, useful to colonists only as a broad pathway toward the salubrious climes of California and the Oregon Territory. In the 1870s and 1880s, however, a number of factors combined to stimulate development of the short-grass country. One was the nation's need for beef, and ranchers from Texas drove their herds northward to the railheads in Kansas, feeding their cattle off the grasslands along the way. The discovery that cattle thrived on these plains led to the extension of the range into the northern plains. Then there was the passage of the Homestead Act during the Civil War. This landmark legislation that permitted settlers to secure acreage virtually free was a powerful inducement. Between 1870 and 1900, westering settlers claimed 430 million acres, much of it on the plains. Adding to the boom were the railroads, then snaking their way across the continent. If they were to survive and prosper they had to encourage settlement along their rights of way. To attract farmers to the plains the railroads established demonstration farms to prove the fertility of the soil, they offered huge blocks of land to settlers at very attractive prices, they even sent recruiters to scour Europe from the shores of Britain to the interior of Russia to bring immigrants to the American West. To clear the plains of Indians, the railroads hired professional hunters to kill off the buffalo by the tens of thousands, thus denying the Indians their primary source of sustenance. Where the railroads left off the United States Army took over. In a series of bloody engagements, American soldiers pressed the Indians harder and harder, rounding up tribe after tribe and imprisoning them on reservations. By the end of the nineteenth century such tactics had largely succeeded. The great emptiness of the short-grass country was filled from the Missouri River right up to the foothills of the Rockies. The sea of grass on which the buffalo had fed was replaced by seas of wheat and corn on which America and even the world would depend for its daily bread.

In 1927, Ole Edvart Rolvaag, the Norwegian-American writer, published his novel *Giants in the Earth,* which told of pioneering days on the plains. In it, Rolvaag's hero, a Scandinavian immigrant named Per Hansa, expresses his love of the land that had come to be his own, thoughts that were undoubtedly shared by thousands of other pioneers, sentiments that are still held by today's farmers in the Heartland. "Once more Per Hansa's heart filled with a deep sense of peace and contentment. . . . Was he really to own it? Was it really to become his possession, this big stretch of fine land that spread here before him? . . . His heart began to expand with a mighty exaltation. An emotion he had never felt before filled him and made him walk erect. 'Good God!' he panted. 'This kingdom is going to be mine!'" ❑

NINE DAYS IN SEPTEMBER: THE KANSAS STATE FAIR

Hutchinson, Kansas, is in the middle of the Midwest. It's the home of the Kansas State Fair, a nine-day extravaganza of agricultural showmanship, the proud culmination of a year's worth of planning and labor, a time to show off the superb fruits of the harvest. First held in 1913, the fair has been dedicated to its original purpose for two-thirds of a century: "To promote industries of the state, especially the predominant industry of agriculture, and to foster better citizenship by promotion of the state's activities, institutions, and youth work." The latter is accomplished by encouraging young people in their 4-H work and rewarding its excellence. The former is recognized with blue ribbons for everything from quinces to currant wine to cattle.

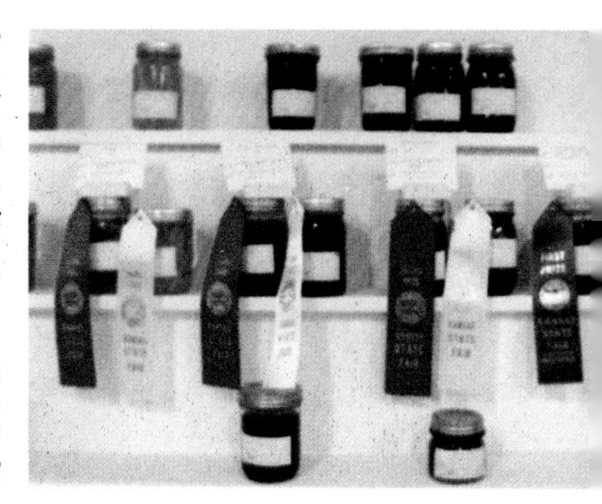

Prize jars of preserves proudly displayed at the state fair.

For nine days, the fairgrounds are covered with a cornucopia of

Woman riding with her child on horse at the annual Kansas State Fair in Hutchinson, Kansas.

produce and a proud parade of prize hogs and sows, steers and cows. It is crisscrossed by thousands of people who have come from every county for miles around to ride the rides, to watch the shows, to cheer winners, or to be winners. They'll watch the marching of one hundred high school bands from all over the state of Kansas. They'll cast critical eyes on exhibitions of poultry, pigeons, and pastries. They'll lust over fancy new models of glistening farm equipment.

Some will compete to see who can shear sheep the fastest, whose cut flower arrangements are the most beautiful, whose preserves are the best, whose fancy stitching the most elaborate. There'll be a "Wheat King" and a "Cookie Jar" winner, a "Best-Dressed Girl" and a "Best-Groomed Boy." There'll be lots of races: stock car races, chuck wagon races, tractor-pulling contests. Big-name entertainers are scheduled for every day of the fair.

There'll be friends from all over the state, whose conversation will be as succinctly specialized as the convention talk between doctors or lawyers: Charolais, Brangus, Limousin (those are cattle); Corriedale, Shropshire, Southdown, Montadale (those are sheep); Appaloosa horses, Duroc swine. They'll talk of piping systems, swine facilities, feed

In hope of a blue ribbon, youngsters lead their prize heifers in front of the judges.

formulas, automated feeding, milking parlors, grinders, hoppers, air dryers, blowers, combines, tractors, discs, harrows, balers. . . .

When the fair is over, the Kansans will go home with their blue ribbons, maybe the bill for a new tractor, certainly some new ideas about how to plant or cultivate or feed or raise or enrich or preserve—because farming is complex and changing, and the good farmer is the man who is willing to adapt.

In state fair country, the art of hand quilting still survives, as this magnificent display attests.

The midway at the Kansas State Fair.

The state fair ends the summer. Soon the chill midwestern winter will settle over the fields, the countryside will button up, the cows will keep to their barns. The planning for the new year will begin, and the hope for even better crops, even fatter cattle, even more blue ribbons at next September's state fair.

AN IOWA FARMER

The Midwest is America's breadbasket, and the farmer is the fellow who provides the dough. As the baker rises before dawn to get the morning buns and muffins into the ovens, so too will you find the Iowa farmer greeting the sun that is rising over his own shop. And what a shop it is! This land is the legacy of behemoth glaciers that once churned across it, leaving behind a soil that is well endowed with minerals, and is rich-black to depths of eighteen inches. By the time the earliest settlers arrived here in the mid-1800s, the ground had been further imbued with a-thousand-times-a-thousand years of grass returning its nutrients to the soil in a never-ending cycle of birth and decay. So fertile were these acres that one could toss a seed to earth and almost watch it sprout.

Those first nineteenth-century Iowa settlers arrived on these prairies with their families, built their houses and tilled their lands with the help of their families, and deeded their acres to their descendants. The family tradition endures to this day. But, with all its rewards, farming has become a hazardous business, one in which the operator is a risk-taking manager who, with his family, does most of the farm work, and who is responsible for the difficult tasks of planning, financing, and management as well. Bill Judge, of Boon County, Iowa, with his wife, Patsy, and two children, is one of these risk-taking managers.

Michener Talks with the Judge Family

MICHENER: I understand your family has operated on this land for about a hundred years.

JUDGE: Almost that long. They were originally immigrants from Ireland. They came through the eastern part of the country and settled here in the latter part of the 1800s.

MICHENER: And they acquired the land a small bit at a time?

JUDGE: Right. By now, we have about eight hundred acres in the family—my father and aunts and ourselves. In the hundred or so years since my family has been here, I guess we've managed pretty well. . . . We're all still here, anyway.

MICHENER: Have you always lived right in this area of Boon County?

JUDGE: I've only gotten half a mile from where I started—so I've stayed pretty close to home.

MICHENER: And why do you stay with farming?

JUDGE: It's a way of life I've come to know, and I enjoy the challenges that go with it.

MICHENER: How about being a farm wife, Mrs. Judge?

PATSY JUDGE: I don't think farm wives are much different from city wives now. We work and go to town to get our groceries, and do other things just like everyone else. So it's really not so different. Although there's a little bit of loneliness sometimes. . . . You're more by yourselves. But I enjoy the farm—I like the changing seasons and the busy times. I like the wintertime, too—we have more time with our family then, more time to do things together.

MICHENER: Patsy, do you get snowed in in the winter?

PATSY JUDGE: Oh, yes. Although being snowed in isn't as bad as the ice storms, when the electricity goes off, and we're sort of secluded for a while. When that happens, we always think that we do lots of neat things like play games and have a lot of fun together, but really we all just get on each other's nerves. . . . And anyway, the telephones usually work, and there are snowmobiles and all kinds of ways to get around. So it's not a big problem.

MICHENER: These days, is it easier to raise children on a farm than in a city?

PATSY JUDGE: I think our city friends envy us sometimes, because our kids don't have all the outside influences that theirs do. But on the other hand, our kids don't really learn to get along with as many other kinds of people.

JUDGE: By being more or less isolated, outside influences—people who use drugs, for instance—are limited. Some of this isolation is a disadvantage: Our kids don't have the activities that would be available in a metropolitan area. But they don't have some of the adverse activities either.

MICHENER: Do the children of farm families tend to go on to college these days?

PATSY JUDGE: Yes, they do. An education is just as important for someone going into farming as for anyone else now, because there's so much management ability needed.

MICHENER: Well, you don't live very far from Ames, Iowa. Back east, we think of Ames as one of the great agricultural centers in the nation.

JUDGE: Well, we think it is. Of course, we're both graduates of the college.

The Farm

MICHENER: Life on the farm must be easier now than it was in your grandfather's day.

JUDGE: Oh, a lot easier! Mechanization has taken the backbreaking work out of the process that goes into producing a crop. Of course, there are a lot more worries now. There's the increased burden of management, because we operate on so much larger a scale than my grandparents did.

MICHENER: What would be the smallest farm you could use?

JUDGE: Well, with an adequate livestock program, a family of our size could survive on two hundred acres.

MICHENER: So the old "hundred acres and a mule" is dead?

JUDGE: Very dead. Next year, my brother and I will be farming one thousand forty acres, and I think we'll be able to handle that without any problems.

MICHENER: How much heavy equipment do you have to have for one thousand forty acres?

JUDGE: Well, each man has to have at his disposal the equipment that he needs day in and day out. If you're underequipped, you're going to be late, which reduces yields, and in the harvest you run the risk of the loss of a crop because of snow or severe winds. We couldn't farm on this scale without heavy machines—they're the necessary tools of our trade.

MICHENER: I've lived on farmland all my life, but I've never seen land as rich and black as this. How did it get that way?

JUDGE: This is prairie soil. It's very high in organic matter, which

Bill and Patsy Judge, a farming couple from Ames, Iowa, talk to James Michener.

gives that black color to the soil. It's good, rich soil. It holds moisture well, conserves rainfall . . .

MICHENER: So you don't have the heavy problem of replenishing your soil with organic matter all the time?

JUDGE: No, it's not a problem, although we make sure that the humus we do produce is returned to the soil.

MICHENER: How are your yields—are they higher than the national average?

JUDGE: Iowa and Illinois vie for the record in corn production yields each year.

MICHENER: What do you grow?

JUDGE: Our program alternates back and forth between corn and soybeans. What is in soybeans this year will be planted in corn the following year, and vice versa. We rotate the crops to restore nitrogen to the soil, and to break up the life cycle of pests such as corn ripworms. That reduces the need for insecticides.

MICHENER: Do you use a lot of fertilizer?

JUDGE: Yes, we do. We use all three major plant nutrients. The nitrogen is derived from anhydrous ammonia, and the potassium and phosphorus are applied in the fall as dry fertilizers.

MICHENER: Do you raise cattle?

JUDGE: Yes. Our cattle are all feed-lot cattle—we don't raise calves. We buy young cattle and feed them until they reach market grade. They're all kept in lots, except in the fall when we run them through the harvested cornfields to pick up dropped corn. And we raise our own hogs, too.

MICHENER: All of your eight hundred acres is relatively flat. Do you have any swampy land?

JUDGE: Some of it is. One of the greatest problems we have in this area is drainage. Before drainage tile was put in, there were places where water stood year round.

MICHENER: So all these fields have underground drainage systems built into them. How are they put in?

JUDGE: Well, they used to use systems of clay tile. They dug them in at least three feet deep to get below the frost level, so in the winter they won't freeze and break up. The tiles collect underground water and carry it to a stream or river or some other outlet. Some of these old tile lines were put in maybe eighty years ago, and of course they were all dug in by hand. Now they're deteriorating; they've just served their time. So they're having to be replaced.

MICHENER: Well, they kept the Judge family in business for eighty years. When you replace them, do you still dig them in by hand?

JUDGE: No. Now there's a very sophisticated machine that operates on a laser beam. It digs the trench, lays plastic tubing, and covers the trench all in one operation. It's a far cry from the spade and the shovel.

Farm Economics

MICHENER: According to what I read in the newspapers, Iowa has more millionaires than almost any other state in the Union, in proportion to its population. I think Idaho has the most millionaires, and Iowa comes in second or third. They say that the reason is the excessive growth in the value of land. And they figure that in an average Iowa county there will be one hundred seventeen millionaires. So in Boon County, your neighbors include one hundred seventeen millionaires.

PATSY JUDGE: If they are, they certainly aren't living like millionaires.

MICHENER: I talked about this with farmers in North Dakota, and they said, "Michener, you're seeing America's only poor millionaires!" They had the land, and it was worth a lot of money, but they couldn't do much with it.

JUDGE: That's true. Farmland is now more an investment than a unit of production. It's inflated in value to the point where, by the time interest is paid and all the other production outlays, the revenue from a crop will not cover the costs.

MICHENER: So the value placed on an acre of your land is so high that you cannot grow enough crops on it to justify the high price?

JUDGE: Exactly. But your land is your employment. If you were to sell the land, you'd no longer be employed. So you continue to produce, and hope that in time it will be worth the money you paid for the land. But on today's market, the price we receive for corn is not quite covering the cost of production, if you include all the out-of-pocket costs plus the interest on the land and taxes and everything that goes into the production of the crop.

MICHENER: In other words, it costs you more to produce the corn than you can get selling it. So what do you do? You feed some to your cattle and your hogs . . .

JUDGE: Right. We put this corn to use in a livestock program, in the hope of gaining a better return than we would by selling the corn as grain. We grow all the corn we need to feed our animals.

MICHENER: So in effect what you're doing is converting your corn into hogs and cattle.

JUDGE: Right. We market our corn as livestock. But we can't do that with our soybean crop. We sell soybeans as grain, then it's processed so the oil is removed, and we buy it back as soybean meal, which is a protein concentrate for livestock feed.

MICHENER: The Judge farm has always been a family farm. Is that type of farming doomed?

JUDGE: We don't think it is here in Iowa. For the most part, this is very intensive agriculture—it's very difficult to farm here without considerable background. And one of the most effective ways to achieve that is to grow up on the farm.

MICHENER: Well, how about the intrusion of agribusiness: a couple of guys from Philadelphia or New York come out and buy up all the farms and operate them as a unit?

JUDGE: We've seen a few attempts at that, and they've failed.

MICHENER: If this farm is so valuable, and the soil so productive, it must pose a great problem when you want to pass it on. How about taxes? Don't they hit you very hard?

JUDGE: That's one of the real big problems. In a farmer's lifetime, land may become a great proportion of his total possessions. And when he passes it on to the next generation, possibly fifty percent of what he owns—his life savings—will be taken in taxes and administrative procedures.

MICHENER: Okay. Let's say I've saved forty-two thousand dollars. Can I come out to Iowa and buy a farm?

JUDGE: It would be a very small one.

MICHENER: I could grow some onions, maybe.

AMERICAN FARMING: THE HAZARDS OF SUCCESS

❑ If the way a nation provides food for its people is taken as an index of its success, then America must rank as the most successful on earth. No other country has ever produced food in such abundance. Paradoxically, this triumph of American agriculture has created a situation that some experts find potentially dangerous: The number of farms and farmers shrink yearly; food production is becoming more specialized and centralized; and the costs of efficient farming have risen to the point where a young farmer, just starting out, must either inherit his land or mortgage his future to the hilt to buy a few acres.

In the heart of the growing and harvesting season, you may be hard put to find locally grown vegetables in some parts of the United States. In many places in the corn belt, if you get a yen for sweet corn you'll have to buy it at the supermarket just like the local farm wives. And it won't be fresh picked, because it will have been trucked from a good distance—New Jersey, perhaps, or New York State. Few corn belt farmers raise sweet corn anymore; they concentrate on the mass production of feed corn or soybeans, cattle or pigs. Today states like Massachusetts possess many acres of unused farmland and import most of the food their citizens eat. More and more, people who relish corn and fresh vegetables grow them in their backyard gardens, while the small farms that once supplied produce and milk to a local region are going or gone.

Farming in the United States has experienced a revolution as far-reaching in its effects as was the Industrial Revolution of the nineteenth century, and our nostalgic notions about the old farm and the rural good life often bear little relation to present reality. In 1950 there were over 6 million farms in the United States, and the average farm size was 180 acres; in 1974 the total number had shrunk to 2.3 million and the average size had ballooned to 440 acres. The population engaged in farming has diminished proportionately, until today only 3 percent of our people are needed to provide food in such abundance that their efforts feed the entire nation, and some one-quarter of the agricultural crop is exported to other countries. By contrast, in the USSR almost 20 percent of the population works directly in farming; almost 30 percent in South Africa; 64 percent in China.

America has achieved this extraordinary abundance through a combination of singular circumstances, beginning with the existence of vast stretches of rich and empty farmland in the Midwest. The early settlers, who broke their light plows trying to turn the thick sod of the plains and prairies, soon had heavier plows that did the job, then gang plows, then combines and a host of increasingly ingenious machines that made cultivation possible on a scale never before attempted. Cheap manufactured fertilizers and the development of new hybrid plant varieties enormously increased crop yields. A complex network of roads, railroads, and waterways moved vast quantities of grain and cattle out of America's heartland, and shuttled oranges away from California and Florida, strawberries north from Texas. Perhaps most significant was the recognition, in the mid-nineteenth century, that successful farming requires educated farmers. The establishment of agricultural schools in land-grant colleges and of government-supported agricultural services gave farmers access to the newest agricultural techniques and to the most advanced products of agricultural research. ❑

American Bonanza

❑ In little over a century, then, American soil and technology has produced an agricultural bonanza. It has also turned farming into an intensely competitive business. Today's farmer needs more than hard work and good weather to produce a profitable crop. He must cultivate sufficient acreage, must own a barn loaded with expensive machinery, and must possess a banker's ability to juggle finances. Above all, he needs money. In the 1970s alone, farm operating expenses soared by over 60 percent, and total farm debt increased from $59 billion to $94 billion. In order to keep competitive, the dairy farmer in that decade installed sophisticated milking parlors and automatic feeding equipment. With much of the burden of milking and feeding off his hands, he had more time to raise larger herds. The midwestern swine raiser, if he wanted to stay in business, was forced to build new confinement facilities to hold the larger numbers of pigs that alone could make his operation profitable. The California lettuce grower contemplated buying a harvesting machine—even if he couldn't afford one—to cut his high labor costs and get his crop into a highly competitive market in the shortest possible time.

Good farmland has become too expensive for most farmers to buy. Its price has doubled and tripled in a decade, forced up by absentee investors and speculators, or bought up for suburban development. Where farmland cannot be forced to yield a good cash crop—in New England, for instance—corn and tobacco fields lie fallow or, in favored spots, are transmuted into vacation havens—resort hotels, ski lodges. And when sons and daughters inherit a family farm, they often discover that its value—assessed for tax purposes at today's inflated prices—makes it just too expensive to keep.

The trend is toward ever greater concentrations of land and capital. The latest statistics show 2.4 percent of all farms producing almost 40 percent of the total United States agricultural crop. Many farms are still family owned and managed, but some family spreads have become so large that they are indistinguishable from the giant-size assemblages that are owned by corporations and farmed like factories.

The American agricultural success story seems to prove that larger is better. But a potential problem exists when there are too many eggs in too few baskets. And, as the rest of the world draws more and more food from the American cornucopia, we may wish that we hadn't covered so many good acres with cement, or retired so many farmers who could still be plowing their own family-sized farms. ❑

The skyline of Chicago with the tall white tower of the Standard Oil Building at left. (Colour Library International, Ltd.)

CHICAGO: CAPITAL OF MID-AMERICA

The monolithic John Hancock Center rises 1,127 feet into the sky over Chicago. (Colour Library International, Ltd.)

In the Midwest, all roads lead to Chicago. It is the heart of the American heartland. The trucks and the cars come funneling through this major city on the prairie at the rate of hundreds of thousands each day. The railroads, which first put the city on the map, are today but a minor factor in the city's wealth, their place having been taken by the airplane. Chicago's major airport, O'Hare International, is the world's busiest. Two thousand aircraft a day, in and out, alternately soak up and disgorge the fifty million travelers who pass through this terminus each year. But O'Hare is just one of the superlatives about which the Windy City boasts. Chicagoans exult in the world's tallest building, the Sears Tower; the biggest single steelmaking plant on earth, Inland Steel; the largest hotel in the nation, the Conrad Hilton; the biggest sewage-treatment system anywhere; America's largest volume of manufactured goods shipped; the tallest apartment building. In fact, a condominium owner on the ninety-second floor of the John Hancock Center—which soars above Chicago's "Magnificent Mile" and incorporates both offices and dwelling places—raised his floors by six inches just so he could claim ownership of the most elevated apartment in the world.

Modern Chicago could not have happened without the fire started by Mrs. O'Leary's fabled cow, which destroyed the ramshackle, wood-built old city in 1871. Whether the lantern knocked over by the cow's

Michigan Avenue, Chicago's elegant, lakefront boulevard. The Wrigley Building with its famous clock tower is at left. (Colour Library International, Ltd.)

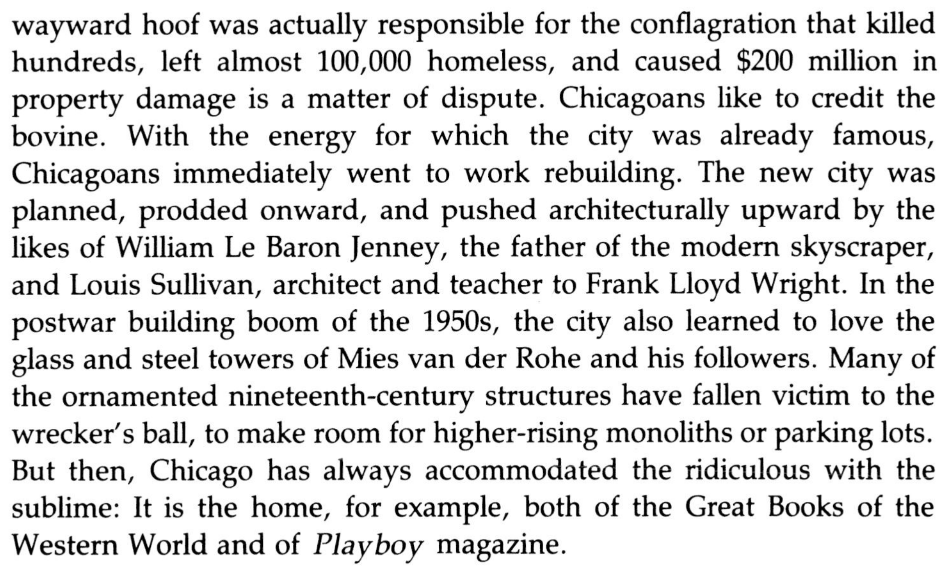

wayward hoof was actually responsible for the conflagration that killed hundreds, left almost 100,000 homeless, and caused $200 million in property damage is a matter of dispute. Chicagoans like to credit the bovine. With the energy for which the city was already famous, Chicagoans immediately went to work rebuilding. The new city was planned, prodded onward, and pushed architecturally upward by the likes of William Le Baron Jenney, the father of the modern skyscraper, and Louis Sullivan, architect and teacher to Frank Lloyd Wright. In the postwar building boom of the 1950s, the city also learned to love the glass and steel towers of Mies van der Rohe and his followers. Many of the ornamented nineteenth-century structures have fallen victim to the wrecker's ball, to make room for higher-rising monoliths or parking lots. But then, Chicago has always accommodated the ridiculous with the sublime: It is the home, for example, both of the Great Books of the Western World and of *Playboy* magazine.

Chicago's O'Hare International Airport is the busiest in the nation.

A stabile by Alexander Calder, one of many examples of art in Chicago's public spaces.

The Art Institute of Chicago on Michigan Avenue at Adams Street ranks among the world's most splendid art museums. (The Art Institute of Chicago)

Chicago in the 1980s looks as if it had been thrust skyward, as if the sheer weight of Lake Michigan, pressing against the shore, had forced spouts of glass, steel, and concrete out of the prairies and into the air. At ground level, one finds a city liberally sprinkled with enormous parks and with grand works of public art—here a Picasso; there a Chagall, a Calder, an Oldenburg. The famous stockyards and slaughterhouses have vanished, gone almost a decade now since the decentralization of the meat-packing industry. The lowing and bleating of a past population of millions of animals is now but a faint memory in the wind. But the raw, hustling energy that Carl Sandburg wrote of is still an obvious presence. ❑

The sculpture garden behind the Art Institute of Chicago is an oasis of quiet beauty. (The Art Institute of Chicago)

Michener Talks with Irv Kupcinet

How might the city be viewed today by one of its own eloquent chroniclers? I think of him as Mr. Chicago—Irv Kupcinet, newspaper columnist, television talk-show host, raconteur, whose love affair with the Windy City is legendary.

MICHENER: Kup, how long have you lived in Chicago?

KUPCINET: All my life, Jim, except for a couple of years at the University of North Dakota. I was a kind of tramp athlete in the Depression days. I went wherever I could play. So I played football at the university, and studied journalism.

MICHENER: You later played for the Chicago Bears, didn't you?

KUPCINET: No, Jim—I played for the Philadelphia Eagles way back in 1935, when you and I were youngsters.

MICHENER: Boy, that league has come a long way, hasn't it?

KUPCINET: Tremendous way . . . The foresight of people like George Hallis [owner of the Chicago Bears], who practically invented professional football, was really remarkable. George never lost confidence that football would be a major professional sport.

MICHENER: What did you get paid when you were a pro?

KUPCINET: In those days we got paid by the game: one hundred twenty-five dollars a game. That was pretty good money in 1935. When I officiated I made only seventy-five dollars a game.

James Michener with Irv Kupcinet, newspaper columnist and television talk-show host.

Northwestern University, one of the many major educational institutions in the Chicago area. (Colour Library International, Ltd.)

MICHENER: Well, they're doing a lot better than that now. Chicago is still a very big sports town, isn't it?

KUPCINET: We're one of the few cities that still has two major-league baseball teams, which we support very well despite their poor records. We have the Bears in professional football, and they sell out every week. We have the Bulls and the Blackhawks who are both doing fairly well. We have Northwestern University, which does not do well at all, either in attendance or in victories. But De Paul University has one of the best college basketball teams. In fact, although we have a lot of great teams here and good support, we have not had a great many winners. The Cubs haven't won a pennant since 1945, and the White Sox last won a pennant in 1959. But the fans here still support their ball clubs.

MICHENER: Tell me, Kup, how does it feel to be "Mister Chicago"?

KUPCINET: I'm delighted to be an unofficial spokesman for the city of Chicago, which I love very dearly, warts and all. I serve on committees, and I'm in very many fundraising activities. It seems we have some event every day of the week where you're called upon to help raise funds, to make speeches. It's part of the responsibility I assume as a columnist. Then, you do have access to a lot of people, and consequently you can do a lot of good things.

MICHENER: I noticed as we were casually walking through the streets that about a third of the people we passed knew you and said, "Hi, Kup." It was no big deal . . . but it was rather warm.

KUPCINET: Well, I've been around for so long, Jim . . . and I do know a lot of people in this town.

MICHENER: When I lived in Colorado, we used to look to Chicago as our capital. We would think of coming east—of Chicago as an eastern city. Does it still function as the capital of the great hinterland?

KUPCINET: I think it does. We're the capital of the Middle West. We're the great city between New York and Los Angeles, and I think we have so much to offer—the theater and the culture and the architecture, in addition to the museums and education. It's a city that people look to in the whole Middle West. It's the capital for the area all the way from Ohio to Colorado.

MICHENER: I first knew Chicago through the writing of Ben Hecht, that marvelous newspaperman, and he portrayed a pretty rough-and-ready town. [Ben Hecht was coauthor of *The Front Page*, a play about newspaper competition in Chicago in the late 1920s.] Have things changed much here since those hectic days?

KUPCINET: We used to have five or six very active newspapers, and the competition between them was called the greatest in the nation. Now we're down to two papers, but the competition is still very tough. And the caliber of the press has improved enormously. So many more college-prepared youngsters have entered journalism. Writers like Mike Royko and Roger Simon and Bob Greene, and some of the others who

The Chicago Sun Times *Building* (ABOVE) *and the* Chicago Tribune *Building* (LEFT) *represent architectural styles as different as are the two newspapers' political philosophies.* (Colour Library International, Ltd., and the *Chicago Tribune*)

write today's columns, are every bit as good as the Ben Hechts of earlier years.

MICHENER: When I was a boy, Chicago was known as "hog butcher to the world."

KUPCINET: We've lost the monopoly we had as the stockyards of the world, the great stockyards about which Carl Sandburg wrote so brilliantly. The meat industry has changed completely, and the stockyards are gone. Today Chicago is a financial community, an educational community. We've had tremendous success in our commodity exchanges. I think economically, Chicago's very very strong; we're not limited to one or two industries, we do very well across the board. Transportation is still tremendous, although the railroads which once made Chicago the railroad capital of the nation are gone. But O'Hare Field is the largest and busiest airport in the entire nation, and airlines have taken up the slack that was created when the railroads disappeared.

We've lost a lot of people who used to come through by train. The Pump Room was once the great melting pot of the nation, because train passengers would stop there for lunch or dinner, and then take their connecting train and go on to the west, or down to New Orleans. . . .

MICHENER: The first date I had with my wife—who is a Chicago woman—was at the Pump Room. And I remember thinking how nice it was of me to have taken her out, because obviously she was a working girl who hadn't eaten for four weeks. I never saw a woman eat so much. And then I took her out again the next night, because she was a

Rockefeller Memorial Chapel on the University of Chicago campus, designed by Bertram Grosvenor Goodhue. Like most of the other buildings at the university, the chapel is faced with Indiana limestone. The tower contains a carillon, one of the largest in the world, which was the gift of John D. Rockefeller. (University of Chicago News Information Service)

Chicago University students at a writing workshop.

marvelous person, and, my God, she still kept eating. And it's been that way ever since. And she weighs maybe one hundred ten pounds. . . . So I'm very fond of Chicago. We had a great time here.

I'd like to ask you a tough question, Kup. You're a macho type, you played professional football, you're a rugged man. I think of the literary figures in Chicago as macho also: Farrell and Studs Terkel and Nelson Algren . . . Sandburg, Saul Bellow. . . . And yet today, the leadership of your city is in the hands of a woman. You have a woman mayor, a woman president of the University of Chicago.

Prominent Women

KUPCINET: The mayor took on the powerful Democratic machine, and she won! She's very very popular, and she's doing a splendid job. Hannah Grey, president of the University of Chicago, is a great educator. She was at Yale University, where she could have been made president, but she came back here, where she had taught previously. The university is a tremendous institution, and Hannah Grey is a fine administrator. And of course don't overlook Northwestern University, De Paul, Loyola, Roosevelt University. We have a great number of educational institutions here.

MICHENER: Do you feel that Chicago has been able to keep the inner city viable?

KUPCINET: We have a serious problem with black neighborhoods that are very underprivileged. I think our school system has been negligent in treating our blacks properly. But we're fortunate in having the largest number of middle-class blacks in the nation, and they're a big influence in creating a stable society.

MICHENER: Are your schools well supported?

KUPCINET: Yes they are, but we have a tremendous problem meeting the requirements of HEW, the Health, Education and Welfare Department's standards of desegregation, and we've been in the midst of a tremendous battle over how to desegregate the schools.

MICHENER: There's a very strong ethnic component in Chicago, isn't there?

KUPCINET: There are a number of strong ethnic groups. The blacks have moved up to about one-third of the city's population—they represent over a million of the three million population of Chicago. And we have a growing Hispanic minority, which is very much neglected in our political scheme. The whites of course have dominated, in particular the Irish; the blacks and the Hispanics have a long way to go to get their share of representation.

MICHENER: I see a lot of new building going on. Is that part of a city plan?

KUPCINET: Everything you see is part of a city plan. There's a great effort to revive the south part of the Loop. We now have a Dearborn Plaza, we're going to have a River City development, there's a great deal of building and planning that's going on today to improve the life of people who live now in subnormal conditions. Chicago is one of the more beautiful cities in the country, and it's going to get even better because we have extensive plans for redevelopment. And all through the city you'll find magnificent architecture.

MICHENER: I've heard that many architects compare parts of Chicago with Paris.

KUPCINET: Yes, it's often been compared with Paris. Michigan Boulevard is not quite as wide as Paris's Champs Elysées—

MICHENER: It's what you Chicagoans call "Boule Mich," isn't it? It's really one of the great streets of the world. I've known it all my life, and with tremendous affection.

KUPCINET: And it borders Lake Michigan, one of the prettiest

Chicago police patrolling an outdoor event. (Colour Library International, Ltd.)

Audience at Chicagofest, a music festival. (Colour Library International, Ltd.)

lakefronts in the entire nation. Our forefathers had the good sense to make it recreational instead of commercial. No big shipping, no commerce at all—it's all for recreational purposes. So we have about forty miles of beaches in Chicago. In the summertime, Chicago looks like the Riviera, with all those white sailboats out there—only much cleaner than the Riviera. And the lake is our great air conditioner. It keeps us cool in the summertime.

MICHENER: What big jobs does Chicago still have left to do?

KUPCINET: The biggest job is in education. Bringing the blacks and the Hispanics into full representation in our society is vital, and it depends on education. Our system needs a great deal of improvement. I don't care to criticize the administrators; I think the circumstances are more devastating than they anticipated. But if we can get our educational system in such a condition as to provide equal opportunity for all, then I think as a city we'll have done our share.

MICHENER: Your public services—health, police, transportation—are in pretty good shape, aren't they?

KUPCINET: Very good shape. A great city is measured by the quality of its police, its transportation, its water. In each one of these, Chicago measures as high as any city in the nation. In education, though, we're not as good as we should be.

COLUMBUS'S MUSEUM FOR LIVING

Just forty-five miles south of Indiana's capital, Indianapolis, lies the small city of Columbus. Close enough to the capital to be a bedroom community, Columbus has sufficient industry of its own so that few of its 36,000 citizens need make the daily trek on U.S. 31 to find work in the big city. Columbus is also a place that is difficult to leave, even for the working day, because it exudes a sense of excitement and endeavor. By rights this relatively small Hoosier city should have the traditional sawtooth-roofed, smoke-belching, stack-crested factory look of the typical company town. But it doesn't. Instead more than forty new and architecturally exciting buildings have been fit gracefully into Columbus's rural scheme. The list of designers is, in itself, an architectural Baedeker. Saarinen—father and son, I. M. Pei, Harry Weese, Casar Pelli, Edward Larrabee Barnes, John M. Johansen, John Warnecke among others have all contributed their talents to Columbus's cityscape. Complimenting the architecture are works of some of the world's most renowned contemporary sculptors: Henry Moore, Jean Tinguely, Harris Barron, and Constantino Nivola.

J. Irwin Miller.

The guiding force in this artistic blossoming on the prairie has been J. Irwin Miller, Columbus's leading citizen and until recently chief executive of the Cummins Engine Company, the town's primary employer. In 1957, Mr. Miller, through the Company's Cummins Foundation, offered to pay the design fees for any new school buildings in Columbus, provided that the plans were drawn up by a leading architect from a list of names he supplied. Later, the offer was extended to include any public building. The result has been not only the creation of architectural gems but also a swelling of community pride. Here are Mr. Miller's comments on this unique and highly successful program.

How It All Started

"It was quite accidental. This town long had a reputation for citizen concern. Well, right after World War II, we found ourselves with a city that had doubled in population. No new school buildings had gone up since the 1920s. And we would be overcrowded unless we built almost one school a year for ten years. The first two schools were built in a hurry—they were prefabs. Obviously these were unacceptable quarters for young people to have their educational experience. And so some of us decided to try to encourage something better. We had a sort of prototype to look to—the State Department program for building United States embassies, which relied on hiring the best architects in the nation. I knew a little bit about that through my friend Mr. Saarinen. I talked with him, and asked why something like this wouldn't work in Columbus. Here, however, we would concentrate on hiring not the current big names but the really brightest of the younger architects. Saarinen, Doug Haskell of the magazine *Architectural Forum,* and Pietro Baluski, dean of M.I.T., formed a committee and picked a panel of six or eight of the brightest young architects. Most of these had never built a

One of the new school buildings in Columbus, Indiana.

Art exhibit in public space.

LEFT: *A church reflected in the window of a building in downtown Columbus.*

RIGHT: *Children playing in one of the new parks in Columbus.*

school before. We then suggested to the Columbus schoolboard that it pick one of these young architects to design the next school. We would pay for the design. We really had nothing in mind other than finding a good design for the next school building.

"After that first building went up, the schoolboard came back and said, 'Hey! How about it? Does your offer apply for the next building too?' So it sort of grew by accident and not by any grand design at all."

On Democracy

"A legitimate criticism could be made of Columbus. And that is that it has a lot of decay in the middle of a lot of good building designs. There isn't a master plan. You'll find blocks without anything significant on them, and then you'll find an isolated marvelous building. But in my opinion, in any democratic community, the process is more important than the product. And it's important that the whole community be involved. That there be genuine participation. That government work in the way it ought to work. A certain amount of mess is essential to a functioning democracy. There has always been an emphasis in this town that the democratic process is more important than the result.

"A great deal of good stuff has been built here outside our program. Churches like the First Baptist and the library were built without reference to the program."

On the Effects of the Architectural Program

"I think there's a direct relationship between good architecture and good schools and a concern for battered wives or pregnant teenagers. An important feature that characterizes any good community is concern about people who can't help themselves or who are left behind and can't keep up. There is an absolutely remarkable group of organizations here that started on a shoestring to aid battered wives, minorities who can't

Colored towers, a striking design and architectural concept.

get scholarships, poor people who are denied their normal legal rights, and the like. I think that there are probably more organizations of that sort, operating on tiny budgets, really serving the people who otherwise can't help themselves, than in any town I know.

"There's an obscure character in a play by Euripides, who said, 'Where the good things are there is home.' If you want to make this home for people, you've got to work on the good things. And that's in a sense what we're trying to do. Everybody must be involved. It can't be done by one or two—it can't be imposed."

Voices of Columbus

MAYOR MAX ANDRUS: As the architectural program started I think it developed a sense of pride in all the people who live in Columbus. I think it is significant that so many older homes are being renovated here. Of course, we have some programs in that area, but many of the renovations are purely voluntary. Perhaps the greatest thing we can point with pride to—certainly we're proud of the setting, the architecture, and the great buildings we have—is the people who occupy these buildings. I feel very strongly that the academic and extracurricular activities offered by the school system, the parks, and the recreation department give young people the opportunity for all types of activity.

MARYLOU SMITH: [Living here] feels great. That's probably the simplest way I can put it. As the town grew in its architecture, I grew. I am not a student of architecture, far from it. But I have learned to appreciate architecture more in the past ten years than ever before. I've watched how these buildings are helping our young people. Especially the schools. I think the schools here are terrific.

The Commons is a terrific spot in town for young people and old people. We have a meeting place there for seminars. And the playgrounds—they're called Chaos One and Chaos Two—are super places to go. I have no children, but they're fun spots for me to go just to watch those kids play.

Now I'm not saying it's all peaches and cream. No, don't get me wrong. We have our problems just like any town has. But we try to stay ahead of these problems most of the time.

Max Andrus, mayor of Columbus.

"WITH GOD ALL THINGS ARE POSSIBLE"

The Ohio state motto was adopted in 1959, just a few years before it became apparent—even to the most fanatic Buckeye booster—that some things were not going to be quite so possible after all. Ohio has big problems: declining industry, old and poverty-ridden cities, pollution, unemployment. And yet, that motto still seems appropriate. It's a fitting heading for the state's history, for the beliefs of a majority of its population and their vision of the future.

Ohio reputedly represents Middle America. Not long ago, a lady in Dayton was discovered whose opinions were taken to be of the essence of mid-Americanness—she was interviewed often and was quoted widely. Although it's questionable whether she and her fellow Ohioans actually speak for mainstream America, certainly the Ohio population accurately mirrors the make-up of the nation as a whole.

Starting in the late eighteenth century, a flood of people came over the Appalachians, down the Ohio River, and up from all the states of the South to settle in the Ohio country. The northern part of the region—once the "Western Reserve" of the royal colony of Connecticut—was soon filled with New Englanders, who cut down the vast hardwood

View of Cincinnati, Ohio, from northern Kentucky. Founded in 1788 and named Losantiville, the city was renamed Cincinnati in 1790 for the Society of Cincinnatus, a group of Revolutionary War officers. It is an industrial, commercial, and cultural center for the states of Ohio and Kentucky. (Cincinnati Chamber of Commerce)

forests, fenced in their fields, and built pretty New England towns with names like Amherst and Andover, Cambridge and New Concord. Cincinnati was a bustling river port by the early 1800s and became, for a while, the third largest city in America. It was cosmopolitan enough to attract the English traveler, Mrs. Frances Trollope, who was impressed by the city's prosperity, although she objected to the low level of public manners and the high population of pigs in the streets. In her scandalous exposé, *Domestic Manners of the Americans*, she wrote that she was "startled at recognizing in almost every full-dressed *beau* that passed me, the master or shopman that I had been used to see behind the counter, or lolling at the door of every shop in the city." Within a few years of Mrs. Trollope, numbers of Germans would also settle in Cincinnati, adding to its distinctive qualities a charm and stateliness that it still possesses.

The New England tradition put its mark on Ohio, too. The first college in the old Northwest Territory, Ohio University, was founded in

An outdoor class at Oberlin College. (Oberlin College News)

Athens in 1804—just one year after Ohio was admitted to statehood. Kenyon College was founded in 1824 by a New Hampshire minister, and Oberlin College, begun by Massachusetts Congregationalists, opened in 1833. The year 1836 saw the publication of the first McGuffey's Readers, written by Ohioan William Holmes McGuffey; with their emphasis on honesty, industry, and thrift, they would shape the attitudes of generations of midwestern schoolchildren. Abolitionist sentiment came west with New Englanders, too. Harriet Beecher Stowe lived for years in Cincinnati, close to one of the main routes of the underground railroad, which passed runaway slaves through a secret network of Ohio farms and villages to Lake Erie and freedom in Canada.

Bordered on the north by Lake Erie and the Ohio River to the east and south, Ohio from its beginnings had easy access to markets in the populous sections of the country for its timber, wheat, and hogs. With the completion of the Ohio end of the great National Road, of the Ohio-Erie canals, and of a railroad network that covered the state from south to north, Ohio became an exporter of the coal from its Appalachian mines, and an importer of iron ore from the iron ranges to the west. By the latter half of the nineteenth century, huge steelmaking complexes were belching smoke into the bucolic Ohio air. Cleveland, Akron, and Youngstown grew into major industrial cities. New waves of European immigrants came to work in the mills, bringing with them new attitudes about the rights of workingmen. The American Federation of Labor and the United Mine Workers both were founded in Ohio in the 1880s.

Although northern Ohio became one of the most heavily industrialized sections of the nation, most of the rest of the state continues to be profitably agricultural. The exception is its eastern portion, the Appalachians along the Ohio River. Here towns have long mixed heavy industry with coal mining, but today there is much unemployment. Steel mills are closing, and mines have shut down. ❑

Sonny Capers works at the steel mill in Steubenville, a town of some 27,000 on the banks of the Ohio. In many respects, Sonny's life resembles a portrait of the American dream. He is a man who enjoys his work and fills his leisure with his family, his home, and an intimate knowledge of his well-beloved countryside.

Sonny Capers Talks about His Life

"One of the things I like best is hunting, especially deer hunting. The woods around my house have probably some of the best deer hunting in the area. I've always liked the outdoors. When I was about seven years old, my dad decided I was about old enough to go hunting with him. So I've been doing it all my life. And I'd just as soon come out here and sit in the woods for three or four hours as I would do anything, anything at all.

"My boy will be nine years old in January. I asked him what he wanted for Christmas, and he said that he would like a good bow that he can actually use for hunting, a bow like mine. I got a five-point deer with this bow last year, and I think that was the most thrilling experience of my life. We use the meat—there's no way you should ever take an animal if you're not going to use it."

Growing Up

"My father was a coal miner. His father was a coal miner. My dad's retired now—he had physical problems that forced him out of the mine into an early retirement. He spent a lot of time in the mine. Every time something broke down in the mine, he'd stay until it was repaired. In the evening, if he wasn't home it was usually because something broke down in the mine and he'd be there.

"I grew up in a small town called Hopedale, about eight miles from here. I always felt when I was growing up that I would like to get into some type of forestry or natural resources. But when I got out of school, I took the easy route: They were hiring at the mill, and I got in the mill, and that's where I stayed until I went to the service. And when I came back, jobs weren't all that easy to find, and I'd put in too much time to leave the mill. But it pays good, and it's really good work, so—that's where I'm at. Working at the mill hasn't hurt me. I make a good living, and we don't do without anything. If we want something, we can usually purchase it and not worry about it."

Pollution

"I don't believe the mills today are the trouble they used to be. I know when I was growing up, if you took a ride down through Steubenville or anywhere in this general vicinity, it seemed like there was a cloud hanging over it all the time. But the pollution today isn't anywhere near what it's been in the past. Let's face it—when you make

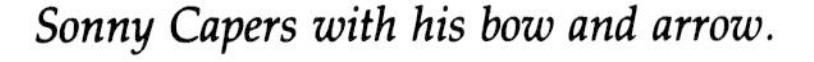

Sonny Capers with his bow and arrow.

Smog and dust surround the activity of a working steel mill. (Frederick Hecker)

steel you're going to have small particles of dirt in the air. There's no way of getting around it. You're never going to clean it one hundred percent."

[In 1970, the National Pollution Control Administration ranked Steubenville first in emissions of dirt, soot, and smoke. The steel mills have since cleaned up a good deal.]

Working

"Naturally, there's danger. When the furnace is turned on and you walk out in front of it, there's danger and you have to worry about it. Although after you've worked around it a while, you learn what to look for, what doesn't look right, and you stay away from it. We have safety shoes, hard hats, safety glasses, and flame-retardant suits. I would never go into an industrial area without a hard hat, protection on my feet, and especially safety glasses. When you walk in front of the furnace, a piece could fall off the roof or the belly and splash you with molten steel or slag. I've had glasses that were all spotted with steel and slag.

"My job is second furnaceman. The job includes charging scrap into the furnace, then hot metal, then blowing it for twenty to twenty-two minutes.

[Sonny's mill produces steel through a relatively new method called the Basic Oxygen Process. The pear-shaped furnace is tilted to receive a charge of scrap metal and molten iron, then brought to an upright position so that a water-cooled tube, or lance, can blow oxygen into the flames, creating an intense heat that burns off the impurities in the metal. Precise amounts of carbon and alloying metals like manganese are added during the "heat," which takes about twenty-two minutes. Charging the furnace, and then emptying it, takes another twenty minutes or so. The entire process requires only about forty-five minutes.]

"After the furnace is blown, the lance is pulled, and we turn down the furnace again to test the temperature. If it's right, the melting foreman will tell me how much manganese he wants to add to the steel, and I'll weigh it up on a scale and then dump it down a chute into the furnace. One heat produces about two hundred eighty-five tons of steel, and if we're operating with no trouble, we can usually get ten or eleven heats in one turn, an eight-hour day.

"The furnace crew works around the clock, in three shifts. From seven fifteen in the morning to three fifteen in the afternoon we call the daylight turn. And then from three fifteen to eleven fifteen in the evening is the afternoon turn. And eleven fifteen to seven fifteen in the morning is called the midnight turn. I work all three of them. If I had my choice of any turn to work steady, I believe it would be daylight. Afternoon turn I don't like because it takes all your evening hours away from you. And I don't like midnight turn, because I just find it hard to sleep during the day. It's hard on my family, too.

"I enjoy the work. It's never boring. It seems like something new happens every day. When you work with steel, you don't lose interest in it because no two heats are alike. If you really pay attention to it, there's a lot to learn. It's not like an assembly line, where you just go and go and go unless something breaks down. With steel, you may bring a heat down and if it's awful hot, you gotta find out why. Something's happening—the computer hasn't picked the charge right, or you've made a mistake or someone else has. There's something wrong somewhere, and you've gotta find out what, because you don't want to put in another heat until you do.

"The guys who work on the furnace are usually pretty close. There's seldom any argument, and we have a good time. It makes the turn go a lot quicker when you get along the way we do."

Family

"I'm thirty-three years old, my wife, Sandy, is thirty-two, Tracy is six, and Troy is nine. In a good year, I'll probably earn around twenty-five to twenty-eight thousand. We don't try to live above our means, but inflation affects everybody, and it bothers us just the same as it does everyone. The higher it goes, the more you have to tighten up, that's all.

Sonny at a Cub Scouts meeting. His son, Troy, is a member of the troop.

We have a cost-of-living clause in our contract, so when inflation rises, our income is raised. But that's not solving the problem—everything just can't be raised and raised, because it's never-ending. There's got to be a point where it stops. I think about the old people on Social Security, who don't get a raise every so often. I just wonder how they make it with these fuel supplies the way they are.

"I like my house. It's comfortable. It's not too big, so it helps on the heating, with fuel being as expensive as it is. One of the things I like about this house is the view. You can watch the seasons change down here in the country. I like spending as much time with the kids as possible. I like to try to help them identify different shrubs, trees, bushes, by their leaves and bark. That's one advantage to living out here in the country—no matter where you go, you're always close to it.

"I'm happy that Troy's in the Cub Scouts—I'm really proud that he's taking an interest in it. At the last den leader's meeting, I was elected committee chairman, and this gives me more opportunity to spend time with him.

"There's a birdhouse hanging in a tree out here at the side of the yard. Troy and I built it one day when it was real cold. He was getting tired of sitting around, and so was I—so we went out in the garage and drew a couple of little plans, and just put it together for a small wren house in the summertime. And it's been occupied every year since we put it up.

"I'm hoping that both children decide to go to college. I'm sure we'll find a way to come up with enough money. . . . And I wouldn't mind it if my son went into the steel mill. It hasn't hurt me. I make a good living."

Energy

"I'm concerned about energy in this country, like everyone else. We're becoming more dependent on oil instead of getting away from it. We have an abundance of coal, and I feel the government ought to take more steps to utilize it. I know everybody here feels the same way I do about it. This area is steel and coal—that's really what keeps the economy here going. We have a problem with high-sulfur coal here—

they claim our coal has a lot more sulfur than western coal. But I'm sure they'll work something out to lower the sulfur emissions—the Environmental Protection Agency and the companies will work together, and they'll find some way to eliminate the pollution. . . ."

Steel

"I feel that the demand for steel is directly related to the economy of the country. If a man's working good, he'll buy a car, say, every four years. If he's working really good, he'll buy one maybe every two years. Naturally that's gonna mean more steel. They say in the 1980s we won't be able to produce enough steel. I believe that the steel companies are going to have to improve and modernize their mills to keep up with foreign manufacturers. Overall, it seems like they've been modernizing a lot quicker than we have—mostly in Germany and Japan from what I understand.

"If I should lose my job in the mill—it's quite possible because there's a lot of plants closing—I would look for another job around here. I'd look for the mines to start back up. I don't think that this EPA situation on high-sulfur coal is going to last forever—there has to be a compromise on it someplace. You just can't quit mining coal. . . . And I think if I left the mill, that's probably where I would go. Try to get a job in the coal mine."

MOTOWN ON THE ROPES

Some interesting figures to emerge from the 1980 census are these: In ten years the city of Detroit's population fell by 321,841, while Houston, Texas, gained almost precisely that number of people, 321,457. Nobody would maintain that the citizens of Detroit, en masse, are packing up their belongings, loading their families into their gas-guzzling early-1970s station wagons, and moving south to Houston. But the fact is that one of the most popular newspapers in Detroit and its metropolitan area is the *Houston Chronicle.* It is sold on newsstands, hawked on streetcorners, and stocked by libraries. It is not that Motown's residents are suddenly interested in Houston schoolboard appropriations or the schedule of the Houston Symphony. It is job and housing opportunities in the booming Texas port city that attract Detroiters to the bulging classified ad pages of the *Chronicle.* In 1980 alone some seventy thousand new jobs became available in Houston. In 1981 about twenty thousand of Michigan's citizens were running out of unemployment benefits each month. Clearly, then, to Detroit's laid-off auto workers and the tens of thousands who once made their livings in allied industries, Houston is the land of milk and honey—or at least a weekly paycheck.

Under the best of circumstances, Detroit would be a city in trouble. Most of its neighborhoods are old and dilapidated. The middle class long ago fled to the suburbs, reducing the city's tax base and increasing its need for expensive social services. The race riots of 1967 left ugly physical and psychic scars; and continuing tensions between blacks and Detroit's ethnic groups, together with fierce competition for employment in a shrinking job market, make the possibilities for new explosions ever present.

At the root of Detroit's deep malaise is the depression in the United States auto industry. Though the nation as a whole has a vital stake in the health of car and truck manufacturing, nowhere does a falloff in car sales hurt more than in Detroit and its immediate suburbs. Plant after plant has closed down, some perhaps permanently, others for long-term retooling, as American automakers reel under the impact of popular imports—small, fuel-efficient vehicles that are relatively cheap to buy, to service, and to run. In the first quarter of 1981, only mammoth General Motors showed a small profit. Ford chalked up a loss of $439 million, while Chrysler—kept alive only by massive loan guarantees from the federal government—lost nearly $300 million.

The effect of such figures on Detroit's economy and quality of life is incalculable, though it is apparent in the long lines at unemployment offices, the groups of jobless men lounging in the city parks, and the daily departures of moving vans headed south. There are, however, other figures that provide an insight into Detroit's crisis. The most telling perhaps is the fact that of Motown's 1.2 million citizens, about 720,000 or 60 percent are receiving some form of public assistance, ranging from Social Security to unemployment benefits to outright welfare. All of this would be mitigated somewhat if there was a feeling that times will improve. That belief is no longer tenable. ❑

Citizens in Detroit's downtown area. (Colour Library International, Ltd.)

Ford Motor Company, world headquarters in Dearborn, Michigan. (Colour Library International, Ltd.)

A New Auto Industry

❑ Most people believe that the American automobile industry will rebound. The new gas-efficient models coming off the assembly lines may well lead to revitalization. But the automobile business that emerges from this crisis will no doubt be a very different one from that of a decade or even five years ago. It will probably be far more

Looking at downtown Detroit, across the Detroit River from Windsor, Canada. (Colour Library International, Ltd.)

An early Ford model housed in the Henry Ford Museum at Dearborn, Michigan. (Colour Library International, Ltd.)

decentralized, with more assembly plants hundreds or even thousands of miles from Detroit. And the old days of the labor-intensive assembly line will give way to high-technology automation. Sophisticated, computerized robots—machines that never take a coffee break, rarely make a mistake, and can work around the clock, month in and month out—will displace tens of thousands of workers.

All of this is cold comfort to the worker who has spent his best years at a GM or Chrysler plant and has now used up his unemployment benefits. As one jobless Detroit worker put it when it was suggested that he move south: "Where are you going to go with no money? You want to sell your home to go someplace else and you can't sell it because nobody's got a job, nobody's got the money."

Back in 1977, Detroit completed a magnificent complex of new buildings, the Renaissance Center, that includes four skyscraper office buildings surrounding a seventy-three-story hotel. The Renaissance Center was to be the symbol of a city's restoration to greatness, the symbol of a new day. That new day has already come, but hardly in the form that Renaissance Center's planners had anticipated. The depression in the auto industry may be making Detroit obsolete. ❑

Michener Talks with Lee Iacocca

In America, transportation essentially means the car. Perhaps no industry has contributed more to American prosperity than has automobile manufacturing. Certainly no industry has had a more revolutionary impact on the way we live. Now the United States auto industry is in tremendous trouble, its future is in doubt. One of the leaders of the industry is Lee Iacocca, head of the Chrysler Corporation. I spoke with

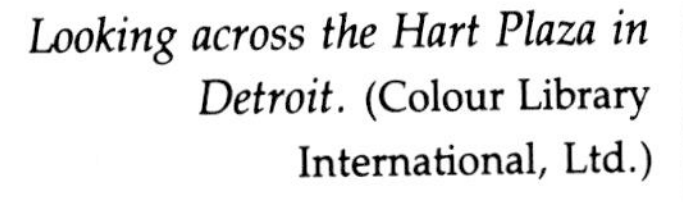

Looking across the Hart Plaza in Detroit. (Colour Library International, Ltd.)

him in Detroit about the past, the future, and how the pride of American industry came to its present condition.

MICHENER: You know, Mr. Iacocca, I am one of those wiseacres who must have given you a lot of trouble, but a long time ago I began to feel that the European and Japanese automakers were the bright ones because they were making small cars. How did America allow that portion of the market to slip out of its hands?

IACOCCA: It was really a question of need. After World War II, Europe needed small, highly efficient cars because gasoline started there in those days at a buck a gallon. Now it's up to two dollars a gallon. We had cheap energy. As recently as 1972 it was only thirty-three cents for a gallon of gas in the United States. We had little incentive to plan cars that were fuel-efficient. Rather than that, we planned our cars around automatic transmissions. We planned our cars around air conditioning—things that even in this day are virtually unheard of in all of Europe.

As a result, the Europeans and Japanese do make the best four- and five-speed straight transmissions and we make the best automatics, because we spent thirty years working on what we did best—and what our market demanded—and they spent thirty years doing other things.

What has really made a difference is one thing: energy. With energy costs rising constantly, the number-one motivation in buying a car is how it does in fuel efficiency. So we're having to redesign all of our cars, all of our plants—and we have to do it within a five-year period. That's why we're having so much difficulty right now.

Lee Iacocca, head of Chrysler Corporation talking with James Michener.

MICHENER: When you were at Ford, you were the genius behind the Mustang, which was a fabulously successful car. What was the cost of gasoline when you brought that car out?

IACOCCA: About thirty cents a gallon. Our biggest problem with the Mustang was to get customers to accept a six-cylinder engine that gave the car fuel economy. They didn't want it. In their view, the car looked so sporty that a V-8 engine was called for. We had to offer all kinds of incentives to get people to take the six-cylinder engine—and that was only fifteen years ago.

Americans Spurned Small Cars

MICHENER: Have you had periods when you couldn't give small cars away?

IACOCCA: Oh, sure. As recently as January of 1979. That's hard to believe, I know. But the fact is that our smallest, most fuel-efficient cars just wouldn't sell. In one month I had to offer an eleven-million-dollar incentive just to move these cars. Then came the crisis in Iran and by March 1979, these same cars were selling at black-market prices. So it's hard to plan the market, but the public sees the light quickly. Maybe we in the auto industry didn't see it quickly enough. But now we can't build small cars fast enough, and it's going to take us through 1982 before we are fully competitive with the small Japanese and European cars.

MICHENER: Could you and Ford and General Motors make small cars as well as they are made in Germany and Japan?

IACOCCA: We think we do now. At Chrysler, for example, we build a car called the Omni Horizon that we think is the equal of any car made in Europe. I believe that one of the finest European cars is the Volkswagen Rabbit. Our car is similar to it, and our quality levels have improved. We build just one model of car in each plant, and that helps. Before we had so many sizes and variants and so many options that it became difficult in a mass-production system to build a good quality car. Now that's changing and our cars are comparable to any.

MICHENER: Have you felt that Congress intruded unfairly into the automobile industry?

IACOCCA: I think the government went too far. They seemed to believe that if a little regulation was good, a lot of regulation was terrific. I really feel that excessive regulation is what's killing us off.

MICHENER: Suppose I were a congressman or a bureaucrat in Washington. Would you resent it if I came out here and said to you, "Now, look, we've got to do certain things about the automobile?"

IACOCCA: No, I think the government's role is clear-cut in some areas—say, air pollution. The free enterprise system won't allow one company to say, "My air's cleaner than the other guy's air." We didn't even recognize the problem. Pollution standards must be set by the government for the social good. The same is true of many safety devices. But now, let's take another situation. When it comes to fuel-efficient cars, and the Japanese are beating our heads in, you don't need a law to tell you that you had better meet the market for expensive gas, and you better meet it quick or you're going out of business.

MICHENER: What role do you see the automobile playing in the private life of an individual, say, a boy or girl of eighteen or so?

IACOCCA: I have two teenage girls. They need wheels. Now they need fuel-efficient wheels. But thereby hangs a tale, because they want fuel efficiency, but they also want a car to be very sporty. They don't want a little econo-box. That was the magic of the Mustang. Long hood, short deck, fast steering, hard spring—you really drove that car. It was good-looking. People identify their life-style with certain types of cars. Older people buy four-door cars, because they want to carry more than two passengers.

MICHENER: Do you think that fundamental attitudes in the United States regarding independence and freedom are related to the car?

IACOCCA: Certainly. This is a big country. Japan, France, or Germany—they are small compared to the United States. We've got fifty states and huge turnpike systems connecting them. The nature of our vacations, the process of getting to work, shopping, all depend on mobility, on a family having at least one car. I think we're getting to the point where the majority of families have two or three cars. Why? For mobility.

MICHENER: What do you see as the relationship between the private automobile and a public transportation system that might carry workers to their jobs?

IACOCCA: I happen to be—even though I've been in the auto business all of my life—a great believer in public transportation systems that complement the use of the automobile. Good bus systems with high-speed bus lanes, and some commuter cars by rail. But when you stop to think of it, few places other than New York and Chicago and some of the other really big cities lend themselves to a rail commuter system because the rails are fixed from Point A to Point B. But I do think we need to do more in the bus area. We, at Chrysler, for example, now have a van pooling company that helps cities and states put together the eight or nine people in a van to go to work from a central area to a plant. That's highly efficient. I think that's catching on around the country. And I think this system makes eminent sense, because it gives the passengers the best of both worlds. They cut down on their fuel bills, and they have a driver, and there's nine people in the vehicle instead of one. It's personal enough so that each passenger can be picked up at home.

MICHENER: Do you have any women executives at Chrysler?

IACOCCA: Not at the vice-presidential level. There are, however, women executives. We're getting more and more each year, giving them opportunities, as we probably should have done more of in the past.

MICHENER: How about equal employment?

IACOCCA: Our company is very heavily black. In fact, twenty-six percent of the Chrysler Corporation is black. That's because of our location of our factories in the metropolitan Detroit area which has a large black population. We've made a lot of strides concerning upward mobility and training for blacks. There are a lot of good training schools in this company.

MICHENER: Can a black get promoted?

IACOCCA: It's not a matter of *can*. The fact is that blacks get promoted every day.

THE SMALL COLLEGE: CAN IT SURVIVE?

Change is a constant in American life. The only thing that never changes in this country is the fact that everything seems to change. I think we're probably better for it, since change confronts us with the challenge to adapt. But there are some changes that fill me with a sense of loss. And one of these is the seeming demise of the small college in the United States.

Once, at a time that was closer to this country's beginnings, all institutions of higher learning were small. And so it was with Antioch College, founded 127 years ago in Yellow Springs, Ohio.

As our population grew, the big university system emerged, providing learning opportunities for more people and offering a choice in educational styles. The small college existed alongside the giant learning center, and each stood as an alternative to the other. But today Antioch, like other small schools throughout the country, is being starved by reduced enrollments, sharply higher costs, and a staggering debt. But Antioch seems to have recovered from what was only a few years ago a life-threatening dilemma, thanks to the steadfastness of its faculty, employees, and students, and to the determination of its president, William M. Birenbaum. I spoke with him about some of the problems that American higher education now confronts.

Michener Talks with William Birenbaum

MICHENER: I have more than a passing interest in Antioch, you know. I married an Antioch girl, so I've been able to assess the kind of education you provide here. What do you think have been Antioch's major contributions to the American education system?

BIRENBAUM: The admission of women to equal opportunity in higher education. The early admission—in 1853—of black people to the private sector of American higher education. The recognition of the relationship between how we learn and how we employ learning in work. The early commitment to international education as part of being a well-educated American. And today, our effort to reach out beyond the normal definition of what a campus is.

William M. Birenbaum, president of Antioch College in Yellow Springs, Ohio.

MICHENER: When I was in school, Antioch was known for its work-study plan. How does that operate, Dr. Birenbaum?

BIRENBAUM: It's based on the assumption that there is an intimate, immediate relationship between what you take into your head and how you use it, and that the use of it has something to do with your capacity to learn more. Every student here is required, in alternate terms, to engage in formal study on campus and, in the next quarter or time period, to work at a job related to that formal study. It's worked pretty well.

MICHENER: Has Antioch's character and contribution derived in any way from the fact that it's a relatively small college?

BIRENBAUM: The beauty of Antioch, it seems to me, is that, although the environment for formal learning here is "small," a student can find work in a large complex hospital, or a large complex corporate organization, or in a large complex urban community. So there's an interplay between the small college community and the small situation in which students live and learn and the larger world.

MICHENER: Would you like to see Antioch quadruple in size?

BIRENBAUM: I don't think size is the question. Being small is often more intricate and difficult to manage than being big. Often the key issues that arise out of very small situations mushroom quickly into the huge, complex political problems of our lives.

I manage an institution in ten different places across the land, with thousands of students, hundred of employees, and mind-blowing sums of money coming in and out. Yet often, when I sit in my office with only one other person, the most complex, overwhelming things happen.

MICHENER: Antioch has campuses, then, across the country—at one time you had about twenty, didn't you?

BIRENBAUM: At one time, there were thirty-two. Like Antioch itself, they all recognized the relationship between work and learning, they were all dedicated to liberal education, and they all had a deep sense of community participation.

Well, when you've got thirty-two communities going and they vary from a Texas village of three or four hundred Chicano people to the inner city of Baltimore to this kind of environment here at Yellow Springs—at that point conceptions of community begin to vary. That's one of the charms of America, and one of her problems: to find out of this diversity the common benchmarks for defining and regulating the way we live together.

MICHENER: Has Antioch ever been a publicly funded institution?

BIRENBAUM: No, we've always been private; the main impulse for our existence has come from persons acting as private citizens. We were born, as so many of the smaller liberal arts colleges in this country were, of a religious origin.

But, as to public funds—some fifteen to twenty percent of our annual operation is funded through money that comes to us in financial aid. A great many grants are given to us in support of research or program development. And my administration and I spend a lot of our time complying with public regulations that deeply shape our lives here. Affirmative action is the most obvious example.

On Higher Education in America

MICHENER: Are many of the small colleges in the United States in financial danger?

BIRENBAUM: I would guess more than half. I testified recently at a Senate hearing on this matter, and heard a demographic group from Harvard estimate that in the 1980s perhaps as many as five hundred of these institutions will cease to be. I think that the institutions that

Bosworth Hall at Oberlin College. Like Antioch, Oberlin is a small college, based on New England models. It was the first American college to hold co-educational classes. Before the Civil War, it was a center for abolitionism. (Oberlin College News)

survive will be those that are most forthright in facing the moral and intellectual problems of our civilization. And some will do it better than others.

Because of its adventuresomeness, Antioch has always been very newsworthy. The reason the press and the media in recent months have been so interested in Antioch is because we're again on a front line, we're already anticipating the 1980s in our own survival struggle. But I know at least ten distinguished colleges that are in as critical a fiscal condition as we are.

MICHENER: And that just might go out of existence? Is this because of declining population?

BIRENBAUM: We're faced with a growing population. By any demographic projection, this country will have two hundred fifty million people as we end the next two decades. And look at our problems—they're more complex, more fascinating than ever before. And who would say that America's found the answers to energy, the environment, political democracy, racism? We've got more people to educate and more interesting educational challenges than ever, and yet much of the present educational establishment is crying gloom and doom about the shrinkage of the profession, about institutions going out of business. Of course, if you think about education in terms of eighteen- to twenty-three-year-olds, you're in trouble. If you think of a college like Antioch as having a potential only for a particular age category or a particular segment of the population, then you may find yourself with a very difficult market situation.

MICHENER: Are these five hundred threatened colleges also being hit by the fact that young Americans are beginning to doubt the efficacy of a college education?

BIRENBAUM: I meet a lot of young people who realize that there are many places in this culture in which one can learn well. What we traditionally call "college" no longer has the monopoly for conveying knowledge. There are many other places.

Of the baccalaureate degrees awarded last year, forty-eight percent were earned by people who had attended more than one institution along the road to the credential. What does that mean? It means that many students are not going in a straight four-year line. They're entering, they're dropping out to study abroad, or to hit the road, or to work for a year. They're transferring at the end of two years, from a city to an urban campus, or from the countryside to the city.

Another example: In New York City, it is a fact that in fields like chemistry or economics, there are more Ph.D.s doing advanced research outside the universities than in them. And, if you're interested in art history or in the performing or creative arts, you're not terribly well advised to bind yourself into a traditional academic institution in New York.

Last year, corporate America spent more money in the implementation of its own corporate educational systems for its own workers than it contributed to all of the colleges and universities in America.

MICHENER: Can America afford to lose these five hundred threatened colleges?

BIRENBAUM: Can America afford to go to smaller automobiles, or to recast the way we live in the cities, and the relationship of cities to suburbs? Can America afford to tamper with institutions which have worked well and brought us to where we are, in order to survive? Then my answer is yes, I think America will survive even though it may lose five hundred private liberal-education colleges. I don't think the disappearance of the institutions will lead to the disappearance of the basic values that these institutions embody. Those values will find a way of continued expression.

The institutional format is changing, and not only for the small private college. Some of the huge public institutions we have now are monstrous in the ways that they have come to distort their purposes. So I'd be very surprised if the public system will be the same in ten or fifteen years.

MICHENER: Well, if the five hundred are threatened, can the big schools take over the burden?

BIRENBAUM: They've already taken over a part of the burden. The whole impact of open admissions, of open access to higher education—a good part of that burden has been assumed by the public sector. In any case, liberal education is not the monopoly of the private sector or of the small college. There are many public institutions whose excellence in liberal education is unquestionable.

MICHENER: Would you advise a young person to go into training to become a college professor?

BIRENBAUM: It seems to me that the excitement of being a teacher is certainly not limited to the professoriate. And although there's much to commend making your living as a formal institutional teacher, there are other ways to teach. The big thing is, I think teaching is neat. I would encourage everyone to cultivate the talent to teach. As a way of making a living, teaching isn't all bad, but it's more and more like other ways of making a living in America: You get unionized, institutionalized, you get captured by salary schedules, ranks, and titles just as if you were working in industry or government.

It's true that some people who've trained as academics are not finding jobs. They are going to have to work elsewhere. But if they're imaginative, they'll find some way to handle that.

MICHENER: How do you see education in fifteen years—in 1995?

BIRENBAUM: It seems clear to me that during the next twenty years we are going to cope more successfully with our biases about technology. People now in my profession who are still frightened by a typewriter or a hand calculator are going to become more comfortable with these and other tools—the computer, for instance.

Second, the university is one of the three oldest continuing institutions—along with the papacy and the British monarchy—in our civilization. I assume there'll always be a Harvard. But I see a much greater separation of research activities from the academic base, and a much closer relationship between programs that formally educate people and places of work. And that may mean that the credentialing—the Ph.D., MA, BA—may no longer be the exclusive monopoly of academic institutions. I think there'll be a much greater decentralization not only of learning but of giving credit for learning—through workplaces, through community life.

MICHENER: Well, will Antioch be here in 1995?

BIRENBAUM: Antioch and the need for it will be here.

ON EDUCATION

I spent about half my working life in education, and have always supposed that when I grew older I would return to it, for it is without question the noblest profession with which I have been associated. I have been shocked in recent years to read of schools in which teachers are assaulted in the halls or raped in the library, because when I taught I held that my first responsibility was to maintain order so that learning could take place. I still believe that discipline is necessary to the learning situation. I do not mean submission or silence, for the effective learning process is apt to be lively and sometimes even obstreperous, but it must derive from evolving patterns which are kept under some kind of control.

Television may produce a new breed of citizen who can function adequately without knowing how to read, but even then reading will remain the master tool of civilized man. It must have priority in elementary education, and those unlucky children who are prevented from reading by psychological blocks or physical handicaps should be given remedial treatment; stubborn or refractory children who refuse to learn must not be allowed to disrupt our schools. I believe in the educability of all human beings, so I would not cut the nonliterate off from a chance at education; but common sense would demand that I place him in a different kind of classroom where he would learn more and obstruct less, because the education of brilliant young people who will one day lead our society is also a responsibility of our schools.

The Socratic method of probing, questioning, and regrouping ideas is still the sovereign path to learning, especially for those sophisticated minds that will produce the intellectual, business, political, and artistic leadership in the five decades following their graduation. Thus, I am concerned about the responsibility of the university to those generations unborn or now playing in sandboxes, especially the black generations and the children of the underprivileged, for whom the university may be their only chance of attainment. Throughout Western history, and even more so in Eastern nations like China and Japan, the traditional way by which men improved their society has been through learning: in ancient China, learning at the desk of some sage; in Greece, learning at the feet of the philosophers; in the Middle Ages, learning in the monasteries; and in recent centuries, learning at universities. No poor boy who has seen his own life expand because of education would want to see the process denied to others.

James Michener at the University of Iowa, Iowa City.

Let me summarize my attitude toward American education by explaining what one suffers when he talks with European critics. They badger Americans with observations like: "Everyone knows that a high-school degree from France or Germany or Israel is superior to the average college degree in America. Professor X taught at Upper Oklahoma State Teachers one year and told us that most of his students barely knew how to read."

I used to argue with such critics but lately have developed a different tactic. I confess everything: "You're right, the European high school does teach more than our second-class college. You're right, we do have students who can barely read. You're right, discipline in our schools is deplorable. . . . But you must not judge your system against ours because we're trying to do something never before attempted. We're trying to educate an entire people. For every young Frenchman or German who can wangle a place in one of your colleges, we provide places for twenty young Americans. When we try to educate so many, some are bound to be poor risks, so naturally, if you compare your best students with our worst, your system is superior. But if you put your top against our top, ours do not suffer. And we produce twenty times as many. Our gamble is to educate everyone who looks as if he could absorb an education, and that's why our society moves ahead. That's why we draw down so many more Nobel Prizes than our population would warrant."

It is not difficult for me to defend American education, for I can tell my critics, "If I had been born in Yugoslavia or Spain, I would have had no chance for an education. From birth I would have been doomed to a limited life. But the American system was constructed so as to identify children of promise and to make something of them."

We now have over twelve million young people in college. We're the only nation in history to have more college students than farmers. We have more college professors than most nations have students. And from this reservoir of trained intelligence we hope to identify those brains that will keep us alive. The loss we suffer trying to educate those who fail is insignificant when compared to the gain we make from those who succeed.

THE WRITERS WORKSHOP AT THE UNIVERSITY OF IOWA

One of the great American universities is to be found in Iowa City, Iowa. With a student population of more than 22,000 in addition to the faculty and support personnel, the University of Iowa is very nearly as populous as a medium-size city—Columbus, Indiana, for example. And still, Iowa is considered a medium-size university by Midwest standards.

The university was founded in 1847 and conducted its first classes in 1855. At that time, there were only three instructors, and out of a tiny annual budget, $115 was allocated for *both* books and firewood. Today she is a Big Ten school and a major instructional, research, health care, and cultural center.

In addition to small colleges such as Antioch, we need great institutions like the University of Iowa, although these huge intellectual centers should be less a training ground for entrance to the Establishment and more a proving ground for true intelligence. This is a philosophy that is upheld at Iowa, the first university in this country to accept creative work in lieu of the traditional academic thesis from graduate students in the arts.

The Iowa Writers Workshop stresses the idea that although writing cannot be taught, talent can be developed. The many workshop students I talked with are enthusiastic about the opportunity they have been given to work with some of America's finest writers, and to learn

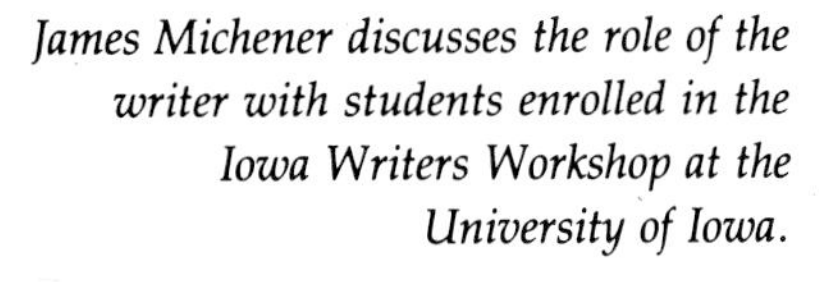

James Michener discusses the role of the writer with students enrolled in the Iowa Writers Workshop at the University of Iowa.

whether they, too, can make their way in the difficult and demanding world of professional writing.

Students Talked about the Program and Their Work

STUDENT: One of the wonderful things about the workshop is the sort of feedback that you get on your work. You can sit up in your ivory tower, and write, and never know whether you're any good. You may think you're wonderful, or you may think you're terrible . . . but what you learn about your work from your teachers and fellow students is a very valuable thing.

STUDENT: A lot of people graduate from college and then go out into the world before coming here. The workshop is less of a classic educational experience than it is one in which the student exercises discipline and independence and good qualities that are refined through periods of working in the world before coming back into school. . . . When you reach a certain level of writing competency, you begin to feel comfortable with your own limits, and then you come here. You have to have a lot of skills developed before you can take advantage of this program. . . . A lot of us are married and some are thirty or older. When we took these two years, we made a special pact with ourselves: A lot of us said, okay, I'll give myself two years, and if at the end of that time I haven't achieved a great deal that would allow me to continue writing full time, I'll find myself another career.

University of Iowa student on campus.

STUDENT: I expect a lot of long years and a lot of hard work, with not that much encouragement. . . .

I hope eventually to be published, but if I think while I'm writing about the possibility of publication, then I feel that someone is reading over my shoulder, and I find that unpleasant. So I just try to write things that please me as much as possible on the assumption, perhaps naive, that if I'm pleased, someone else will be pleased, too. . . .

I'm at a stage now where I have more important things to worry about than whether I can get published. I have a hard enough time deciding about how I feel about what I write.

STUDENT: One of the things that's so pleasant about Iowa is that work that is regarded as frivolous elsewhere is taken seriously here.

Michener Talks about Michener

MICHENER: I'm a professional writer. I work at my job very diligently and take it very seriously, so I feel a great sympathy with each of you. I wonder where you may be twenty or thirty years from now. And I'd be very pleased to answer any questions that you might have.

STUDENT: You're probably as financially successful as any serious writer in America, and I'd like to know how that's affected you. Has it impinged on your writing?

MICHENER: Well, you know I never wrote anything until I was forty years old—which means that success came to me when I was fairly mature and fairly stable, and it came very slowly. My first books were no great sensations at all. So I never had the problem of fame or great wealth knocking me in the head. I was pretty mature at that time, and I took it very easily.

STUDENT: Why would a publishing company take a chance on a book from a forty-year-old person who had never written anything before?

MICHENER: That's a very good question. I submitted it anonymously, because I guess I was afraid of rejection. I never had any great hopes for it, really. I knew I was moderately competent, and I let it go at that. I think it was miraculous that they took it, and even more miraculous that they kept on taking my books.

STUDENT: Which was your first book?

MICHENER: *South Pacific.* It was a good way to start.

STUDENT: I've read that early on you decided that if people watch television more and more, they're going to want some substantial alternative—that is, good books.

Television Changes Reading Habits

MICHENER: I realized that if television did catch on, there would be a substantial number of people who would want to read more than they ever did before—that they would want to read long books which gave them more substance than they were getting from television. And so I consciously worked toward a larger form. I said, "I'll gamble my whole life on the fact that people will want to read large books like *Hawaii* and *The Source* as an antidote to some of the really dreadful television shows." I gambled on this. I gambled consciously and I was proved correct, and for that I am very grateful.

. . . I think an artist is stupid if he works against the grain of his own personality and his own capacity. I can do certain things, I can do them moderately well—but I don't believe that that leads to formula. It leads to competence. Of all the books I have written, most people have never even heard of half of them. I've written very widely on Asian art, I've written on politics, on sociology, on sports, on the analysis of our society. I wrote all of these things in order to keep from merely writing big best-sellers. I've always protected myself by writing a different kind of book when I've finished one of these big successes. And I would recommend that for anybody. The problem of becoming typed, or of writing to formula, is always a great danger to a writer. You have to fight against it.

Michener explains his views on the author's craft to writing workshop students at the University of Iowa.

STUDENT: How do you get so much done? How much do you produce in an average day?

MICHENER: You know, I don't think of myself as prolific. I rented a house in Maryland to do my last book, and on the shelf there were the works of Walter Scott, of George Eliot—and those great writers did five times as much as you and I do. And although I don't begin to compare in output with those people, I am known as a fairly prolific writer. How have I been able to do it? Very simply, I had some very good education. I went to a great college, Swarthmore, and in my last two years there I never was in a class of more than four students, nose-to-nose with a great professor. I went to Harvard, I went to Ohio State, I went to a great university in Europe, St. Andrews. I would be ashamed of myself if I were not able to work, because I sure had great teachers.

STUDENT: That doesn't have much to do with your discipline though. What about that—the day-to-day stuff?

MICHENER: You have to have the discipline to get up in the morning and go to work, and write a book which nobody's asked you to write, and which you don't know whether anybody will read. . . . If you look at the five or six great successes I've had, how many of you would choose any one of them as a subject for an important novel? Archaeology in Israel—what kind of subject is that? Or geese on the Chesapeake Bay? But the job of the writer is to take whatever subject you choose and make it interesting. I'm not good at dialogue, I'm not good in plotting, you notice I don't care how my novels end, I don't care about winding up characters. But I do believe that if I put my mind to it, I could describe a kitchen chair in about four paragraphs, and *make* you read to the end of those four paragraphs.

I have tremendous respect for American writers like Philip Roth, who's so good at words, and Vonnegut, who's so good at imaginative things, and Joe Heller, who has such a wonderful sense of humor. Okay, they can do that. I can do what I do.

You should be aware of the problems of publishing today. I suppose you've been told that the big publishers no longer accept manuscripts just mailed in, as they say, over the transom. Your job of getting published is rather more difficult than mine, because I did mail my book in over the transom. It's hard to get an agent, because good agents don't want to take you on until you've published something. But you've come to one of the best places in America to break into publishing. Any of your professors here would command attention if he or she sent one of your manuscripts to a publisher and said, "You know, this kid is worth looking at."

Publishers have to publish, and all of us grow older and we're not going to be here indefinitely. Somebody's going to come up out of your group to take our place, and it might as well be you.

THE TWIN CITIES: PLACES THAT WORK

On almost everyone's list of America's ten most livable urban areas, the Twin Cities of Minnesota—Minneapolis and St. Paul—rank high. For these two cities, standing side by side on opposite banks of the Mississippi, offer a lesson to all the nation on what urban life might be like. It is not that the Twin Cities share none of the problems of places like New York, Los Angeles, or Boston. Here too there is poverty, though less widespread than in many of America's metropolitan regions. Here too there is unemployment, though diversification of industry, together with a considerable number of enterprises in the booming high-technology fields, have made the jobless relatively few in number. Here too there are racial tensions between whites and a small number of blacks and a somewhat larger population of Chippewa Indians. Yet, tensions here are muted, not because minorities fear to fight for their rights but because in recent decades conversation has proved to be a better tool to advance justice than confrontation. When the late Hubert Humphrey was mayor of Minneapolis in the 1940s, he led the city in the passage of America's first municipal fair-employment practices law that established a model on which similar ordinances in scores of other cities were later based.

It is almost as if the two million people who live in the Twin Cities and its surrounding communities, having battled with the burdens that the long winter—with its bitter cold and frequent snowstorms—imposes, were somehow gentled by the struggle. Minnesotans claim they love the cold, and judging by the fact that snowmobiles are as ubiquitous as Fords and that cross-country skiers and ice skaters appear

Lake of the Isles, one of twenty-two lakes and lagoons in the City of Lakes. Downtown Minneapolis is in the background. (Minneapolis Convention and Tourist Commission)

to be as numerous as grasshoppers, there is probably much truth in this claim. Yet to see a businessman in St. Paul striding along on a subzero day clad in nothing more than a suit and a lightly lined raincoat is to know that there is much bravado in the Minnesotan's attitude toward winter. "Do your worst," they seem to say to the elements. "I am more than your equal. I can subdue you, master you, and turn you to my purposes."

Hints of bone-crunching cold may come to the Twin Cities as early as October, and a distinct chill may remain in the air well into May. Given a climate much like Scandinavia's—whence the ancestors of a great many Minnesotans came—Twin Cities dwellers take a particular delight in flowers, in color, in sunlight; indeed in anything that enhances the glory of the all too brief summer and lightens the gloom of the long winter night. Minneapolis alone boasts no fewer than 153 parks, lovingly landscaped, and twenty-two lakes open to community recreation. In the downtown areas of both cities, a network of enclosed pedestrian bridges, one story above street level, connect scores of office buildings, shopping malls, restaurants, and entertainment areas, so that in winter workers and those seeking the amenities of urban life need not bundle themselves up and face the peril of the slush-covered streets. This ability to stay indoors while shopping at department stores and boutiques or while rushing from dinner to the theater has played a considerable role in the Twin Cities successful efforts to maintain their downtown areas as both economically and culturally viable.

Equally important has been the high quality of the cultural attractions themselves. The Tyrone Guthrie Repertory Theater in Minneapolis is world-famous, as is the Minneapolis Institute of Art and the Walker Art Center. Both St. Paul's Civic Center and Minneapolis's Nicollet Mall—an eight-block-long shopping street lined with trees and giant pots of flowers—are in the forefront of urban architecture and landscape design.

Both cities benefit from their relatively small size. They are communities built to the human dimension. This permits the individual to live in command of his surroundings rather than be overawed by his environment. Minneapolis, the cultural capital of Minnesota, has a population of fewer than 450,000; St. Paul, the political capital, has barely more than 300,000. Population density is quite low, and private homes are more the rule than large apartment complexes. Add to this the relative homogeneity of both cities' populations—Minneapolis is

Winter scene in Minneapolis. (Minneapolis Convention and Tourism Commission)

Sunset outlines power plant near the twin cities of Minneapolis and St. Paul.
(Colour Library International, Ltd.)

largely made up of Scandinavian-Americans; St. Paul's citizens are more often than not German or Irish in background—and there are the makings of settled communities. ❑

Fraternal Twins

❑ Though the two cities are twins in the sense of physical closeness, they are fraternal rather than identical. To cross the Mississippi from Minneapolis to St. Paul is to move into a distinctly different environment. St. Paul is basically a working-class town, heavily unionized, strongly Roman Catholic, staid, and serene. The residential streets are quiet, the houses mostly modest, the lawns well tended. Only once a year, at Winter Carnival—the Mardi Gras of the North, local boosters call it—does St. Paul bubble with excitement, as natives and thousands of tourists alike marvel at intricate ice sculptures, quaff gallons of beer, and join in celebration. Yet it is all quite decorous, almost subdued when compared with the bacchanal that New Orleans, at the other end of the Mississippi, celebrates at just about the same time of year.

Minneapolis, on the other hand, is a wealthier town, a more sophisticated community, historically more liberal in its outlook and willing to try both social and cultural experiments. No one is surprised in Minneapolis to find the wall of a parking lot covered with a giant-size reproduction of the score of "Gaspard de la Nuit" by Maurice Ravel. Citizens of Minneapolis are more likely to applaud experimental drama, abstract art, or the spicy cuisine of the Orient than their neighbors across the river.

But on one thing, all Twin Cities residents—indeed all Minnesotans—agree. They are fanatically devoted to their major-league teams: baseball's Twins, football's Vikings, and hockey's North Stars. These are obvious sources of civic spirit. Yet in the northland that the Twin Cities dominate, there is a less obvious but no less real source of pride that is manifest in the openness of a people who live in a society that works. ❑

THE GREAT RIVER

❑ Hernando DeSoto found it, for the white man, in 1541. The Chippewa Indians named it "Mississip," which means simply "Great River." It begins as a trickle in northern Minnesota and, joined by its tributaries, meanders 2,348 miles to find the Gulf of Mexico. On it is carried the lifeblood of the nation: grain, coal, vegetable oils, gasoline, chemicals, sand, crushed rock, steel, cement, minerals, petrochemical products—whatever can be made or grown or mined.

The midsection of America is webbed with rivers almost as numerous as the lines in the palm of one's hand, and most of them meet and mingle in the waters of the lifeline of the continent, the mighty Mississippi. From the east, the Wabash, the Cumberland, and the Tennessee rivers meet the long Ohio and spill their joint waters into the Mississippi at the town of Cairo, forming the boundary of the southern tip of Illinois. In the early nineteenth century, this was the watery pathway that carried pioneer farmers westward to the plains and prairies and south to Arkansas and Missouri. From the west, the Montana-born Missouri River, longest in the United States, gathers in the waters of a myriad of other rivers before it meets the Mississippi at St. Louis. Add the Wisconsin, the Illinois, the Minnesota, the Arkansas, the Canadian, the Red—within an area of 1,250,000 square miles bordered east and west by the Appalachians and the Rockies, almost every river eventually finds its way into the Mississippi.

Barge on the Mississippi.

Thomas Jefferson negotiated the purchase of the Louisiana Territory from the French in 1803. He was not sure exactly what he had bought in the way of land for the price of $15 million; and to find out what lay in that vast unknown wilderness, he sent Lewis and Clarke on their momentous expedition. But Jefferson's principal concern in making what many at the time denounced as an extravagant expenditure (and the French minister, Talleyrand, praised as a "noble bargain") was to ensure free passage for American shipping on the Mississippi and an American port on the Gulf of Mexico. Without that passage and port, the frontier farmers in the burgeoning Ohio territory and in the regions west of the Appalachians would have been bottled up in their isolated settlements. For many, there was no way to move their goods except by floating them downstream, on a barge or flatboat. ❑

The River Passages

❑ Until the coming of the railroads, Americans had been largely a water-borne people. Wherever it was possible, goods and travelers moved by boat. Shallow-drafted keelboats, with men to push long poles against the current and sails to catch the wind, could be forced upstream, although this was a slow and arduous process. Flatboats and barges were heavy and clumsy, but they could move large cargoes down the river currents. Flatboats were basically barges with square roofed shelters built on their decks. A French traveler on the Mississippi was astonished at the sight of a fleet of the clumsy craft: "I could not conceive what such large square boxes could be," he wrote. "On ascending the banks of the river, I perceived in these boats several families, bringing with them their horses, cows, fowl, carts, ploughs, harness, beds, implements of husbandry; in short, all the furniture needed for housekeeping, agriculture, and the management of a farm." A flatboat journey from Pittsburgh to New Orleans might take six weeks or longer. At the docks in New Orleans, the boat was broken up—since a return journey upstream was impossible—and its timber sold.

But it was steam power that turned the intricate network of inland waterways into major arteries of commerce. The first steamboats were sailing on midwestern rivers as early as 1811, and by the 1820s some hundred paddlewheelers made regular stops at tiny riverport villages. Steamboats plied the Mississippi from New Orleans north, and sailed the waters of all the Great Lakes. With the opening of the Erie Canal in 1825—linking the Hudson River with Lake Erie over 360 miles to the west—water-borne traffic surged through the lakes. Detroit, which had been a small fur-trading post, became a major port by the 1830s, a stopover city for westbound emigrants who found work in the booming lakeside industries and left with replenished wallets to stake out the plush acres of the Great Lakes plains country.

Churning up the Missouri and Mississippi rivers, steamboats carried

Captain piloting his barge on the Mississippi near Hannibal, Missouri.

settlers into the heart of the western wilderness. Cabin passage from St. Louis to Fort Benton in the foothills of the Rocky Mountains was expensive—about $150—but it saved weeks of hard and often hazardous travel. Mississippi steamboats carried thousands of new residents all the way north to St. Paul, and returned downriver with cargoes of furs replacing passengers. ❑

Mark Twain and the Mississippi

❑ In the heyday of the barge and keelboat traffic, the river heroes had been the boatmen, rowdy roustabouts who boasted, like the legendary Mike Fink, that they could "out-run, out-jump, out-shoot, out-brag, out-drink, and out-fight any man on both sides of the river." By Mark Twain's time, the steamboat had become the choicest mode of travel, and to be a steamboat pilot was, according to Twain, "the grandest position of all." Twain himself became a pilot after he persuaded Mr. Bixby, of the steamboat *Paul Jones,* to "teach me the Mississippi River from New Orleans to St. Louis for $500. . . . I entered upon the small enterprise of 'learning' twelve or thirteen hundred miles of the great Mississippi River with the easy confidence of my time of life. . . . I did not consider that [it] could be much of a trick, since [the river] was so wide." ❑

Hannibal, Missouri

❑ Twain chronicled the life of the people in the Mississippi region with a gusto and humor, and a sharp eye for their absurdities, equaled by no other writer of his time or ours. Twain was born in 1835 in the small hamlet of Hannibal, Missouri, on the western bank of the Mississippi River. His tales of growing up in Hannibal have provided generations of readers with an American fantasy of boyhood in paradise—albeit one threatened by the lurking evil of Injun Joe and old Pap Finn, Huck's drunk father.

Twain's description of a hot Hannibal day seems to touch a memory in all of us, even if we've never left the sidewalks of a modern city: ". . . The white town drowsing in the sunshine of a summer's morning; the streets empty, or pretty nearly so; one or two clerks sitting in front of the Water Street stores, with their splint-bottomed chairs tilted back against the walls, chins on breasts, hats slouched over their faces . . . a sow and a litter of pigs loafing along the sidewalk, doing a good business in watermelon rinds and seeds . . . and the fragrant town drunkard, asleep."

Hannibal has grown since Twain's time, from a tiny hamlet of less than a thousand pre–Civil War Americans to a bustling community of almost a score times that number. Yet the town hasn't changed all that much since Twain's day. And the nineteenth-century myth of childhood, the one Twain created, still lives. Kids still fish the banks of Jackson's Island where Tom, Huck, and Joe Harper went to become pirates. And maybe someone soon will catch a catfish as big as the one Huck Finn got. That was a six-foot-two monster. It weighed two hundred pounds—"As big a fish as was ever catched in the Mississipp, I reckon," said Huck.

Children still grow up in Hannibal pretty much the same way they did in Twain's time. Some of them talked to Michener about their town and their predecessor, the boy Sam Clemens, who left Hannibal to become the world-famous author Mark Twain. ❑

Voices of Hannibal Students

STUDENT: Mark Twain left Hannibal to broaden his horizons, but even though he left, I think Hannibal stayed a part of him. You can see it in his writing.

Main Street in today's Hannibal, Missouri.

Tom Sawyer's fence.

Students in a Hannibal classroom talk about Hannibal and Mark Twain.

STUDENT: I think Twain was bored with Hannibal, and he wanted to fulfill his dreams, so he went out in the world.

STUDENT: Hannibal is a nice town to grow up in, but there are not as many opportunities here as there are in larger cities, and I feel that may have been one of the reasons Mark Twain left.

STUDENT: I'd say if I ever moved away I'm sure that eventually I'd come back here and settle down again. But I'll probably just live here the rest of my life.

STUDENT: In the summertime, practically everybody is a river rat, and if you want to find out where your friends are, you go down to the river.

Boys from Hannibal fishing in the river as Tom and Huck did in Twain's imagination.

A Barge on the Great River

No longer the simple wood scow of a century ago, the modern barge is actually an assemblage of many barges, lashed together by steel cables, pushed by a powerful towboat, and hauling cargoes that can equal in volume the contents of hundreds of railroad freightcars. Barge captain Al Rogers talked with me about life on the river today:

"People tell me the romance is all gone from the river, but I don't believe that. People come out here and work for a while, and then they think they're not satisfied and they go somewhere else. But they turn up again. They always come back. I suppose you get hooked on it.

"The river has always been a challenge to me, and I think the challenge keeps people here."

"You never find any two trips the same," says Captain Rogers. "Wind and weather change the look of the river from moment to moment. Storms and floods change its physical character, fill deep channels with sand, carve out new passages from solid earth. Still, we have managed to make the Mississippi more docile, even if we haven't

Students at Hannibal High School.

yet tamed her. We've built levees as high as twenty-four feet, we've dredged new waterways to contain the floodwaters that once ravaged the land. And we maintain shipping channels that run the entire length of the Mississippi, and channels as well on its major tributaries. As a result, freight traffic has grown to such an extent that, by 1975, the Mississippi River freighted almost half of all the water-borne cargoes carried on all the inland waterways in the United States."

The St. Louis Arch—Gateway to the West

The city of St. Louis rises where the mightiest of waterways joins the muddiest (described by those who know her as "too thick to drink and too thin to plough")—where the Mississippi meets the Missouri. The French trader Pierre Laclède selected this site in 1764 to establish a post from which to trade with the Indians who lived upriver. He wrote, "I have found a situation where I intend to establish a settlement which, in the future, shall become one of the most beautiful cities in the world."

St. Louis's Gateway Arch is as beautiful, certainly, as Laclède's vision must have been. This soaring structure of stainless steel, designed by the great Eero Saarinen, has become a famous symbol not only of the city, but even more, of the limitless lands that lie to the west.

The midwestern city of St. Louis, Missouri, as seen through the beautiful and spectacularly simple Gateway Arch. (Colour Library International, Ltd.)

THE SOUTHWEST

VULTURE MINE, A GHOST TOWN

One of the most enduring symbols of the American Southwest is the abandoned gold or silver mine. In Arizona, I visited a long-defunct mining town, one of hundreds in the Southwest. This one was called Vulture Mine, an inauspicious name for what was once one of the richest gold mines in the country. In its day it produced more than $30 million in gold. Even today, when the only metal a visitor can see is the tin on the roofs, locals will tell you that there is more than $600,000 in gold still to be mined here.

Ghost town of Tomboy on Imogen Pass trail near Telluride, Colorado. (Colour Library International, Ltd.)

Tombstone at Boothill, Arizona, once site of a mining boom town. (Colour Library International, Ltd.)

Everywhere in the vast and beautiful desert landscape of the American Southwest, one is offered the possibility of great wealth, just out of sight—in the land, or in the future. In the early days prospectors helped to settle the Southwest. They came from the East, or they came from California—where America's original gold rush had run out of steam by the 1860s—in search of gold, silver, or copper. Boom towns sprang up all over. Oatman, Bisbee, Jerome, Tombstone—the list goes on and on. More often than not, boom went bust when the veins ran out or ran so deep into the earth that they could no longer be tapped, as happened here at Vulture. The miners moved on, then moved on again—across deserts and mountains and over vast distances. Moving on—that's a vital element in the story of America's Southwest.

There is a tree near the Vulture Mine. It is called "the hanging tree." It symbolizes the rude, swift justice that characterized the mining frontier. The life of the miner was hard; it was competitive; often it was brutal. Claim jumping and its attendant brawls were facts of life for the free-lance miner. It's said that four hundred men were killed in the first fifteen years of operation at the Vulture Mine. Some presumably met with accidents; others certainly were the victims of greed that the very words "gold" and "silver" evoke in the breasts of men. There is a story that the prospector who discovered Vulture Mine's gold was circled by a vulture as he picked up his first nugget. He shot himself years later at that very spot. In Western ballads, the vulture always gets the last laugh.

Every ghost town has its story. That's what's left when everyone and everything else is gone. The Southwest is as full of stories as it is of ghost towns. The yarn is as much a part of the heritage of desert and mountain America as are the deserts and mountains themselves.

THE MINING FRONTIER

❑ The nation's appetite for gold was first whetted in 1849 with the discovery of the vast bonanza in California's Sierras. But by the end of the 1850s, the easy pickings in the California gold fields were exhausted, and those forty-niners who had not already struck it rich, or given up the hunt in favor of farming or ranching, headed eastward across the Sierras into Nevada, New Mexico, Arizona, and Colorado. The smell of gold was in the air, and their instincts were sufficiently acute to pick up the scent. As early as 1853, a few of the forty-niners had begun to drift east. That year a strike was made along the Gila River in southern

Arizona, and within months a wasteland was transformed into the boom town of Gila City. Some twelve hundred prospectors and suppliers converged on the Gila. There was, in the words of one observer, "a saloon to supply the necessities of life and later . . . a grocery store and a Chinese restaurant for the luxuries." There were also brothels and gambling halls dedicated to divesting the successful prospector of his hard-earned hoard of gold dust and nuggets. For a time, Gila City basked in its reputation as the wickedest town in the West—a sobriquet claimed by many another mining town—but by the mid-1860s, the gold was gone. The miners departed, leaving behind but "three chimneys and a coyote," as one passerby observed.

There were other mining communities, scores and scores of them, with stories similar to Gila City's: Wickenburg, Tombstone, Diamond City, Bannack all grew like weeds for a decade or so, then sank into decrepitude. But nothing, *nothing* ever came close to Virginia City, Nevada, with its Comstock Lode.

Henry T. P. Comstock—known to his friends as Old Pancake—was a man who dreamed of riches, and dreaming was what he did best. He styled himself a prospector, perhaps because not even Old Pancake could admit that his true vocation was loafing. And, indeed, he did prospect, in his fashion. He liked to loll about on his mule, sniffing the air and glancing this way and that. If something glinted in the sun and if Comstock was in the mood for activity, he might dismount, mosey over, and investigate the source of the glimmer. Old Pancake had come to Nevada because, like others, he had heard tales of gold. He stayed because it seemed to be as good a spot for loafing as any other.

One day in June 1859, Comstock was astride his mule while the animal ambled along an eastern slope of the Sierras. There Comstock came across two fellow prospectors—Patrick McLaughlin and Peter O'Reilly—working a spring. Normally Old Pancake would have just passed by, might even have waved his hand in greeting had he the energy. This time, however, something impelled Comstock to rein in his mule, to dismount and approach the men. The writer Dan De Quille described the scene: "Comstock . . . saw at a glance the unusual

One of the main buildings at Vulture Mine.

quantity of gold that was in sight. . . . Conceiving at once that a wonderful discovery had been made, [he] straightened himself up and coolly proceeded to inform the astonished miners that they were working on ground that belonged to him."

Normally such an assertion, in such circumstances, would have ended in gunplay. McLaughlin and O'Reilly must have been particularly peaceable sorts or perhaps Comstock was possessed of some awesome persuasive powers, for instead of plugging Old Pancake, they reached agreement with him. Comstock and two of his friends—James "Old Virginny" Finney and Manney Penrod—would share ownership of the claim with them. (Old Virginny's portion was soon bought out by Comstock for a bottle of whiskey, but the hapless prospector achieved a degree of immortality, if not riches, for it was in his honor that Virginia City was named.)

Comstock and his partners did find quantities of gold in the quartz rock they mined. Often, however, they came across another metal they could not identify and that was extremely difficult to separate from the quartz. Curious about what this metal might be, they dispatched a sample of the quartz to an assayer in California. It was the assayer's report that touched off a treasure hunt of unprecedented dimensions. Basing his findings on the small sample at hand, he predicted that each ton of the quartz would contain no less than $1,000 worth of gold—a bonanza in itself—and, quite unexpectedly, $3,000 worth of silver. Within a year, ten thousand miners and hangers-on were in the area. The shantytown of Virginia City had been established and was roaring, complete with the usual amenities: bars, gambling dens, bawdyhouses, dance halls. In addition, there were lawyers to help prospectors file claims, undertakers to bury claim jumpers or their victims, and six physicians who had booming practices treating gunshot wounds, venereal diseases, and arsenic poisoning—this last because the local rivers contained large doses of the deadly poison.

Comstock and his partners were not to profit much from their find. Others, more sophisticated and with a supply of ready cash, were the real beneficiaries. One of these was George Hearst—father of William Randolph Hearst, the newspaper tycoon—who received news of the assayer's report even before Comstock did. He rushed to Virginia City from California and divested McLaughlin of his claim for a mere $3,300. Comstock himself sold out to another investor for $10,000. The thousands of prospectors who flooded into Virginia City established their claims but lacked the money and technical know-how to exploit them, and one by one, the claims were bought out—first by speculators, then by businessmen with the capital to work the mines. Many of the original prospectors became day laborers, working deep inside the shafts where temperatures rose to 120°F. The Comstock Lode eventually made scores of wealthy investors even richer. Before it gave out in the 1880s, Comstock produced at least $300 million in gold and silver. Then one day, the cost of production began to exceed the value of the product. Comstock—like so many other bonanza mines in the mountain West—went bust. ❑

HOUSTON, NEW BOOM TOWN OF THE SOUTHWEST

When the Trailriders come to town to take part in the Livestock and Rodeo Show, Houston, Texas, reverts, if only for a moment, to its pioneer beginnings. To hunker down with the performers as they camp in the middle of downtown Houston's Memorial Park, to listen to the twanging guitars and quiet voices humming old cowboy ballads, is to be taken on a nostalgic journey of the mind back to the Southwest of a century ago. Yet these are twentieth-century Trailriders, and when they open for their two week-long shows, it will not be in some dusty corral but in Houston's plush Astrodome, the very model of

Today's trailrider may be more showman than cowboy, but each rider who participates in the annual Trailriders' Parade covers at least sixty miles on horseback of the old trails that lead to the city.

The modern buildings tower above a statue of Sam Houston, fighter for Texas independence and first president of the Republic of Texas.
(Colour Library International, Ltd.)

The Astrodome, which houses sports and other entertainment events. (Colour Library International, Ltd.)

an up-to-date stadium that only the modern American technological mind could conceive of, much less build.

Ghost town and boom town: Both are part of the Southwest, but it is the latter, like Houston, that represents the present and the future. The biggest city in the Southwest, the fastest-growing major metropolis in the nation, Houston is a living monument to individualism and enterprise. It has no fixed boundaries, and the very idea of a zoning ordinance is enough to make the average Houstonian wince. It just grows, and grows, and grows. There are predictions that this metropolis will be America's largest city by the year 2000, in area if not in population.

Houston is often called the Chicago of the Southwest. Like Chicago, the town was built by railroads. Like Chicago, it is a major port, thanks to the Ship Channel that gives it access to the Gulf of Mexico. Again, like Chicago, it was a major cattle center. Now, however, oil is what makes Houston the booming city it is—the petrochemical capital of the world. Oil is found literally in peoples' backyards, and a barbecue pit hard by a towering rig, a dozen or so yards from the patio, is hardly an unusual sight here. Oil has changed Houston and all of Texas from a poor rural region scratching out a pittance on cotton and cattle into an American colossus.

From the dining room of Houston's Petroleum Club atop the Exxon Building, where Houston's rich meet for lunch, the talk is all of oil. But Texas oil is actually on the decline now. The great discoveries are made elsewhere, on the North Slope of Alaska and in the oil shale fields of the Northwest, to say nothing of Europe's offshore fields. Still the state of Texas, with its impressive production of crude, with its vast petroleum and natural gas processing plants, continues to provide one-third of the nation's energy. And Texas oil money and Texas oil know-how underlie much of the world's petroleum production.

That Houston glorifies in its future is perhaps one reason why it celebrates, with such gusto, its past—both real and legendary. It's no accident that the Texas school system insists that all students study state history. Nor is it merely a desire for a day off that impells the Houston schoolboard to release children from their studies on the day the Trailriders come to town and parade. Texans love their legends, and even as they count their high-stake chips in the continuing game of oil, they affect clothing—ten-gallon hats and intricately worked leather boots—more evocative of the nineteenth century than the twentieth.

Penzoil Building, offices of one of the many petroleum corporations located in Houston. (Colour Library International, Ltd.)

Perhaps no place in Houston better demonstrates Texas's split personality than the San Antone Rose Bar, with its mechanical bucking bronco—a bone-breaking entertainment that has spread from Texas to saloons all over the nation. Some of the workers in the refineries near the bar find the bronc relaxing; tourists find it a challenge.

The Trailriders and the rest of the rodeo and livestock show at the Astrodome are an echo of the frontier in the most modern of settings. I am more and more captivated by certain imaginative things done by cities, and the Astrodome is one of them. I find it a brilliant concept, equivalent in purpose, if not in architectural design, to the Colosseum in Rome—both essentially sports palaces handsome enough to be worthy of great cities. This air-conditioned palace uses enough electricity to light a town of nine thousand people. Beneath the dome, some five to six hundred thousand people will watch the rodeo and livestock show during its fortnight's stay. The West has always provided itself with its own show. This is part of a long tradition that started with Buffalo Bill's

Construction workers share in Houston's building boom, itself a spinoff of oil money that has brought vast new wealth to the city.

LEFT: *Rodeo rider and clown.*

RIGHT: *Wagon races at the rodeo.*

Wild West Show in the late 1800s, a show that featured among its performers the legendary sharpshooter Annie Oakley and the great Indian warriors Sitting Bull and Geronimo. The West has always been its own mythologizer. Rodeos are part of the West and part of the myth. The fact that this one is inside the Astrodome only testifies to the strength of a regional tradition that adapts to the present and a contemporary culture that wants to take its past along with it.

Like the Astrodome, the Houston Ship Channel is another example of far-sighted imagination brought to fruition. The 1914 opening of this fifty-mile-long, thirty-six-foot-deep, four-hundred-foot-wide channel to the sea gave Houston the potential of becoming a major port. Today the harbor is America's third largest, its docks capable of servicing the largest oceangoing ships. Evidently, even in the early years of this century, Houstonians had already developed Texas-size ambitions. As Will Rogers once said, "Houston dared to dig a ditch and bring the sea to its door." What Houstonians will do next is anybody's guess. But one thing is certain; whatever it is, it will be big, and broad, and handsome, and profitable; a fitting tribute to the burgeoning city and its Lone Star State.

Monument to the astronauts of Apollo 11 *who landed on the moon, July 1969. This beautiful and unusual structure is in downtown Houston.*

The observation tower adjacent to the Hyatt-Regency Hotel is an example of contemporary architecture in Dallas. A network of highways links the different sections of this vibrant and growing city. (Colour Library International, Ltd.)

THE BIG D AND ITS NEIGHBORS

Nothing illustrates Texas's bigness better than the Dallas/Fort Worth Airport, which lies midway between the two cities. Approximately the size of Manhattan Island, this agglomeration of runways, terminals, hangars, parking lots, looping roads, and the like is larger in area than all three of New York City's commercial airports put together, with room left over for a fourth landing field of prodigious expanse. Local talk has it that innumerable passengers changing planes at Dallas/Fort Worth have landed there with all of their faculties perfectly intact only to be driven absolutely mad by the sheer bafflement involved in finding their way from one terminal to another. Be that as it may, the airport is certainly a symbol of the astonishing growth of the Sunbelt in general and the Dallas/Fort Worth area in particular. Today, the two cities, which are some thirty miles apart, and the many suburbs they dominate boast a combined population of more than 2.5 million—and among these residents are many of the wealthiest people in the United States.

Dallas, with more than 900,000 citizens, is the seventh largest city in the nation and the second largest in Texas. If Houston is bigger and growing somewhat faster, citizens of Dallas take comfort in their firmly held belief that in terms of wealth, culture, commerce, and the amenities of urban life, their city far outclasses any other in the entire Southwest. Indeed, Dallas is the state's and region's major insurance and banking center and it boasts thriving aerospace and computer industries as well as a major symphony orchestra, an acclaimed local theater group, an impressive summer opera program, and that perennial National Football League power, the Dallas Cowboys. Oddly enough, the Cowboys, the delight of every true Dallas resident, play their home games not in the city's famed Cotton Bowl but at a nearby suburban stadium.

A visitor coming to Dallas in search of whooping and hollering cowboys, herds of cattle lowing their way through the streets, and other appurtenances of the Old West is certain to be mightily disappointed. For the face that Dallas presents to the world is more that of an eastern than a western city—blue-suited businessmen quietly making impressive financial deals and svelte ladies (reputed to be the most beautiful and fashionable in the entire nation) hurrying to luncheon appointments at restaurants where the bill of fare is more likely to be *nouvelle cuisine* than old-time barbeque. It may well be that the term "Big D," Dallas's nickname, stands for "the Big Dollar," for the accumulation of wealth is far and away the favorite pastime of the city's elite.

Of all America's major cities, Dallas is probably the most conservative. Despite a large population of poor blacks and impoverished whites, it is the city's business elite that runs the show. Almost to a man, members of the establishment are conservative and look upon social change as a fundamental threat to their status, power, and wealth. It was in Dallas that Lyndon Johnson was spat upon during the presidential campaign in 1960; it was in Dallas that Adlai Stevenson was physically attacked three years later; and, of course, it was in Dallas that John F. Kennedy was assassinated. Though his murderer was identified as a left-wing fanatic, the slaying reinforced the city's image as a place of political extremism. Since that tragic November day almost two decades ago, Dallas has been trying, with indifferent success, to shed that image.

As in politics, so too in religion. Dallas is sometimes called the "Vatican of American Fundamentalism." One city block near the downtown area holds no fewer than ten churches, all of them fundamentalist to one degree or another. The largest Baptist and Presbyterian churches in the nation are located in Dallas, and the city's religious leaders work closely with businessmen to maintain a conservative tone.

For all its obeisance to such traditional values as fundamentalist religion and rugged individualism, Dallas is certainly of the modern world. Its museums are filled not only with representations of the Old

View of downtown Dallas, the second-largest city in Texas. (Colour Library International, Ltd.)

West but with the works of modern and contemporary European and American masters as well; its Theater Center contains the only public auditorium ever designed by Frank Lloyd Wright; its fashion industry rivals that of New York; and at night the city offers revelers everything from country music bars to plush and elegant supper clubs. Yet, despite its patina of culture, there is much about Dallas that bespeaks the open, raw, and brutal competition for money. It is this aspect of the city's life that has made it fascinating to Americans from every region and every walk of life. Each Friday night, millions upon millions of Americans settle down before their television sets to watch a continuing drama that centers about the accumulation of wealth and power. It is no accident that this weekly national pastime is entitled "Dallas." ❑

Fort Worth

❑ Though only thirty miles from Dallas, Fort Worth, in style and substance, might well be on the other side of the moon. A city of almost 400,000, it comes much closer to the average American's idea of the Old West than does its much larger and wealthier neighbor. Though Dallas long ago became the dominant city in the region, many travelers have found Fort Worth to be a more appealing—more human—place. There is money there—lots of it—but the flaunting of wealth is almost unknown. And though in sheer numbers of museums, theaters, orchestras, and the like, Fort Worth is no match for its neighbor, there are many who would hold that the smaller city has shown considerably more taste in its purchase and display of cultural attractions than has the larger one. Finally, Fort Worth, which began as a cowboy's town—a cattle center—exhibits a casualness that confirmed Dallas residents find baffling. Traditionally there has been considerable enmity between the two cities: the larger Dallas a bit authoritarian, ideological, and forthrightly money-oriented; the smaller Fort Worth relaxed and thumbing its nose at the display of power and wealth. Between the two cities there seemed to be an unbridgeable chasm, symbolized by thirty miles of open plains. Now the open spaces that had separated Dallas from Fort Worth are dotted with houses, factories, office buildings, restaurants, stadiums, shopping centers, and general suburban sprawl. This region has been dubbed "Mid-Cities" and it ties Fort Worth and Dallas into what the Census Bureau calls a single "urbanized area." For residents of Fort Worth the linkage has been a mixed blessing. True, their city has boomed. New hotels, new office buildings, new restaurants are everywhere, but some fear that the new proximity will lead to the blurring of Fort Worth's distinctive character, that the money ethos of Dallas will swamp their city. For the moment, however, Fort Worth remains a place of great charm, a town that seems to move along at a cowpoke's unhurried lope; a city that speaks with a slow drawl that soothes rather than excites. ❑

OIL: AN INDUSTRY THAT CHANGED THE WORLD

❑ The multibillion-dollar petroleum industry that has become the major preoccupation of the industrialized world and the single most potent weapon in the arsenal of the Third World had its beginnings in a discovery in the 1850s that was so modest as to be almost obscure. To the few hundred citizens of Titusville, a village in western Pennsylvania, oil was something they knew more than enough about. The black, viscous substance was everywhere, seeping up through the soil to ruin crops, seeping down into wells to befoul the water supply. In their view, the stuff was a pestilence, a plague of nature that threatened their very livelihoods. There were, of course, legends that the oil might have medicinal properties. The Seneca Indians, who had once lived in the region, were said to have quaffed the stuff and rubbed it on their bodies, but whether their health actually benefited was a matter of conjecture and debate. True, a few local entrepreneurs, trading on the Indian legend, had bottled the petroleum and had attempted to market it under the name Seneca Oil as a cure-all—with indifferent success. And then there was a professor of chemistry at Yale who refined some Titusville petroleum and discovered that it would burn brightly in a lamp.

It was this chemist's work that first intrigued a few financiers, for whale oil—the nation's primary illuminant—was becoming both expensive and rare. If the oil could be brought out of the ground cheaply and in quantity and refined into kerosene, a substitute for whale oil would be available and a new and profitable industry born. A fast-talking one-

Drilling for oil from the ocean floor near Houston. (Colour Library International, Ltd.)

time railroad conductor named Edwin Drake convinced the consortium of financiers that he was the man to drill for the oil, and off he went to Titusville to pioneer many of the techniques that would later become standard in the oil drilling business. Drake brought in the world's first oil well in 1859.

During the next few decades the kerosene industry boomed, making fortunes for industrialists like John D. Rockefeller, and laying the groundwork for today's massive, worldwide petroleum business. In those days kerosene was the only major product to be refined from petroleum; most other byproducts were considered waste. With the rise of the gas lighting business, and later the discovery of the electric light, it looked for a while that the petroleum boom would go bust. But even as kerosene was beginning to decrease in value, a long-scorned byproduct of the refining process, gasoline, was beginning to show some potential. In the 1880s and 1890s, European inventors were putting together a new kind of motor—the internal combustion engine—and experimenting with self-propelled road vehicles. That gasoline was a superb fuel to drive these engines was soon well accepted, but it was also widely assumed that the world's supply of petroleum was too limited to service a fast-growing automobile industry. ❑

A New Oil Boom

❑ An American promoter named Edward Doheny changed all that. In 1893 he discovered a vast pool of petroleum beneath the small city of Los Angeles. Around the same time he convinced a railroad to try petroleum as a fuel for its locomotives. The experiment was a great success, and a new oil boom was on. Soon Los Angeles oil was fueling not only trains but, refined into gasoline, it was being used to drive the internal combustion engines of automobiles. A symbiotic relationship quickly

Oil refinery outside Houston.

developed between the two new industries. As more oil was found, more cars were built; as more cars were built the scramble to discover new supplies of oil became even more frantic. By the turn of the century, the petroleum industry had grown into a little giant.

That little giant began to take on the aspect of a behemoth in 1901 when a mining engineer named Anthony Lucas brought in Texas's first gusher, Spindletop, near the city of Beaumont. Spindletop had its genesis in the fervent belief of a Beaumontian and amateur geologist named Patillo Higgins that there was oil in great quantities in the land around the city. In the 1890s Higgins began drilling on his own—coming up with dry hole after dry hole and losing a small fortune in the effort. By the end of the decade, Higgins was broke and could no longer afford to continue his explorations, but he did convince Lucas to take up the work. From the fall of 1900 until the following January, Lucas supervised drilling operations on Spindletop. On January 10, 1901, as his drill bit plunged 1,160 feet into the Texas soil, riggers heard a low rumbling from the bowels of the earth, and then there was a kind of explosion. They ran for cover, reaching safety just as jets of rock and mud surged up from below and cascaded into the air. Then came the petroleum: gallons, tens of gallons, thousands of gallons—black gold roaring from the depths and shooting skyward, like a fountain from hell. Only after ten days had gone by, and nearly a million gallons of oil had been wasted, were Lucas's men able to cap the well. The Texas oil boom was on. It would help make the automobile a practical device for America's millions. It would change the face of Texas and the American Southwest. It would alter the economy of the nation and revolutionize the politics of the world. It is a revolution, that, for good or ill, continues yet. ❑

SANTA FE: A BLENDING OF CULTURES

Santa Fe has been called the most human of all American cities. It was built with people, rather than institutions, in mind. It exemplifies the architecture of the Southwest, with earth-colored buildings no more than two stories high, buildings that seem to catch the special quality of light here. Artists come to Santa Fe by the hundreds. Perhaps it is for the light, perhaps it is for the clean mountain air, certainly it is for the ambience of welcome extended to all who paint or sculpt or write. Some call Santa Fe "proudly provincial." Perhaps it is, but most assuredly it is relaxed—an old city in an old part of the country; a great lady of the provinces who has long since learned to wear her age with charm and grace.

The Trails of the Conquerors

❑ A sense of history pervades New Mexico's capital, Santa Fe, as it does all of the state. But it is a vastly different history than the East

San Miguel Mission in Santa Fe, New Mexico.

Indian traders outside Palace of the Governors, Santa Fe. (Colour Library International, Ltd.)

Coast American or the midwesterner calls his own. Here there are no Pilgrim Fathers or woodland Indians to revere, no carefully preserved memories of the Revolutionary War, for the heritage of New Mexico is that of the highly sophisticated Pueblo Indian tribes overlaid with the richly embroidered fabric of Spanish and Mexican America.

The first Europeans to arrive in New Mexico—indeed in the Southwest itself—were four hapless would-be conquistadors out of Spanish Mexico, whose ship was wrecked on the Texas coast. According to these survivors of the tragedy, they were held captive for six years by Indians, then finally escaped and wandered through portions of what is now New Mexico before picking their way to safety in 1536 into Spanish-held Old Mexico. The leader of this ill-fated expedition was one Alvar Nunez Cabeza de Vaca. Perhaps he hallucinated in the desert sun, because upon returning to Mexico he reported to the authorities that he had seen, during his journeys, cities where gold was more common than clay—the legendary Seven Cities of Cibola. Mexico's Spanish masters, always eager for new sources of treasure, took Cabeza's bait. In 1540 Captain General Don Francisco Vásquez de Coronado organized an expedition that set out for the American Southwest. The Spanish grandee was to spend years trekking through the desert and plains, but all he garnered for his efforts was frustration. There were no cities of gold, no Eldorado, no Cibola. Yet the expedition was to have a lasting effect upon the American West. Some of the horses the conquistador brought with him escaped and were, in turn, captured by Indians, who had never before seen such animals. These horses formed the basic breeding stock from which the Indian herds grew. They would drastically alter the customs and practices of many Indian tribes that gave up farming on the edges of the plains to become horse-borne hunters of buffalo and cavalry without peer in the world.

As for Coronado, the closest he came to gilded cities were the villages of the Pueblo Indians. Had the Spanish adventurer been less hungry for treasure and more of a scholar, he might have found these settlements well worth the journey, for the Pueblo Indians were the inheritors of a great culture—then existing in only attenuated form. In ages past, their ancestors had lived in fortresslike cities perched in high, inaccessible canyons beneath the towering peaks of the Rockies. Typical was the Anasazi village in Chaco Canyon, New Mexico, a five-story high, semicircular structure facing onto a great plaza. Within its walls, this town, now known as Pueblo Bonito, contained some eight hundred rooms that housed about twelve hundred people. This and other such villages were the sites of complex and prosperous Indian civilizations. Farming on the hillsides and hunting brought the Anasazi a comfortable way of life which enabled them to create arts and crafts of exquisite beauty—particularly in the form of lushly decorated pottery. But this golden age of the southwestern Indian was not to last. A series of droughts forced the abandonment of Pueblo Bonita, as it did the other great apartment villages of the regions. The Indians left their great centers to the ravages of nature and established smaller, more economically viable pueblos in which the traditions of the settled tribes of the area were carried on, though in not so grand a form. ❑

Spanish Colonists

❑ It was these later pueblos that Coronado passed through on his fruitless quest for gold, a quest that carried him all the way to Kansas before he gave up. Four decades would pass before another Spanish expedition headed north out of Mexico. Though the members of this party certainly kept a sharp watch for treasure, they also examined the land through which they passed, and when they returned home to Old Mexico they reported that the soil and climate to the north was suitable for grazing both cattle and sheep. This impelled a young Spaniard named Don Juan de Onate to form a party of colonists who, in 1598, established the first European settlement in New Mexico, San Juan, on the banks of the Rio Grande. A decade later, in 1609—just about the time that English colonists were establishing Jamestown on the Virginia coast—a second party of Spaniards founded Santa Fe, which quickly became the focal point of Spanish life and administration in the regions north of Old Mexico.

As Santa Fe grew and prospered over the next two centuries, a new nation was taking shape along North America's Atlantic Coast. In the late eighteenth century, when the United States achieved its independence from Britain, its citizens almost immediately began pushing inland. Inevitably the time would come when the two cultures would meet. It was in 1806 that the fateful confrontation took place. Led by a young lieutenant named Zebulon Pike (for whom Pike's Peak in Colorado is named), an exploratory party of American soldiers blazed a trail west from the banks of the Missouri into Colorado and then south to Santa Fe. Following in Pike's footsteps, along what would come to be known as the Santa Fe Trail, came grizzled, wilderness-wise merchants out of Independence, Missouri. They had goods to sell, and the people of Santa Fe—long limited to purchasing items brought up from Mexico—were happy to see them. But the Spanish authorities were anything but pleased. Fearful of American economic competition and political influence, they barred trade with the merchants from the east, and those traders who fell into their clutches were summarily imprisoned. Yet, as always happens in such situations, smuggling flourished. When Mexico threw off Spanish rule in 1821, and New Mexico became a province of the new nation, trading became easier, though tariffs were high and bribes to officials of the Santa Fe administration were often necessary to grease the wheels of commerce. Such practices were hardly conducive to mutual respect, and the citizens of Sante Fe looked upon the trailriders as sharpers, lewd in their conduct and sly in their trading practices. The Americans, for their part, returned the compliments; one trader, Josiah Gregg, remarked that the New Mexicans were "cunning, loquacious, . . . sycophantic [and] cringing," given to both "bigotry and fanaticism."

Sentiments such as these were not limited to Mexican officials in Santa Fe and American traders; they reflected an overall deterioration in relations between the two countries in the 1830s and 1840s. Texas's struggle for independence and the controversy between Mexico and the United States over the Lone Star Republic's desire to join the Union made the very word "Mexican" anathema to most Americans. In the aftermath of President James Polk's declaration of war on Mexico in 1846, American troops surged westward from the middle border to overrun the lightly defended outposts of Mexican rule in North America. When the war ended two years later, Mexico was forced to cede its claims to vast North American territories. Texas, New Mexico, Arizona, Colorado, Utah, Nevada, and California were now under the Stars and Stripes. By force of arms, the Indian and Hispanic worlds of the Southwest were merged with the alien Anglo-Saxon society of the United States. The creation of a unity out of these very different cultures has been a goal of the last century and a half. Only now, with the slow emergence of Mexican-American and Indian political and economic influence does that goal seem possible to achieve. ❑

Restoring the Past

Sante Fe's Plaza was laid out in 1610 by the Spanish governor Don Pedro de Peralta. It fronts upon the graceful governor's palace, also built in 1610. This city therefore has the oldest public building in the United States, the Palace of the Governors, and one of the oldest churches, the San Miguel Mission. From its earliest days Santa Fe has been a capital, first of Spain's New Mexico province, then of the Mexican province, then of the New Mexico territory and, finally, beginning in 1912, of the state of New Mexico. The city also marked the end of the *Camino Real*, the Royal Highway, a tortuous trail, despite its grand designation, that wound the fifteen hundred miles from Mexico City. And the Santa Fe Trail from Missouri ended here, this the primary trade

LEFT: *Palajemo working in the restored* placita *and* (RIGHT) *Palajemo and Michener standing near* ornos, *or ovens.*

link with the east until the first railroad arrived in 1880. Santa Fe incorporates more of our beginnings in the Southwest than any other city. In this lovely town the magic of many cultures and past ages seems to emanate from the buildings themselves. Nowhere is this more evident than on the outskirts of town, where an enterprising twentieth-century settler, George Palajemo, originally from Finland, has devoted his life to preserving the colonial heritage. With the help of the Smithsonian Institution, the now eighty-year-old Palajemo has created a living Spanish ranch that is both a museum and a working enterprise. I spent several pleasant hours chatting with him.

Michener Talks with George Palajemo

MICHENER: How did a man from Finland get to New Mexico?

PALAJEMO: It was very simple, really. I fell in love with a girl from New Mexico. Met her in New York, and she brought me here. This is her family ranch.

Church on the ranch.

MICHENER: The ranch is very old, I understand.

PALAJEMO: It is one of the most historic ranches in New Mexico, but it has been in my family only since 1932. It comprises about a thousand acres and originally was a sheep farm. But about fifty years ago, cattle raising became the primary source of income for the ranch.

MICHENER: The original settlers who came to this area with Onate—were they Spanish or Mexican?

PALAJEMO: They were Spanish. Many of them were born and raised in Spain before migrating to Mexico. When they came north they brought with them their animals and all their tools and implements for farming. New Mexico was really the first Spanish colony north of Mexico itself.

MICHENER: How did the original Spaniards who settled here make their living?

PALAJEMO: Basically, sheep farming. They produced wool, and eventually there was some weaving. Wool and blankets, really.

MICHENER: If their only exports were what sheep provided they must have had rather meager lives?

PALAJEMO: I should say so. Really it's remarkable that they were able to survive in those circumstances, because they faced so many difficulties. There were, of course, the Comanches and Apaches roaming around. They could attack the colonists any time. They would raid the ranches and steal all the produce. That in itself made life here very dangerous. Also, the farming was not easy. The climate was unpredictable, the soil quite poor. So I have the highest respect for these Spaniards.

MICHENER: After a time the Spanish did establish rather good relations with the Indians, didn't they?

PALAJEMO: With the Pueblo Indians. At times the Spanish and the Pueblo Indians actually lived together. The Spanish would escape into the pueblos when the nomads were raiding too successfully.

MICHENER: So what developed was a Spanish culture side by side with an Indian culture.

Palajemo and Michener talk in front of the altar at Las Coloridas Chapel.

Old paddle wheel, restored to working order.

PALAJEMO: Yes, for the most part the Spanish and the Pueblo Indians were very friendly. The Indians learned something from the Spanish, like making adobes, using clay ovens, and other things. And the Spanish learned from the Indians. They got corn, squash, and other agricultural products they had not known about in Europe.

The Restoration

MICHENER: When did you first get the idea of converting your family ranch into a museum?

PALAJEMO: It really began in 1952. The Museum of New Mexico asked me to reconstruct the defense tower—called in Spanish *Torrione*—on the ranch. The ruins were here. And when the museum asked me to do it and gave me a model, I proceeded. And then I began to think that there were other reasons to continue this preservation work.

A major reason was to preserve the countryside, to have a completely preserved environment. Here the old life-style and the old traditions would live. It would help the Spanish-speaking people understand their culture better and to appreciate it more. And it would inspire the younger generations to preserve their heritage.

MICHENER: Have you brought in buildings from other parts of New Mexico?

PALAJEMO: Yes. I had to in order to re-create a part of the northern New Mexico countryside as it was a couple of hundred years ago. I had to bring in a little bit more than was here originally. Mostly buildings of log construction. The adobe buildings are, of course, originals or built right here. You can't move adobe.

MICHENER: In the development of the museum, whose money did you use?

PALAJEMO: We are fortunate that the family has been able to finance most of it. And the plan is for the family to endow it and secure its future. We feel that it's very important that there is this sort of a preservation project which will continue. We hope that it will continue to be not just a museum with collections, but actually a replica of the countryside. I haven't mentioned it before, but this is actually an educational institution. It is not a museum in the sense that it is open every day to the public. We could not do that because it is so big. The security would be very difficult. Groups, however—schoolchildren, college students, and societies interested in history—come here. All told, about twenty thousand people a year visit the ranch.

MICHENER: You have a staff of about seven, I understand. Up to now, has your family paid their salaries?

PALAJEMO: Most of it. But there has been some public support. Grants and foundation support and contributions from the public.

MICHENER: Aren't you affiliated with the Smithsonian Institution in some way?

PALAJEMO: Yes we are. As a living historical farm and agricultural museum we are sponsored by the Smithsonian. And we have festivals here. A spring festival and a harvest festival. These festivals have turned out to be very important for us. They give us a chance to open the museum to the public and to have all the exhibits functioning. We then show the old traditions, even religious processions; an the music and the dance. Festivals have been a wonderful tool for us.

MICHENER: I understand you have a project much like this one in California.

PALAJEMO: Not exactly the same thing, but a historic preservation, yes. My family had a graceful old house in Pasadena, a house with eighteen rooms, and this is now the Pasadena Historical Museum. In the park around the house we had a Finnish sauna. And there we have a Finnish art museum

MICHENER: What do you see as the future of Spanish as a language in this area?

PALAJEMO: It's finally being recognized as very important. As you know, language is the main force of a culture—the mainstream of the culture. In order to save the culture, you have to save the language. And people here are beginning to understand that relations with countries

south of here—Mexico, Central America, South America—are all going to be very important for the North American future.

Mariachi band strolling through the streets of San Antonio.

SAN ANTONIO AND ITS MEXICAN-AMERICANS

The inner city of San Antonio is one of the loveliest I've ever seen. What has been done here to protect the San Antonio River as it meanders through town, and the terrain surrounding it, is most commendable. The river gives a focus to the downtown of one of the most interesting cities in Texas, a city whose history evokes the entire range of southwestern culture. Today, San Antonio's Mexican heritage is reflected in the fact that Hispanics number more than half of the population. So San Antonio is a good place in which to look at the recent history of a fast-emerging minority, our Mexican-Americans.

It is estimated that there are over seven million Mexican-Americans living legally in the United States. Estimates of illegal immigrants from Mexico number in the millions as well. The assimilation of our Mexican-American population has been slow and troubled. For many years they have ranked among the poorest of our population, with a meager share in the democratic dream.

Those sixteenth-century Spaniards who came as conquerors to the Southwest managed by dint of backbreaking toil to scratch a living from the parched earth. Three centuries later, however, their descendants themselves were conquered by Anglo-Americans surging westward across the continent. In the backwash of the Mexican war, numerous old Spanish and Mexican land titles were just swept away, and a population once proud and dominant was reduced to penury. In the decades to come, waves of poor immigrants from south of the Rio Grande fled from revolutions in their homeland. Poverty piled on poverty.

The Mexican-American population of the Southwest became the labor force that underlay the Anglo-owned agricultural complex of the region. Living in rural and urban *barrios*—essentially Hispanic ghettos—the Southwest's Mexican-Americans, often called Chicanos, long suffered severe discrimination in both educational and occupational opportunities. Recently, however, there have been changes in the old patterns of discrimination in the Southwest. Many think that Mexican-Americans have reached a crossroads in their history here in San Antonio, where the nation's first Hispanic mayor of a major city was elected to office in 1981.

Juan Patlan on Growing Up a Mexican-American

Juan Patlan, head of the Mexican-American Unity Council.

One of the groups working to bring about true integration of Hispanics with the Anglo community is the Mexican-American Unity Council. Juan Patlan, head of the council, describes the work of his organization and his hopes for San Antonio, and reminisces about his life as the son of a Mexican-American migrant farm worker. Patlan's father, Juan, Sr., recalls the grimmer era of the 1930s and 1940s, while Mary Valenzuela speaks of what the Unity Council has meant to her.

Juan Patlan Speaks

"We were migrant farm workers. I remember that we used to get in the migrant stream at the end of the school year, and we'd go pick cotton around Corpus Christi, and we'd follow the cotton crop all the way to the Panhandle. A lot of times my dad couldn't bring us back to school until October or November. Somehow we made it through school. I graduated from high school in 1958, and then I had a few odd jobs. I worked in a steel mill in Chicago and came back to San Antonio in 1960. I got a job as a route salesman selling corn chips, and after a couple of years I'd raised enough money to be able to go back to school. I went to a junior college first; then I took another year to work some more and raise some more money. Then I went to the University of Texas in Austin to finish my education.

"In my home town, we were all poor families, migrant farm workers, and it was kind of rough—but never so rough that we didn't have enough to eat. It was rough going to school, too, especially since at the beginning we didn't speak English. We had to learn English from nothing. We grew up in homes where nothing but Spanish was spoken, and all of a sudden we were put in school at the age of seven, and we had to speak English. We went to a segregated school—but it was really a special place. We made our first friends there; we met our teachers there and began to learn from them."

San Antonio's unique ambience owes much to citizens like these three men.

San Antonio woman prepares tortillas, the traditional bread of Mexico.

On Bilingual Education

"Bilingual education is very important in our lives. It makes it easier for our children to learn. It helps us to maintain our culture. Some people think that our kids should learn in English, because not to learn in English is not to be patriotic. And some people honestly feel that you retard the learning process by teaching kids in a language other than the language that they ultimately will have to learn—which is English. But we feel that we can maintain our culture and still be good and very patriotic citizens. And bilingual education is one way of keeping that culture."

The Influence of His Father

"My father has played a tremendous role in shaping my own life. He was very strong for education. He made sure that all of us got an education. He himself is a very well read man in spite of the fact that he had very little formal education. He has read most of the classics in literature, and so he has a very broad view of life and politics and human beings. And since my early childhood, he used to talk to me about what it is to be a man and how a person should conduct himself or herself, and the importance of getting an education—the importance, above all, of understanding that a person has rights. I learned from him that a person should fight—not physically but with ideas—to promote his own freedom and pursue justice. My father had a tremendous impact on me, and I guess he is the reason why I am an activist."

Juan Patlan, Sr., Remembers

I was born in Saltijo, Mexico. My parents came to Texas in 1913. We were really poor people. I used to go out into the streets to shine shoes, but I don't have any shoes, no hat either. We used to go out to West Texas to pull some cotton. In the wintertime, we would work here in the fields, in carrots, cabbage, onions.

"In 1929, I got married. My wife and I raised nine children, six girls and three boys. Wages were very low then. For pulling cotton they used to pay fifty cents, sixty cents a hundred pounds for clean cotton. If you make three dollars a day, that's six hundred pounds—not many people picked six hundred pounds. At the most, four hundred pounds, which was two dollars. That was about all we could make.

"When our children started growing up, I owned a truck. I used to carry my wife and my children in the truck to the cotton fields, and we would pick cotton down in Corpus Christi, and then I would bring my family back home so they could go to school. Then I would work on the fields, and haul carrots to the packing sheds, take people in the morning to the fields, and in the afternoon bring the people back home. My children worked very very hard with me—all of them.

"When my wife and I started having a family, she and I promised that we will send them to school, because we thought that the language was a big barrier between the Anglos and the Mexican-Americans. During the time that our children went to school, they were taught separately from the Anglos. Some friends of mine brought a suit against the school for discrimination, and I believe that from that time many things have been changed, because now all the children go together. Only the children who don't speak English at the beginning have teachers who can teach them in Spanish, and then teach them English. But there is no discrimination now, everybody is together. For which we feel very good. My oldest son decided he wanted to go to college, and we all helped together, my wife and my children all worked mighty

From the carnage within this building came the cry "Remember the Alamo" that rallied Texans to their ultimate victory. Now a tranquil site in the heart of San Antonio, the Alamo in 1836 was a place for martyrdom in the fight for Texas's independence. A mission turned into a fortress, the Alamo withstood a siege by Mexicans for thirteen days before being overrun.

hard, and he went to San Marcos and then he went to Austin, but he never finished. Why? Because we never have enough money. But anyway, he took good advantage of that education and helped send the other boys, like Juan, and one of our daughters.

"We had a very, very hard time with Juan. When he was about three years old, he got polio. We took him to the hospital in San Antonio, but after almost a month we took him out because he was getting worse. So we brought him home, and we started to make another kind of cure. I don't know if any of you remember a book by Sister Kenny. The farmer I was working for gave me her book, and we started doing exactly what the sister said to do. And after one year, Juan began crawling around and walking again. I took him to the doctor here, and he couldn't believe it.

"Things are very different now in this town. When I came, it was a very rough time for Mexican-Americans. We used to walk three, four miles from the town to the fields; our children used to walk two miles to school every day. Now everyone has a car. In the schools we have teachers and principals and a school superintendent who are Mexican-Americans. Wages are better now. Out on the farms they pay three dollars and twenty cents an hour. During the Depression we used to work here in the city for seventy-five cents for ten hours. Nobody believes that, but it's true! Of course I'm retired now—I don't work anymore."

The Mission of San Jose, as seen through an archway of the Alamo, was built by Franciscan friars in 1720. One of the first missions in Spanish North America, San Jose was a focal point of clerical effort to convert the Indians to Christianity.

How Juan Patlan Serves His People

After I finished my education, I was working in San Antonio for a life insurance company, and somehow I just didn't feel that that was the thing for me to do. That was when the War on Poverty programs were starting. In 1967 I went to work for a youth program. Then some of my friends and I began to think that maybe we should form our own organization to do the kinds of things that really should be done, to build our own Mexican institutions, to do housing and economic development. So we formed the Mexican-American Unity Council in November of 1967, and after a year we got our first grant from the Ford Foundation. Now we have social services and training programs and investment companies under one roof. We feel that social services by themselves are not enough—we're getting too used to having everything for free. And we have a responsibility to strengthen our community, to give them access to learning good skills, to the experience of running a business, to dealing with a bank and forming capital.

"The Mexican-American community in the last few years has really

Parade in San Antonio.

come of age in terms of political power. There have been a number of efforts just to organize people and make them aware, educate them, and convert them into a real political group that has to be reckoned with. The MAUC is a community development organization, and our mission is to be a stimulant to develop our community in every possible way.

"Our investment and our involvement in building the Hyatt Regency Hotel in San Antonio typifies what we do. We have invested in the hotel for profit, but also because our investment creates building-trades jobs. We train young people in the building trades. And after training them, we place them here in the hotel—or on similar projects. The hotel also gives us the opportunity to get minority businessmen in some of the retail spaces. So the hotel ties in with everything that we're all about: with business development, with capital formation, with job opportunities.

"One of the best experiences that we've had is in training high school dropouts, both male and female, in the building trades. It's been a tremendous success because we were able to convince the local building-trades unions that they should be part of it. So we have union craftsmen who have been in the trade fifteen or twenty years as instructors. And they take these kids under their wing and teach them all the skills that

Trained in workshops sponsored by the Mexican-American Unity Council, many construction workers now have jobs at a new San Antonio building project.

they know, and teach them about job responsibility—and how to do the best job that they can and take pride in their craft.

"Our Youth Project gives our young people a trade. In the early days, the issue was whether we would take the social service approach, make it easy for our kids. Or do we come down hard on them and tell them, If you're not here at seven o'clock, you're going to get docked. So now we are teaching our kids responsibility—that they have to be responsible for their actions."

Young Mary Valenzuela, a construction worker.

Mary Valenzuela, High School Dropout and Carpenter

"I dropped out of high school in the tenth grade, and from there on I just stayed home. I used to babysit my sister's kids for about twenty dollars a week. Then I got a call from one of my friends about the Mexican-American Unity Council. And so I went in and filled out an application, and they accepted me within a week. I was a painter at first—I painted for a year, and I liked the job. But paint and me didn't agree. So I've been working as a carpenter. They taught me how to read blueprints, and I helped out doing the layout for the cement—and I liked it even though it's a man's job. But it's really not that hard. And they're showing us how to do framing.

"They call me 'Mikey' because I'm doing a man's job. If I talk like a girl they won't pay attention to me—I have to talk like a man. And they don't look at me as a girl—they look at me as Mikey.

"It feels nice to be told, Hey, you can do it! By the end of the day, your muscles hurt, but you feel proud that you put up so many walls and you did so much for a building that's going to be there permanently. And later on in life you can come back and tell your kids, Hey look, your ma helped with this."

Juan Patlan on Housing and Economic Development

"Housing is a tremendous problem in this [the Mexican] part of the city, and our Housing Services Program has been a pioneer in rehabilitating homes for people with low incomes. We've made small grants and low-interest loans available to them—and out of about fifty loans we've had only one delinquency, which is a fantastic statistic. We're building the 'Palacio del Sol'—the Palace of the Sun—one

The bright colors of a Mexican-American mural enliven the wall of a San Antonio housing project.

hundred and six units of housing for our older people. And many other things that are now on the drawing board, so that—if we're able to carry them through—a whole area of San Antonio will be completely turned around and revitalized in the next five or six years.

"The pictures you see on the facades of the public housing projects are another sign of the vitality and the dynamism in this community. The Housing Authority is an institution that's been here for years and years, but it was not in the hands of people who really cared about the community. Before, the drawings and paintings that are now on the walls would never have been possible. They were never even thinkable. So that's another of the many, many signs of change. This community now has a lot of pride, and a lot of commitment.

"While we're doing many important things throughout the Mexican-American Unity Council, the part where I think there will really be a payoff is in our economic development department. Already we have two investment companies that have about ten million dollars available for investment and lending. We have the investment in the hotel. We have some other investments planned. I think we're going to make some major breakthroughs in making investments that create a large number of jobs. That will return us a very healthy profit so that we can keep on doing the kinds of things we have to do."

THE USES AND MISUSES OF WATER

Bernard De Voto said, "The Southwest begins where the average rainfall drops below twenty inches." The most precious resource in the Southwest is water. If farming depended on rainfall alone, there would be no farming in America on the western side of a line drawn from north to south through the middle of the Dakotas, Kansas,

Nebraska—all the way down to Laredo, Texas. With the exception of the most northwestern of our states, the western half of our continent depends for its water not on rainfall but on an artificial system of dams, canals, channels, and pumps that reroute streams and rivers, and on wells that tap deep into underground sources. And increasingly, there is not quite enough water to go around.

At the same time, there has been an enormous population shift to the sun belt—to oasis cities like Phoenix and Tucson in Arizona where demands on the water supply are growing with astronomical speed. Many who move to Arizona from other parts of the country where water is abundant still use water as a recreational resource. It is astonishing to learn, for example, that there are more boat owners in proportion to the population in Arizona than in New York State.

In the desert near Tempe, Arizona, there is a four-and-a-half-million-gallon ocean. Called Big Surf, it's an artificial two-and-a-half-acre lagoon, nine feet deep at its deepest. Every ninety seconds, hydraulic machinery sends a manufactured five-foot wave roaring and rolling up onto the beach. Big Surf is, according to its makers, the world's largest filtered swimming area.

A suburb not far from Phoenix, Arizona, boasts the largest fountain in the world, a fountain that regularly hurls jets of water hundreds of feet into the desert air.

And outside of Tucson, in the desert near Casa Grande, the underground water table is tapped to keep the city's growing population supplied and to provide farmers with water for irrigation. Overpumping the underground water causes the water table to drop—in parts of Arizona, it has sunk by as much as 450 feet. The result: large sinkholes that perforate the desert floor.

We waste water in the desert to the point that, perhaps sooner than later, there will be no more to drink, to bathe in, or to irrigate the crops that we nurture in our arid regions.

LEFT: *Surfers bathing at Tempe, Arizona, near Phoenix.*

RIGHT: *Children playing in the manmade lagoon at Tempe.*

LADLING OUT THE COLORADO RIVER

❑ When Brigham Young and his band of Mormons arrived in Utah in 1847, they soon found that there was not enough rainfall to water their crops. So they dug irrigation ditches—among the first such structures built by white men in America (the southwestern Indians had been irrigating for centuries)—to carry water from a nearby river to their fields. By 1865, the Mormons had over 150,000 acres under irrigation and had constructed 277 canals. Unlike the "gentile" settlers who would soon be farming, mining, and ranching throughout the semiarid regions of the Southwest, the Mormons declared that "there shall be no private ownership of the streams that come out of the canyons. . . . These belong to the people."

The question of water ownership has been a burning issue in the Southwest for one and a half centuries. In the East, with its never-failing streams and rivers, settlers from the beginning had practiced a form of water use derived from their European forebears: The person who owned land on the banks of a stream or river was entitled to withdraw reasonable quantities of water for his own use.

In the West, however, streams often vanished by midsummer, and rivers ran low or ran out. Gold-rush miners, who needed quantities of water to sluice away sand and soil from their gold ore, came to use a law of "prior right." Thus, the first miner to stake out a claim on land near a creek had the right to use the water from the creek; and if the water ran low, miners on neighboring claims had to yield the available water to the first miner. Farmers and ranchers who followed the miners into the West adopted this "first come, first served" system; and water rights became a form of property that could be sold separately from the land. By the early 1900s, thousands of rights had been registered by farmers, ranchers, businesses, factories, single homes, water companies, whole cities—anyone who could claim a need for the water near his property. Water allocations existed for every body of water within the populated regions of the West. And if the water in a particular stream or river dwindled, the state determined whose rights were among the first, and cut off all the rest. ❑

Reclaiming the Waters

❑ Congress recognized the necessity for increasing the available amount of water in the Southwest when it passed the Reclamation Act of 1902, which authorized the Department of the Interior to begin a series of irrigation projects. Even back then, when the desert and semidesert, the rugged Rockies, and the coastal plains of the Southwest were relatively bare of population, the pressing need for water was acknowledged. One of the first projects was the huge Roosevelt Dam, with a storage reservoir that backed up water from Salt River, a distant branch of the Colorado River, to irrigate the acres of fruits and vegetables that would soon be planted near the city of Phoenix. The Colorado River has been the principal source of "reclamation" water since the movement to irrigate the Southwest began. Its magnificent wild waters follow a long and tortuous pathway from their mountain birth in the cool reaches of the Rockies to their final flow into the Gulf of California. But the 1,450 miles of river carry a volume of water that is smaller than that moved along the Hudson, only 315 miles in length.

Every drop of Colorado River water has been given away—by act of Congress, by the courts, by treaty, by regulations promulgated by the states. In fact, on paper more water is allocated than the river actually holds. If certain groups—the Indians, for instance—were to demand their legally guaranteed water rights, the Colorado might run dry.

Hundreds of dams have been built along the Colorado and its tributaries. Many were erected, to control floods or permit navigation, by the Army Corps of Engineers. Utility companies built others to dam water for power generation. More than half the Colorado dams are multipurpose: They are used to store water for irrigation, to control it

The Colorado River, near the Parker Dam, on the Arizona-California border. (Colour Library International, Ltd.)

during periods of flood, and to harness it for hydroelectric turbines. The storage dams are connected to the fields and faucets of the Southwest by networks of canals, pumps, pipelines, and tunnels; and these systems supply water to farms, factories, and cities often many miles distant.

To irrigate the fields of northeastern Colorado, the Colorado—Big Thompson Diversion System actually shifts water to the eastern slopes of the Rockies that would, if left to itself, flow down the western slopes. The system accomplishes this immense diversion by pumping millions of gallons up-slope and through the thirteen-mile long Alva B. Adams Tunnel, a conduit that slices through a mountain.

Two enormous water carriers, the All American Canal and the Colorado River Aqueduct, feed southern California. Of all the consumers of Colorado River water—and they include the states of Wyoming, Utah, Colorado, Nevada, New Mexico, Arizona, and the nation of Mexico—California absorbs by far the most: some 1.61 trillion gallons in 1975. New Mexico, the smallest user, took .094 trillion gallons. Mexico, using water diverted to it along the Alamo Canal, got only .54 trillion gallons.

The Colorado is in a sense bankrupt, since it owes far more water to its users than it takes in. Nevertheless, a vast new water supply scheme is in the works to keep Arizona's major cities, Tucson and Phoenix, water-solvent in the coming years of higher population growth and diminishing ground-water tables. The huge Central Arizona Project will channel enormous volumes of water three hundred miles to the east of the river, where it will fill the swimming pools of Phoenix residents and augment the rolling waters of the Big Surf lagoon. When the project is finished, some experts believe the Colorado will at last run out. Instead of trickling slowly into its last exit in the Gulf of California, it will have disappeared far north of the Gulf, leaving some of the southernmost diversion channels bone dry. If that happens, the question of what rights Los Angeles has to Colorado River water will be even more bitterly argued than it is today. But other questions will also have to be answered—perhaps the principal issue will be whether the best use of

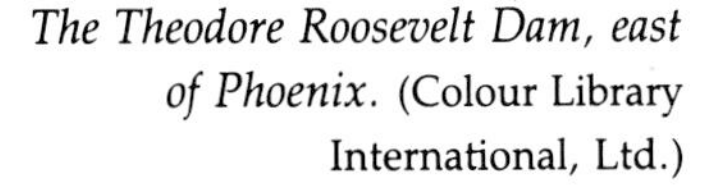
The Theodore Roosevelt Dam, east of Phoenix. (Colour Library International, Ltd.)

Little Colorado River Gorge in the Grand Canyon. (Colour Library International, Ltd.)

our resources is to build large cities and cultivate thousand-acre vegetable fields in the desert. ❑

The First of the Great Dams

Water has always been a central political issue in the Southwest, and its battles have been fought hard both in the southwestern states and in Washington. In 1935, when the first of the great dams, the Hoover Dam, was built to stem the devastating annual floods of the Colorado River, the state of Arizona sent its national guard to the damsite in a futile effort to halt—by force of arms, if necessary—the diversion of Colorado River water from its natural course through Arizona into the parched but populated regions of southern California. Arizona lost that particular battle, and for almost half a century now the Hoover Dam has stood, hailed as thing of beauty and a miracle of engineering. Its benefits are manifold, and its power is awesome. It holds a two-year supply of the great Colorado River in check. It stores enough water in Lake Mead to flood the entire state of Massachusetts to a depth of six feet, and backs up the Colorado 110 miles to the edge of the Grand Canyon.

As impressive and important as the Hoover Dam may be, the construction of six more large dams on the Colorado has raised serious questions. Some observers feel that these dams pose a fundamental threat to the environment, that man is altering nature in such a way that he may destroy important natural resources. One vision of the future Southwest pictures the Colorado River turned into a vast network of lakes and channels spread through the mountains, its waters funneled to far-off cities and agricultural operators miles and miles away.

View of the desert near Phoenix, Arizona, with Superstition Mountain in the background. Irrigation has transformed land like this into fruitful fields.

Eighty-five percent of the water in the Southwest is consumed by agriculture. We may very soon have to decide whether farming in this semiarid region, which requires ever more expensive and ever scarcer water, is a prudent use of our desert domains, in light of an almost certain water crisis to come.

POWER TO THE NAVAHO

There is a spot in the Southwest that is unique in all the United States—a place where the corners of four states touch one another. Near that spot, the junction of Arizona, New Mexico, Utah, and Colorado, we have built one of the largest coal-fired power plants in the world. Considered a monumental achievement when it was completed in 1970, it is now called one of the dirtiest. The air pollution generated by the Four Corners Power Plant was observable even to our astronauts in space. The National Parks Service notes an impairment of visibility as far away as Mesa Verde National Park. A perpetual plume of smoke drifts from the Four Corners across Navaho Land.

For the Navaho Indians, Ship Rock is the rock with wings, rising out of the desert fifteen hundred feet straight up into the air, like the sail of a mythical ship. Ship Rock and the Four Corners Power Plant tower on either side of the new Navaho agricultural community and the irrigated acreage near it.

The Navaho Nation holds an annual festival at Ship Rock. With 160,000 members, the Navaho are the largest of the Indian nations. Their reservation, which extends into New Mexico, Arizona, and Utah, covers 25,000 square miles. The Indian story of deprivations and hardships, injustices suffered and promises broken, is well known. But in recent years, for the Navaho at least, things have changed. Important balances of power have shifted. Indian land that was previously considered worthless has gained sudden value as a source of water and minerals.

The Navaho reservation contains not only extensive high-grade coal reserves but a good share of the United States uranium supply as well. For the first time since they were forced onto the reservations, the Indians possess a source of real power.

Flying together, the United States and New Mexican flags symbolize the double culture of our southwestern states.

History of the Navaho

Some five hundred years ago, a nomadic hunting and gathering people wandered away from their ancestral home in northwestern Canada and Alaska, and came to the southwestern desert region. They called themselves the Dine, "the People." They found themselves in a land with little water or vegetation and scant game for hunting—a region that had long been inhabited by an Indian civilization of great sophistication. This was the Pueblo culture, a people who built complex villages, some of them in the sheer sides of canyons, wove intricate patterned cloth from wild cotton, produced fine pottery and baskets,

LEFT: *Four Corners power plant.*

RIGHT: *Ship Rock, near Four Corners in New Mexico.*

Rugs and blankets like this beauty are increasingly prized by collectors of Indian art.

and sustained themselves with a subtle system of agriculture that took advantage of every drop of rain that fell and every ounce of moisture in the soil.

The Navaho raided the Pueblo villages and learned Pueblo ways. They adapted the Pueblo religion and the fine arts of weaving, basketry, and plant cultivation. In the process, they often improved on them.

The Spaniards came a century or so later. Their villages were also raided, their sheep and horses stolen to become the basis for the flocks and herds the Navaho would raise. Sheep especially were valued for their meat and their warm wool; and as Navaho flocks grew, the People wandered ever farther in search of grazing lands. Unlike the Pueblo, the Navaho learned to live in seminomadic fashion, building isolated wood-and-mud shelters—called hogans—near their pastures, creating a social order whose basis was the extended family rather than the tribe.

In 1846 the United States, having already annexed the Republic of Texas, declared war on Mexico and seized the region that would become the states of New Mexico and Arizona. New settlers followed the army into Navaho territory, and it was soon made brutally clear to the People that the old days of peace—punctuated by an occasional profitable raid on a white farm or village—were over. For now, every Navaho foray into white territory was quickly followed by a punishing cavalry attack. The Civil War, which left the region unprotected by the army, gave the Navaho the opportunity to fight back—to raid, loot, and destroy American settlements. Reaction from the American government was quick and forceful. A band of white volunteers under Colonel Christopher "Kit" Carson, the famous hunter and scout turned Indian fighter, was dispatched with orders to round up the Navaho and drive them out of their lands and into a forty-square-mile patch of wasteland in eastern New Mexico, the Bosque Redondo near Fort Sumner. Carson harried the Navaho, burnt their crops and hogans, slaughtered their sheep, and starved them into surrender. In 1863 the People set out on their "Long Walk" three hundred miles to the east, an event they still remember with bitterness. ❑

Time of Troubles

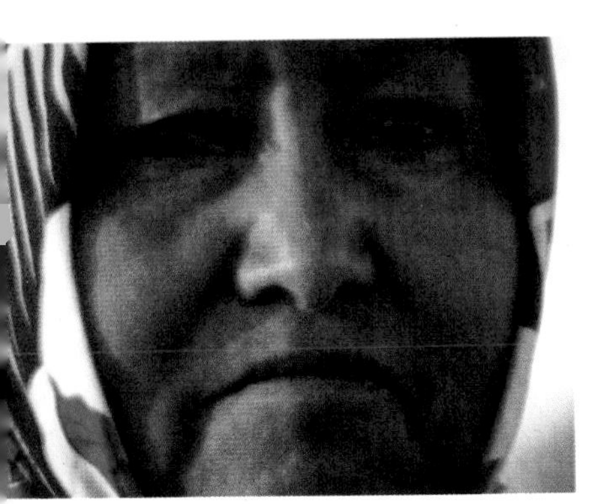

Navaho woman.

❑ It was in the arid wastes of Bosque Redondo that the Navaho developed a tribal consciousness. They languished there for four years, and when it became overwhelmingly obvious that they could not support themselves on the barren soil of the place, the Bureau of Indian Affairs sent them back to a reservation in what had been Navaho country.

At the time of the Civil War, the Navaho numbered about twelve thousand. Only nine thousand were left to return to their homeland in 1868.

Today most of them still live on their reservation. Over a century of reservation life and of dealing with a white bureaucracy has made the

Navaho children in New Mexico.

Navaho finally a canny and cautious citizen. The Navaho Tribal Council is the governing body of the People. Since the 1950s, when oil, gas, coal, and uranium were discovered within the boundaries of the reservation, the council has been responsible for administering a rapidly growing fund of royalty payments. A huge steam power plant, using reservation-mined coal as its fuel, has been built in the northeastern corner of the reservation; and it, too, pays money into the fund.

The Navaho own massive quantities of minerals. They have rights to the use of much of the water from the Colorado River irrigation projects. In the very near future they may be faced with an impossible choice: either to maintain their traditional way of life, which is even today far more intact than that of any other Indian tribe; or to opt for technology, with all the benefits and the dangers that may bring. Some Navaho feel that a compromise is possible. Others fear what will happen when "too much money" erodes traditional restraints and turns the Navaho into a people like any other in these United States. ❑

Interviews with Representatives of the Navaho Nation

Peter MacDonald is the elected head of the Navaho nation. He is also responsible for the formation of CERT, the Council of Energy Resources Tribes, which is sometimes referred to as a domestic OPEC.

On the Navaho reservation near Ship Rock.

Rose Morgan is a young Navaho staff researcher at the Navaho Community College in Ship Rock. Dr. Bahe Billie is the young Navaho dean of the Navaho Community College, and the first Ph.D. of the Navaho nation. The three offered their views on the Navaho's present and future.

MACDONALD: From today into the 1980s and 1990s, I see the Navaho progressing more and more into self-determination, becoming more and more self-sufficient. The reason I'm very optimistic about the Navaho's future is because today we have a large number of our young people going into various universities, studying technologies in the areas of the resources that we have. And if we manage these resources and develop them in our own way, within the context of our own future, we can gain a great deal in terms of employment, better health and educational facilities for our people.

Another thing we have here, under the Navaho, is great agricultural potential. We are now putting under irrigation one hundred and ten thousand acres of land, and this I know is going to be very important to help us become self-sufficient, and to provide employment and other economic programs for the Navaho nation.

Peter MacDonald, the elected head of the Navaho nation.

We are not without problems. Every step, every gain that we make, we have to fight for. We have to deal with the paper tribe, whose ancestral home is on the banks of the river Potomac and extends down to our own area office. These people are the bureaucrats who are constantly trying to make decisions for our future. As a matter of fact, it's just like fighting the old wars back in the 1800s. We still have to watch our flanks, our front, our rear, and make sure that we don't get surprised at any time along the road of progress. So, instead of fighting with Remington rifles and the bow and arrow, we're now fighting in courts and state legislatures. And I think that as we become successful in fighting these wars, we can affect our future in such a way that our people and their children, and their children's children, will have a future. I feel that with the great agricultural potential that is here, with the existing energy resources that we have, and with the large number of young people—as you know, the average age of the Navaho is seventeen and a half—with these young, enthusiastic people going into universities and colleges, learning more about the uses of these resources, gaining knowledge in the technical fields . . . I feel that the future for the Navaho is very bright.

ROSE MORGAN: There have been many changes on the Navaho reservation, and among the people. Urbanization. Education. And after education, people begin to rely on wage work, and wage work brings you to the borders of the reservation where there are more jobs available. People are living closer together, in communities, whereas ordinarily Navaho do not tend to live in clusters. Traditionally, the Navaho people lived very isolated from one another—perhaps ten or twenty miles from the nearest neighbor. When the Navaho acquired sheep from the Spaniards, they worked to multiply them, to see them increase. So it was very important to have many acres for grazing, because sheep were their livelihood. Traditionally the Navaho have led a pastoral life, and through the years their sheep have increased, and the vegetation on the land has been overgrazed. So each individual Navaho family was issued a permit specifying a certain number of sheep that the family could have; this was one way the government thought we could revegetate the land. So today there are not so many sheep, and not that many traditional families whose lives are based on sheep. Now the younger generation seems to be turning more and more toward agriculture.

Example of an enduring Navaho art. A Navaho silversmith wears a necklace she has designed in turquoise and silver. (Colour Library International, Ltd.)

Evolving Traditions

I think that the kinship relations among Navaho families are still very strong. I know that a lot of young people will disagree with me, but through doing research and going out into the remote areas, I find that the clan system is still strong. In the Navaho kinship system, the mother's clan is the child's clan. And everyone in the mother's clan is considered as related, and other whole clans are also related to the mother's clan. This results in a very extended family. When a Navaho introduces himself, he always says which clan he belongs to. And children are not allowed to marry inside their clan or inside related clans, because clan members are considered brothers and sisters. Today, many young people are marrying inside their clan, or marrying a white person. They just run off and go ahead and get married, and live off the reservation. But eventually, they all seem to come back. I've never heard of anyone dying and being buried outside the reservation. They always come back.

The Navaho are one of the few American Indian tribes that have increased in population—I think we're the largest Native American group. And a lot of us are still full-blooded Navaho—I myself am a full-

Navaho Indians display pride in their heritage at this local parade.

blooded Navaho. I think one of the reasons why we grew was because of our isolation. Illnesses couldn't spread from neighbor to neighbor. Whereas the Pueblos and other tribes live in villages together, and when an epidemic hit them, it wiped out sometimes half or three-fourths of the people. And we have a national pride that has helped us avoid assimilation, acculturation through the years. The Navaho people don't boast about how proud they are to be Indians. They are quiet, they sort of keep to themselves, but they're proud among themselves, within their families. They don't show off to the outside world.

There are many things in the Navaho culture that do not change. One thing that the Navaho will never lose is the respect for nature. We look upon nature for our very livelihood, for our arts, our culture. From the sheep we take the wool, and from the wool we make our rugs. And from the plants around us we have learned to take out the dye. We have different plants that we use to make our baskets, and we are noted for our baskets. And also our minerals: the silver, the turquoise that we use in our arts.

But many things have changed. Automobiles and trucks have taken the place of horses and wagons. I know of Navaho families who get a new truck every year—they might live in a log hogan, but they always have a new truck. And when you consider the distance between the families, having an automobile or truck is very important—to get to school, to get to work on time.

Then there are our resources. When they took us away from the land in 1863, they thought we had silver and gold here, and they looked for these minerals but couldn't find them. So five years later, we came back. Little did they know we had all these other resources, though. Uranium, coal, oil, water.

Our coal has been used mainly for power generation, but it makes electricity for cities that are not even in this state, much less in the reservation. I believe over half the Navaho homes don't even have electricity. And we are getting prices for our coal that were negotiated back in the 1960s and that are a lot less than prices today.

Another change: The younger generation seems to be turning more toward agriculture. The Navaho Indian irrigation project is one of our major resources, or will be when we have better trained people. Our land was overgrazed, but we had available water, available land. So the irrigation project was put here. But after it was given to us, well, they wanted some water diverted elsewhere; so the water in our area is really overallocated—I don't think that there is enough water to irrigate the whole proposed one hundred ten thousand acres of land. But even so, with skilled management for the irrigation project, we could go into mass production, into canning, into feed lots. We need people trained in these areas.

Boom in Education

One of the significant changes among the Navaho is education. In the beginning, Navaho children were not allowed to return home during the school year. Then, when education was not so enforced anymore—in the 1940s and 1950s—people sort of slacked off, and there were a lot of dropouts. Then the Navaho nation implemented a division of education in Window Rock, and steps were taken to motivate Navaho to get more education. They had a teacher-training program that multiplied the number of Navaho teachers. And then we got the Navaho Community College, around 1968. Its main campus is down in Arizona, with extension classes and a major branch college in Ship Rock. I think the college is unique in the way that it emphasizes Navaho culture and at the same time directs students toward modern careers—agriculture, farm management, engineering.

We really need well-trained people. For example, the college at Ship Rock was supposed to be training the manpower for the irrigation project. We were supposed to have developed and trained people to have management skills, to see them in offices, as foremen. But the people who went to the irrigation project were just hired as laborers. And so many of them quit and went to the power plant, where the money is. They get paid every week. The traditional people say that a lot of money is not good, it will just make you go off the cliff. . . .

I think it is time we started listening to the older people, because they think in terms of one hundred and fifty years from now. They're almost like prophets. But if we don't listen to them, and just keep going along with whatever the outside society offers us, I don't think that we will survive. In a very short time, we will just be part of the state, we will no longer be a nation within a nation.

Miss Indian U.S.A.

DR. BAHE BILLIE: My grandfather used to say, "A man and a family has to have an ax," but now the new saying seems to be that a man has to have an education. At one time, Ship Rock had only one boarding school, which was run by the federal government. Now we find three schools right in Ship Rock, and the government makes the fourth. So

Navaho men ride in a local rodeo.

you can see there is improvement. There are many opportunities for Navaho. They have created their own college in Arizona, the Navaho Community College, and now they're extending it to different communities. I'm very sure that other Indian tribes are doing similar things.

GLITTER GULCH AND THE STRIP

❑ Las Vegas hurls its neon glow into the night where once there was only sand and the occasional lizard or rattlesnake. Here even the Mormons, a people of incredible tenacity, couldn't make a go of it. They arrived in 1855 and tried to farm the "meadowland" (Las Vegas means "The Meadows" in Spanish)—a small patch of green watered by artesian springs in the middle of the great western desert. After two years they gave up, abandoned their homesteads, and returned to greener pastures in Utah. The army built Fort Baker here in 1864. In 1905 the railroad came through, sold off cheap lots along its right-of-way, and a town of sorts began to emerge. By 1909 Las Vegas had eight hundred people, eleven saloons, and two churches.

RIGHT: *Las Vegas nightclubs specialize in breathtaking costumes—like this performer's—and in star-studded floor shows.* (Las Vegas News Bureau)

Las Vegas patrons gamble night and day. Nevada's legalized gambling is licensed and controlled by state and local authorities. Ten million visitors come to Las Vegas annually to try their luck. (Las Vegas News Bureau)

ABOVE: *Reno was the gambling center of Nevada until after World War II. This arch, Reno's best-known symbol, welcomes visitors to "casino row."* (Greater Reno-Sparks Chamber of Commerce)

The Sands Hotel in Las Vegas, one of the city's many luxury hotels. (Colour Library International, Ltd.)

The town would have remained a small desert community like its widely scattered neighbors in the dusty reaches of southeastern Nevada but for two events: the construction of the Hoover Dam twenty-five miles south of Las Vegas, which began in 1931; and the legalization of gambling—by local option—legislation that was passed in the same year.

The dam was built near the Nevada town of Boulder City, which did not permit gambling within its precincts. The thousands of construction workers imported to work on the dam had very little to do in their off hours, and they preferred doing it in Las Vegas where the saloons welcomed them and the city did not frown on public displays of cards and dice.

Gambling flourished in the wide open spaces of the West. Prospectors and miners, cowboys in town after long lonely weeks on the range, farmers who traveled miles to buy provisions—they all needed more exciting diversions than drink or tired dance-hall girls. Most men came into town with money in their pockets, and they weren't afraid to take a chance on losing it in the hope of winning a bundle. Then, too, a "friendly game" was almost the only form of social activity in the small-town saloon, and the saloon was the only convivial meetingplace in town.

Gambling had been declared illegal now and again in Nevada, but the fact that it was against the law did not prevent a flourishing underground gambling industry. In 1931, despairing of eliminating gambling, tired of the corruption that surrounded it, and hopeful of gaining some of its profits for state coffers, Nevada once again lifted the statewide gambling ban.

Throughout Nevada, particularly in the cities of Reno and Las Vegas, gambling "clubs" opened. Often they were little more than a bar, a wall lined with slot machines, and a few round poker tables. But in the late 1930s, a new Reno club set the style for the glittering future in Nevada. Harold's Club was a splendid gambling palace, its rooms lit up so all the world could see that no hanky-panky took place with the cards or roulette wheels. It advertised everywhere, promising thrills and possible fortunes to every man and his wife (babysitting was available). It wasn't long before playing the slot machines and gaming tables at Harold's Club became a perfectly respectable thing to do.

Reno remained the casino gambling center of Nevada until just after World War II. By then air conditioning had made it feasible to build huge hotels in the desert, and they began going up all over Las Vegas—at first in the city's downtown section (now renowned as Glitter Gulch), later in an area along the highway called The Strip. The huge profits to be made in casino ownership soon brought the mob in. "Bugsy" Siegel built his Flamingo Hotel in 1946; in 1947, when he was flamboyantly assassinated gangland style, investigators began to look into the extent of mob control of the gambling industry, and the state of Nevada decided to require the licensing of casino owners. Despite regular protestations by the Nevada gambling commission, however, even today there seems little doubt that much of Las Vegas gambling is controlled or financed by criminal syndicates. This fact has not prevented other, more respectable organizations from muscling in on the lucrative casino game. Caesar's Palace was partially financed by the Teamsters union. In 1969 Howard Hughes built the Las Vegas Landmark Hotel, featuring a 240-foot swimming pool and a sky-high twenty-ninth-floor casino. The Hilton Hotel Corporation, the Del E. Webb Corporation, MGM, the Union Pacific Railroad, and other giant corporate entities own casinos in Las Vegas.

Las Vegas at night is even more brilliantly lit than at high noon under the desert sun, and the action continues twenty-four hours a day. Along with gambling the town offers luxurious accommodations, first-class restaurants, the world's most expensive entertainers, and an atmosphere that seems reminiscent of the milling, raucous, rough-and-ready scene in a western mining town in the full flush of its prosperity. Perhaps it's this anachronistic feeling that pulls some fifteen million visitors into the mirrored, windowless casinos every year. Or the chance to rub shoulders with the rich and powerful who come by the hundreds. Or the unlikely possibility of hitting a lucky streak at blackjack.

Las Vegas, Nevada, at night. (Colour Library International, Ltd.)

Las Vegas's spectacular success has already spawned one imitator, the mushrooming casino complex in Atlantic City, New Jersey. And the thought of all that money, much of it subject to heavy state taxes, is sparking a gleam in the gloomy recesses of many a state capital. As inflation continues and state revenues shrink, it would be lovely, some think, to be partially funded by big-time gambling. Old-fashioned notions—that gambling is a sin, that those who can least afford it are most vulnerable to it, that inevitably it attracts crime and corruption—are forgotten or suppressed. Las Vegas beckons. ❑

OUR MAGNIFICENT NATIONAL PARKS

To stand atop the Grand Canyon in Arizona is to be awestruck by one of the most splendid views in the entire world. It is a wonder unparalleled not only in the American Southwest, but anywhere on earth. The walls of the Grand Canyon have been carved over millennia by the force of the great river of the Southwest, the Colorado. When I stand on the rim of the canyon and peer down upon the meandering river, more than a mile below, I know that I am in the presence of something we must preserve.

James Michener at the Grand Canyon.

One of the reasons I maintain a home near Chesapeake Bay in Maryland is that it is often possible to see deer browsing in the fields not far from where I am working. I never cease to thrill at the sight of these splendid animals who share the woods with me. What have they been worth to me? Untold values in relaxation and the appreciation of nature.

But someday soon the pressure of population will force these deer to move on. A good society does not require that the deer live on my lawn—but it does require that they live somewhere. This planet, devoid of its natural inhabitants—animals, birds, fish—and devoid of its ancient geological landscapes like the Grand Canyon, would be a desolation.

It is quite possible that men require deer and canyons to keep them human, just as it is possible that we need cleaner air and quieter cities to keep us sane. There is a balance between beauty and business that must not be ignored, and we cannot destroy one without diminishing the other. I believe that the quality of a good life depends in large measure on how man reacts to his natural environment. It is easy to see this when perched upon the Grand Canyon's rim.

A Gift from the Past to the Future

❑ Perhaps no nation on earth contains as many of nature's wonders as the United States. Certainly no other major nation has done more to protect and preserve vast areas of natural grandeur and beauty. In a way, this is odd, for Americans have long had a reputation as doers, exploiters, and users rather than as preservers and conservationists. One has only to glimpse thousands of acres of raped landscape, from which strip miners have extracted coal or copper, to be made acutely aware of how ill we have used the land in all too many instances. But we are a huge nation, and those areas that we have set aside as national parks, national monuments, national recreation areas, and the like, have been carefully, lovingly tended and maintained.

Though the National Park Service has under its aegis some 117,840 square miles, with sites that range in size from the almost 3-million-acre Glacier Bay National Monument in Alaska to the postage-stamp-size Thaddeus Kosciuszko National Memorial in Pennsylvania, it is the great national parks—particularly those in the West and Southwest—that attract the greatest enthusiasm and millions of visitors annually. Here in Arizona is the Grand Canyon National Park, with its two billion years of geological history carved out by the Colorado River. Next door in New Mexico there is the Carlsbad Cavern National Park, its sixty-million-year-old caves studded with weirdly shaped and colored stalactites and stalagmites. To the north in Colorado is the Rocky Mountain National Park, its snow-capped mountain summits straddling the Great Divide. Westward, in Utah, there is Bryce Canyon National Park, where wind and water erosion have fashioned multicolored rock formations that seem to echo such manmade edifices as cathedrals with towering spires. These are but a few of the 320 sites scattered throughout forty-nine of the fifty states, and in territories as distant from the American mainland as Guam, where the National Park Service holds sway. Yosemite in California, Yellowstone and Grand Teton in Wyoming, Crater Lake in Oregon, Glacier in Montana—these are all names that set the naturelover's mouth watering in anticipation of a journey to their wonders or with joyful remembrance of a trip taken perhaps years and years ago.

The fact is that America's National Park System has been a success of overwhelming proportions—and indeed, overwhelmed is what is happening to the system. Annually, nearly 300 million visits are paid to its parks, historic monuments, battlefield sites, and recreation areas. And

Natural entrance to Carlsbad Caverns National Park, New Mexico. (Colour Library International, Ltd.)

Tucson Mountain Park at Gates Pass, Arizona. (Colour Library International, Ltd.)

herein lies the controversy that is becoming more acute with each passing year. True, a great many of the visitors spend only an afternoon or even just an hour touring urban sites or such small self-contained attractions as Texas's San Antonio Missions National Historical Park, or the Pipe Spring National Monument in Arizona, site of an early Mormon fort. But millions, literally millions, flood into the major national parks each year, particularly in the summer. Their cars choke the roads to the primary natural attractions and spew fumes into the atmosphere to endanger the fragile ecological balance of the areas they traverse. Their tents and recreation vehicles crowd campgrounds that can reasonably accommodate but a fraction of their number. Their litter sometimes makes instant slums of woodland trails. And, with increasing frequency, some of their number commit crimes against one another or against the environment. Alcohol, narcotics, and other drugs have become familiar problems in the campgrounds. From June through September, park personnel are forced to contend with many problems usually associated with the nation's old, decaying cities. Park rangers have become law enforcement agents; this sometimes deprives the vast majority of visitors of their services as guides to a wilderness experience. ❑

Conservation or Recreation

❑ The success our national parks have had in attracting hordes of visitors has generated a fierce argument between those who are primarily concerned with the conservation mission of the park service and those who believe its primary function is to provide recreation facilities to the American people. Many conservationists, though not all, are in favor of severely limiting access to the parks by banning private automobiles from their precincts and doing away with the concessionaires who provide urban amenities within the wilderness setting. In the view of these conservationists, only buses—in limited number—should be allowed inside the parks, to ferry visitors from one major attraction to another. Those who wish to camp within the parks or seek out remote corners of natural beauty should have to do so on foot, backpacking their way in and living in a style consistent with the natural setting.

The recreationists see such proposals as the attempt of an elite to deny the great majority of Americans a precious part of their natural heritage. They point out that many, if not most, of the visitors to such places as the Grand Canyon are middle-aged, elderly, or young children with their parents—people who have neither the skill nor the vigor to tramp the mountain trails. Such people, they say, have as much right as the young, strong, and dedicated to enjoy the glories of the park system.

Upper Yosemite Falls and Merced River in Yosemite National Park, California. (Colour Library International, Ltd.)

Some of the recreationists, far from advocating the limiting of access, insist that access should be greatly expanded with more roads, more hotels, more concessions—more of everything that will make the national parks comfortable and inviting to the average American.

In a way, this continuing controversy echoes and parallels the battle between environmentalists and developers in so many aspects of American life. One side insists that we must pull back from runaway development lest we destroy the ecological balance upon which all life ultimately depends. We are, say the environmentalists, like irresponsible children who have come into a vast inheritance that we spend at an alarming rate with scarcely a thought to the well-being of future generations. The developers reply that their opponents greatly overstate the peril. Land and its resources, they say, are there to be used, not just

Ojo Caliente Spring, Midway Geyser Basin, Yellowstone National Park. (Colour Library International, Ltd.)

Moose at Grand Teton National Park, Wyoming. (Colour Library International, Ltd.)

by those they characterize as an arrogant, self-proclaimed intellectual elite, but by all of the people.

At the moment the balance of power seems to be moving in favor of the developers and recreationists. The Reagan administration in Washington has taken a strong position in favor of expanding the role of private concessionaires within our national parks and in increasing access. The argument, however, is merely in its formative stages. Three or four years hence, the conservationist view may again be dominant. In any case, it is certain that the controversy will continue. For our national parks the stakes are high. A total victory for the developers might turn the parks into something much like Disney World—a prettied-up, plastic echo of nature rather than nature itself. A total victory for the conservationists might effectively close down some of the most awe-inspiring natural wonders in the world to tens of millions of Americans who lack the time, interest, and vitality to tramp their way into the backlands. ❑

When I stand at the edge of the Grand Canyon and survey the magnificent landscape around me, I am reminded of the words of the Indian poet N. Scott Momoday, who speaks of the history of a landscape as the history of an idea. That idea, he says, is man's idea of himself. It is like a memory in which we find a landscape that is incomparable, a time that is gone forever, and the human spirit, which endures.

The American spirit is very much like the incomparable landscape. It is my conviction that both will endure.

THE FAR WEST

(Colour Library International, Ltd.)

WESTWARD TO THE PACIFIC

The West. For longer than we have been a nation, the very word has been a symbol, a metaphor for unlimited possibilities. From the rapidly developing urban centers and farmlands of the eastern states, settlers moved ever farther west, at first leapfrogging the high plains beyond the Missouri to put down roots along the Pacific Coast and then finally filling in the grasslands. The pioneers moved west seeking furs, seeking gold, seeking land. They wanted new lives, free from constraint, rich in opportunity.

In western Nebraska there is the Scott's Bluff National Monument, along what was once one of this land's greatest highways: the Oregon Trail. Later it also became a major route for riders of the famed Pony Express. Here at Scott's Bluff, along the banks of the North Platte River, weary pioneers caught sight of such majestic trailmarkers as the bluff itself, a massive outcropping of rock thrusting skyward that seemed to one traveler to resemble "the ruins of some vast city erected by a race of giants." Then there were Chimney Rock and Courthouse Rock (the last so named because its outlines were said to echo those of the courthouse in St. Louis) that thrust up from the endless plains like beacons in the middle of the sea of the unknown West. Covered wagons—prairie schooners, they were called—found safe harbor for refitting at Fort Laramie in what is now Wyoming, the last stop before the Great South Pass through the Rockies.

Fort Laramie was the great way station along the road to the Far West. Built in 1834 as a trading center for white fur trappers and Indians alike, it became a supply depot for the growing tide of migrants moving west in the late 1840s and 1850s, a place to pause, to gather strength for the perils of the journey ahead. Here began the last great leap across the

James Michener at Scott's Bluff along the Oregon Trail.

Fort Laramie, Wyoming, was founded as a trading post in 1834. It was bought by the American Fur Company in 1836. And in 1849, it became a U.S. Army post, which later became a major stop for people moving westward. Troops occupied the fort until 1890.

mountains to the promised lands of California and Oregon. The trip was fraught with danger from the hostile environment and from the sometimes hostile Indians, the Native Americans upon whose lands the settlers trespassed.

Many never saw their promised land. But in spite of the high risks, the settlers kept coming, pushing ever westward to the fertile Oregon farmlands and those veins of California gold.

The Westering Urge

The first citizens of the United States to see the West Coast of North America and lay claim to at least some of its territories in the name of the recently founded Republic were the captain and crew of the vessel *Columbia* that sailed into Oregon's Nootka Sound in 1792. The *Columbia* was a "sea-peddlar," its mission to buy furs from the Indians and then traverse the broad Pacific to China to dispose of the cargo there at high prices. Much of Oregon's coast had already been explored by the British on earlier fur-buying expeditions, but this did not keep the captain of the *Columbia* from his own exploration. Upon discovering the mouth of a great river, which he dubbed the "Columbia" in honor of his ship, he claimed the territory for his nation.

American claims were underscored more than a decade later, when Captains Meriwether Lewis and William Clark, leading an expedition of exploration through the recently obtained Louisiana Territory, pushed beyond the borders of this vast western realm to Oregon's Pacific Coast where, in 1805, they built Fort Clatsop and settled in for the winter while preparing for the long journey home. Though the stay was uncomfortable, it was evidently not entirely devoid of pleasures, Clark remarking in his diary at one point that "an old woman & Wife to a chief of the *Chunnooks* [a local Indian tribe] came out and . . . brought with her 6 young Squars (her daughter & nieces) I believe for the purpose of Gratifying the passions of the men of our party."

American claims to the Oregon country (an area that includes modern-day Oregon, Washington, and British Columbia) were echoed by British claims to the same region. In 1811 the American fur trader John Jacob Astor attempted to nail down United States possession of the area by dispatching a ship around Cape Horn to Oregon, where, at the mouth of the Columbia, his agents built Fort Astoria. This effort quickly came to grief, a casualty of the War of 1812 between Britain and America. Faced with the threat of being overrun by the far more numerous British fur traders in the area, who were employed by the Northwest Company (soon to be merged with the famous Hudson's Bay Company), the Astorians sold out their holdings to their rivals and fled the region. Though in the years to come the Oregon country would be technically ruled by a joint Anglo-American commission, pending resolution of the disputed claim, actual control was in the hands of the Hudson's Bay Company representing the English Crown.

Luckily for future American interests in the Oregon country, the chief British representative in the region was a great bear of a man named John McLoughlin, a physician turned fur trader, chief factor of Hudson's Bay's Fort Vancouver. A man whose stern visage belied his gentle disposition, McLoughlin was constitutionally incapable of carrying out one of his primary duties: to keep Americans from settling the Oregon country. Not that in the 1820s and 1830s there seemed to be much pressure from the Americans to make good their claims. Most Americans would probably have agreed with a report of Congress that stated: "Nature has fixed limits to our nation; she has kindly interposed as our Western barrier, mountains almost inaccessible. . . . This barrier our population can never pass."

One who did not agree, however, was a Bostonian of fanatic Anglophobe views named Hall Jackson Kelley who in 1831 organized an

A view of the landscape outside Fort Laramie.

Oregon society to encourage emigration to the distant territory. The next year Kelley actually set out for Oregon, and after many detours arrived there accompanied by a band of horse thieves. McLoughlin, normally the kindest of men, assumed that Kelley shared the bad habits of his companions and, rather put off by the Bostonian's Anglophobia, treated him quite shabbily. At the first opportunity, McLoughlin put Kelley aboard a passing ship bound for the East Coast. ❑

Missions to the Indians

❑ Kelley's mission may have been a failure, but even while the Bostonian was languishing in a hut outside the walls of Fort Vancouver, a few other Americans were picking their way west to the fabled Oregon country. For most of these hardy few, religion—the conversion of the Indians to Christianity—was the motive for their trek. In the mid-1830s, a kind of missionary fervor was sweeping the East and Midwest. Its genesis lay in the fact that four Indians of Oregon country tribes had appeared in St. Louis with a group of fur-trading mountainmen. A rumor swept the United States that these Indians had come to St. Louis specifically to recruit missionaries who would lead them out of the depths of ignorance and into the sunlight of the Cross. Missionary societies sprang up to convert the heathen of the Far West; vast sums of money were collected and preachers recruited, with Methodist Jason Lee

The trail town of Cody in northern Wyoming. (Colour Library International, Ltd.)

A restored covered wagon. This was the method of transportation for many settlers heading westward.

as their leader. In 1834 Lee and a small band of missionaries joined a party of mountainmen who would lead them overland along what came to be known as the Oregon Trail. After arriving at Fort Vancouver, the preachers were convinced by John McLoughlin to build their mission in the fertile Willamette Valley which would soon become the center of American life in the Oregon country.

Jason Lee had come to Oregon to convert the heathens; he stayed to become a preacher-farmer and a propagandist for American colonization. By 1837, thanks to his efforts, the first white women and children arrived in Oregon. Lee wed one of the women, then quickly departed to the East to testify before Congress on the worth of Oregon and to find new settlers, fifty of whom later accompanied him on the long sea voyage around the horn to the Oregon coast.

In spite of Jason Lee's boosterism, American settlement in Oregon amounted to only about two hundred souls as the 1840s began. Yet slowly, word was spreading throughout the East that Oregon was a virtual paradise of year-round warmth and free-for-the-taking soil of amazing fecundity. Something approaching Oregon Fever was building, a situation partly generated by a long economic depression in the East. In 1841 the first of many wagon trains was formed in Independence, Missouri, and set out for the West Coast; about half the pioneers would settle in Oregon, the rest headed southward to California. An even bigger wagon train, with some one hundred emigrants, moved west along the Oregon Trail the next year, and in 1843, the travel west increased dramatically when a wagon train with about one thousand pioneers braved the Rockies and the rushing rivers beyond. Indeed, in the decade of the 1840s, more than 44,000 Americans would move across the plains and the mountains, the deserts and the wild waters of the western rivers, half of them bound for Oregon, half for California. From an imperceptible presence in 1840, America made good the nation's claim to the Oregon country. This fact of life Britain accepted in 1846 with the establishment by treaty of the United States–Canadian border at the forty-ninth parallel, granting to America the territory that makes up the present states of Oregon and California. ❑

IN TODAY'S WEST, IT'S THE COAL RUSH

The cowboy, that Americana archetype, can still be found riding the range in today's modern West. But, like the Indians before him, he is now being challenged for his land by another invader from the East, one whose impact on the region and the lives of its inhabitants promises to alter drastically the culture of the West.

The fertile farmlands and grazing pastures of the West cover coal reserves estimated at 1.3 trillion tons in Wyoming, Montana, Colorado, and Utah alone. In addition to coal, there is more oil in the shale deposits of these states than in the entire Middle East, plus enormous deposits of other vital minerals, such as uranium and copper.

Development of the West's vast resources will have tremendous impact on the lives of the people who live here. The energy needs of the nation are being pitted against the human needs of the region. To extract these subterranean riches requires mining operations on an unheard-of scale. Converting the most accessible mineral, coal, into electric power has already produced air pollution in the once-pristine places where these coal-fired plants operate—at the Four Corners Plant, for example, or the new plants at Colstrip, Montana.

Land, which we once thought limitless here, can be used for only one purpose at a time: You can ranch it, you can live on it, or you can mine it—but you can't do all three.

Michener Talks with Jack Horton

Jack Horton, former assistant secretary of the interior.

Jack Horton, a former assistant secretary of the interior, operated a working ranch in Wyoming. He died not long after our interview.

MICHENER: When we talk about minerals in the western states, let's pinpoint it. Coal, for example—what states have these enormous coal deposits?

HORTON: The states that run north-south, starting with Montana: Montana, Wyoming, Colorado, New Mexico, plus Arizona and Utah. There is no question that this area of the West can provide solutions to the nation's energy problems in the years to come. There are six to eight hundred years of energy reserves, using only the coal that is there in my state of Wyoming alone. But there's also oil and gas, uranium, and coal shale. Enormous deposits.

Wind River in Wind River Canyon, Wyoming. (Colour Library International, Ltd.)

MICHENER: You mean six hundred years of usable energy that can be converted into electricity—and it's just waiting there to be taken out?

HORTON: That's right. But of course, there is a plethora of problems associated with it. Who owns the coal? How can it be extracted safely? What about the water needed to extract it? And the rights of the ranchers—how will they be protected?

MICHENER: Well, won't the pressure from the other states put such a heavy burden on you that you'll have to dig this coal out?

HORTON: I think Wyoming and the other states are prepared to dig the coal—and the uranium and the oil shale—and contribute them as a raw resource to the rest of the nation. The critical issues, however, are: How should that energy be converted—should it be turned into gas or liquid, or burned for electricity? And should Wyoming and the other states bear *all* the costs—the environmental and social costs as well as the extracting costs?

MICHENER: What do you mean when you speak of the social costs of extracting this coal?

HORTON: These are the costs the community must bear when a large influx of people comes in to mine and transport the coal and convert it into electricity. So we're not talking about just the costs of digging out a ton of coal, or the cost of equipment and shipping; we're talking about schools, hospitals, police, transportation facilities, sanitary facilities—the entire base of a new community that must come into being to support these people.

MICHENER: In other words, the coal is there, but to get it is going to revolutionize the Wyoming way of life.

HORTON: It has already changed several communities—Rock Springs, Gillette . . .

MICHENER: But won't you get great profits from extracting this coal? Why don't you pay your own social costs?

HORTON: Profits are important, both for the state and for local communities. But the way of life is a value that stands even higher.

MICHENER: Well, speaking as a northeasterner myself, why don't we in the Northeast just demand that this coal be dug out and turned into the energy we need?

HORTON: For one thing, it's our state, and a good deal of the coal is ours. A lot of the coal is federal coal, it lies under federal lands; but there's still a state government, there are still the communities with whom negotiations have to take place. I think any action by the federal government to demand the coal would be met with an antagonism and resistance by the people here. The federal government now is providing new initiatives for the conversion of energy into what are called synthetic fuels. They are pushing for much faster development of energy here. It's very clear that the states, if they can't accommodate to the timetables and the tonnages, will seek the only other refuge they have available to them, which will be the courts. The courts will have to referee any conflict between the states and the federal government.

MICHENER: What is the typical pattern of land ownership in the West?

HORTON: In most of the western states, most of the land is owned by the federal government, in the form of National Park Service lands, Forest Service lands, Bureau of Land Management lands. . . . When you total these in any state, it often comes to sixty, seventy, or eighty percent of the entire landholdings in that state.

MICHENER: But you own your ranch land, don't you?

HORTON: Our land is a composite of deeded land, which our family owns, and state grazing land, which the state of Wyoming owns. And immediately to our west is the Bighorn National Forest, which is federally owned. And although there's no coal on our land, just five miles to the east there's a very large coal deposit—in fact, it's the thickest coal deposit in the world: a coal seam two hundred forty feet thick. And in the future, that land may become the location of a synfuel plant.

Michener Talks with Wally McRae

Wally McRae's ranch is in Forsyth, Montana, just up the road from the Colstrip power plant. Wally McRae is a rancher, just like his father and his father's father before him. In spite of many offers to buy him out, Wally McRae is one of those ranchers who prefers to keep his

Cattle crossing range on McRae's ranch.

way of life. In order to do just that, when coal first began to be stripped out of Montana's grazing lands, he and other ranchers formed the Northern Plains Resource Council, which, along with other groups in the area, has attempted to slow down the push for strip mines and power plants in Montana.

MICHENER: Mr. McRae, you're a working cowboy, are you not?

MCRAE: Part of the time I am. I guess I spend a lot of time following a cow around.

MICHENER: Where is your ranch?

MCRAE: It's in southeastern Montana, not too far from the Northern Cheyenne and the Crow reservations. It lies between the Rosebud Creek and the Tongue River, which drains into the Yellowstone.

MICHENER: That's General Custer land, isn't it?

MCRAE: Custer and his soldiers were the last big group of tourists to come into this country—they went right through my place. I don't think that the greeting they got from the Indians was too hospitable. . . .

Portrait of Wally McRae, Wyoming rancher.

MICHENER: So you've grown up with the Indians around you?

MCRAE: About half the students in my high school were northern Cheyenne. For years my family had grazing leases on their reservation, so I've kind of grown up with them.

MICHENER: I met a rancher from your part of the land once, and I asked him, "How much land do you have?" He grabbed me, and he said, "Michener, you never ask anybody west of the Mississippi how much land they have."

MCRAE: He was probably right, there is a kind of lack of propriety—it's like me asking you how much income you got off your book *Centennial.* If you asked me how many men I hire, I'd say, "One, full time." Well, that sounds very small. But if I told you the number of acres I have, that would sound very large. This is a sparsely vegetated area, and it takes a lot of grass, a lot of country to run a cow on.

MICHENER: What do you raise? Grass or cattle?

MCRAE: The crop that I raise is grass, and as far as the cattle go, they're a harvesting machine that has four legs and a couple of horns and harvests the grass crop that I raise.

MICHENER: Do you succeed or fail according to your grass crop?

MCRAE: Yes, and even further back than that. We're dependent on how much rainfall we get, so water is the limiting factor. It always has been in the West.

MICHENER: So to you the cow is something to harvest grass?

MCRAE: She's the machine that I use to harvest the protein in that grass, to turn it into something that's fit for human consumption, because grass isn't.

MICHENER: Is this an efficient way of converting natural resources into consumable resources?

MCRAE: I think it's probably the most efficient way there is.

MICHENER: Do you raise any sheep?

MCRAE: My family has in the past. But the sheep business is pretty much in a decline in Montana now, mostly because of coyotes and other predators. Also you can't hardly hire a sheepherder any more. And if you've got a bunch of sheep in the pasture, and no herder and no dogs, the coyotes are going to get the sheep. Coyotes aren't dumb; they appreciate a lamb chop or two once in a while. And then, I don't know anything about sheep, except by reputation. I think that they're a lot more inclined to just naturally turn up four legs and die than a cow is.

MICHENER: How did your family get here to Montana?

MCRAE: My grandfather came from Scotland on a sailing vessel to Brownsville, Texas. He worked his way north with a trail herd. He herded sheep for a few years, put a stake together, and bought some sheep which he promptly lost in the notorious winter of 1885–86. But then he bought one hundred sixty acres of unsurveyed land from a French Canadian fur trapper, and that started the original ranch. My other grandfather lived just up the creek from my grandfather McRae. He was also a Scotsman.

MICHENER: When you sell your cattle, are you pretty much at the mercy of the market?

MCRAE: Well, I'm a lot more at the mercy of the market than the market is at my mercy. Historically, the livestock business has been one of ups and downs. It's a tough business.

MICHENER: Any of your neighbors go bankrupt?

MCRAE: Not lately. But in your book *Centennial* you talked about the homesteaders that came in. They didn't understand the country, and they didn't appreciate its capabilities and its limitations. They just didn't understand about the water situation.

Industrial Predators

MICHENER: I don't meet many cowboys, Wally, who have written and published books of poems. You have a poem here about a cowboy who has been driven off the land and is making his money as a miner in a coal mine:

Where did you get that yellow hard hat?
In the mines. In the strip mines.
And the union badge? Where did you get that?
In the mines. In the strip mines.
The steel trailer house for you and your spouse?
In the mines. In the strip mines.

What mines are you talking about?

MCRAE: Oh, everybody that lives around here has their own neighborhood strip mine or power plant or something. Unfortunately, if you're trying to run cows and you're also sitting on top of the Fort Union formation, which is the largest known coal reserve in the world—well, there's a conflict there. Because the very basic resources that it takes for me to grow grass are being damaged and diminished by the extraction and conversion of coal.

MICHENER: Are we sitting on coal right now?

MCRAE: I would guess that right below us, probably thirty-five feet down, is a twenty-foot seam of coal. It's a funny thing—the seam we're

The Colstrip power plant, a major energy source and employer for the region.

sitting on is called the MacKay seam, named for my grandfather MacKay. In the 1930s, when he had a tough time keeping his ranch together and his five daughters spent their time running the ranch, he mined coal for a supplementary income.

There are ranchers today who want to do the same thing. They want to take out that resource below their surface, and improve their ranch. But the difference is that when my grandfather mined the MacKay seam, he did it underground, with a pick and shovel and a little drilling outfit. It was a very small operation.

But these aren't small operations now, they're massive. Strip mines, not underground mines.

MICHENER: But if you have enough coal on your land to take care of the city of Chicago for a hundred years, isn't the pressure going to be tremendous to get that coal out from under your land?

MCRAE: The people who are looking covetously at that coal have got to understand that it's a one-shot deal. They may be concerned about that energy, but there's another kind of energy they should think about, one that's measured in calories. That's my business, producing calories, feeding people. I think it's a whole lot more important for people to have a stable, reasonable source of food than it is to waste electricity or waste gasoline.

I'm not too optimistic about our chances in keeping on doing ranching, but the fellow that takes over my outfit, he's going to have a hell of a fight on his hands. A lot of times, people question my patriotism. They say I'm turning my back on the rest of the United States. And if I was firmly convinced that Chicago or the upper Midwest or the Pacific Northwest needed the coal under my ranch, hell, I'd give it to 'em! But that isn't the case. I don't think they need it. Maybe I'm naïve, but I think it's a ripoff by the energy companies. I just don't feel obligated to see a life-style destroyed, and a whole lot of countryside destroyed, and the water used up and the air polluted and the land torn up, for somebody to run a damned electric toothbrush.

MICHENER: But if we took the coal out and restored the land and returned it to what it was, wouldn't that be some kind of compensation?

MCRAE: I'm not convinced that the land can be reclaimed, except by God. I think that we tend to believe that technologically we're omnipotent, and we're not. I haven't seen any reclamation that impresses me. But even if they can reclaim the land, they can't reestablish the rural communities that were destroyed, they can't solve the boom-bust that the West is notorious for. We've always been on a mineral extraction binge in the West, and I don't think we can survive another one. And we can't allow the amount of water that energy development is going to need to be taken out of the Yellowstone or the Missouri. I just don't think we can do it.

MICHENER: Are there people around here who are eager to have their land mined?

A derrick at Colstrip symbolizes the search for wealth underground.

MCRAE: Yes, and they don't understand me, and I don't understand them. There's never been a time when I or my father or my grandfather couldn't have sold the ranch for more money than it was worth, gone somewhere else, and done something else. And yet there are people who are willing to have their ranches and their family's ranches destroyed, for the buck. I don't understand it.

MICHENER: Are you going to allow the railroad to come through the middle of your ranch?

MCRAE: I think that the courts will probably allow the railroad to come through my ranch. I don't see any way that I can stop the railroad, but if there's a way, I will. Because I don't think it's necessary.

MICHENER: If it's held that the public really needs your land, will your courts uphold eminent domain—will they legally take it away from you?

MCRAE: Yes, they can and will. You know, it's almost humorous. The energy companies and the utilities talk about how they epitomize free enterprise, and yet they're the first ones to run to the government for every kind of help they can get. A subsidy, or the right of eminent domain. They're not at all hesitant about using the powers of government when it's to their benefit, but no one complains more about government regulations than do the coal companies, and the oil companies, and the railroads. It's just expediency—whatever suits the occasion. And they're not at all hesitant to use, or to threaten, eminent domain.

MICHENER: So you visualize a continuing struggle for some time?

MCRAE: There are a lot of us that are faced with the same thing. You know, there's an old cowboy joke that says we didn't hire out to be anything but a tough hand. And I think we realize this. Anytime that you decide that you're going to resist the federal government and the railroads and the energy companies and perhaps the majority of public opinion in the United States—then you better damn sure hire out to be a tough hand. Because if you think that your chances of winning are good, then you're naïve.

But I don't think there's a darn thing naïve about us in the Northern Plains Resource Council, which is our organization in Montana. But we feel an obligation to resist and to point out that we're not expendable, that Montana isn't expendable, it's not for sale. Maybe then people will take a long look and think, Am I wasting some of this energy? Can I conserve a little bit?

You know, if you could market the sun, if there was a royalty on the sun, there would be all kinds of solar energy development. There's great potential in using renewable energy.

It's gonna be a tough fight. It's an important fight. And maybe it's a fight that's been fought before and lost. I think of this region as having had other fights and other tragedies take place in it. The coldly calculating elimination of the Indian was a tragedy. Conning the homesteader into coming into this area was a tragedy. And I'm just as convinced that substituting a one-shot extractive coal development deal for long-term agriculture is just as tragic a mistake. I just hope that it doesn't happen again.

Too Many Demands on Too Little Water

As heated as the battle for the mineral resources in the West may be, a much larger fight threatens to eclipse it in importance, one that will determine the course of all further development, whether for energy or agriculture, home or business. It is the fight for the most valuable western resource of all: water.

Since the earliest days of the settling of the West, water rights have been the source of countless feuds, and just one hundred years ago, in some parts, a barrel of water sold for more than a barrel of oil costs today.

Although the United States seems to have plenty of water at the moment, it has always been scarce in the West, and it is here in the West that the nation's great energy resources are located. Present and future energy development will require enormous amounts of water—water that in many cases just isn't there. The lack of water places definite limits on growth and development in the West, whether for energy production or for agriculture.

I went back to Jack Horton to ask him how he sees the water situation in his part of the country.

MICHENER: Water availability is a growing problem in the West, is it not?

HORTON: There are so many competing demands for the water—growth of population, increased energy use. In my state of Wyoming,

Mount Moran and Jackson Lake in Wyoming. (Colour Library International, Ltd.)

water rights are held by the state, and they're allocated under a first-come, first-served system, which essentially gives water rights to the first person there. Nearly all the water in the state has been allocated.

MICHENER: So if I wanted to start a city of, say, two hundred thousand in that beautiful land in central Wyoming, one of my first problems would be, where do I get the water?

HORTON: What you would have to do would be either to find unallocated water, probably in federal storage reservoirs, or to buy water rights from an existing user, probably a rancher. And then the governor of Wyoming would have to approve the transfer of the use from agricultural purposes to your purposes—building a city.

MICHENER: Are the western states handling their water well?

HORTON: The traditional system worked quite well up until the last five or six years. Then the energy industry moved in on a large scale, and not only water quantities but water uses came under intense controversy. The development of energy and the conversion of energy into electricity has generated enormous comment and debate, but the issue below the surface clearly is water, and that certainly will be the paramount issue in the years to come.

MICHENER: The Indians in your area are also involved in the water controversy, aren't they?

HORTON: Yes. The question is how much of the land, and particularly how much of the water for the land, they should have. The issue is now being contested in the courts, and it is so complicated, so full of

Construction on the outskirts of Gillette.

emotional pressures that it will undoubtedly reach the Supreme Court.

In 1908 the Supreme Court gave each reservation the amount of water necessary to support that reservation in its domestic life. But those water rights have never been quantified. No one knows how much those rights should be on a per-acre basis. And while those rights have not been used over the decades since the reservations were created, many other users have come along, particularly agricultural users, and they are now using that water. The issue before the courts is this: Are waters now being used by a rancher downstream specifically owned by a reservation upstream?

MICHENER: If the 1970s were a decade in which our courts grappled with busing and integration, the 1980s could well be a decade in which our courts grapple with land use and water use and energy use.

HORTON: I think there's no doubt about that. And I think if the federal government does not respect the ownership of waters in the West by the western states—and it appears now that they will not—then there will be strong political pressures to go to the courts.

MICHENER: Do you remember the Johnson County Wars that flourished in the end of the last century, when ranchers in Wyoming took the law into their own hands? Do you see range wars developing in the 1980s and 1990s?

HORTON: Of course the issue in the Johnson County War was not simply land, but the control of the land by the people who controlled the water. It's still the same issue, although the character and complexity of our conflict will be different.

❑ [The Johnson County War in 1892 was an eruption of long-simmering hostilities between the cattle barons—owners of immense cattle herds and huge spreads of grazing territory—and the small ranchers and farmers who feared the power of the barons to seize land. The war began when the barons brought in a team of Texas gunslingers whose mission was to kill off any cattle rustlers they could catch. It ended—after the Texans were besieged by three hundred infuriated Johnson County residents—when President Benjamin Harrison called out federal troops. Although the war did not overtly involve land and water issues, the root cause was most certainly the resentment of the struggling small landholder at the often ruthless gobbling up of acreage and water by the big cattlemen.] ❏

Boom Town

MICHENER: Wyoming is a very large state, many times bigger than any east of the Mississippi, but it has a population of only about 350,000. It's very thinly populated, and there are no large cities. Can this population pattern, and the way of life that goes with it, be maintained?

HORTON: It's very clear that we're on a downward scale in terms of the rural quality of life. Many of us would like to keep the state much as it's always been. But change is coming, and we would like to mitigate the bad impacts of large influxes of people.

MICHENER: Take an area like Gillette—what's going to happen to it?

HORTON: Gillette and Rock Springs are the two cities in the state that have experienced enormously rapid population growth because of coal and oil and gas, and what will undoubtedly be the scene of new gasifica-

View of Gillette, Wyoming. This sprawling neighborhood attests to the ever-present need for housing.

tion and liquification plants. And we've seen the inundation of the social services there; of the use of schools, medical facilities, sewers. There were enormous demands made on these cities, far beyond their capacities. But Gillette has recently done an outstanding job of learning how to accommodate these kinds of pressures, with help from the state.

MICHENER: But if the government needed a gasification plant in the Gillette area, bringing in perhaps ten thousand workers with maybe three times that number in their families—that's thirty thousand people, one-tenth of the whole population in Wyoming. . . . What would happen then?

HORTON: The size of Gillette would double, and all of the services in the city would have to be doubled.

MICHENER: Who would pay for that?

HORTON: Well, some people think the federal government should pay for it, because they're the ones behind the new push for synthetic fuels. Some people say the state should pay for it, because in fact the plant would bring an increase of revenue to the state treasury. I feel that the federal government should be primarily responsible for mitigating the pressures that they themselves have created. And it's my belief that the industry which is developing the energy should also accommodate a great proportion of the costs, along with the state.

MICHENER: Could you visualize Wyoming becoming a rural slum?

HORTON: Many would call places like Gillette and Rock Springs rural slums right now. Many believe the federal government will inevitably colonize the West in its enormous push for energy. We are now looking to the rest of the nation and the federal government like the American eagle—with an olive branch in one hand and arrows in the other. We're welcoming the national use of our resources, but we're saying, "We have to live with you and you with us. Pay attention to our environment."

Oil Drilling Comes to Gillette, Wyoming

❑ Since 1883, when the first commercial well was brought in, oil has been gushing up from the harsh, mountainous Wyoming soil in amounts that equal a bonanza for the oil companies and for the owners of oil-bearing land. The oil has also provided a small but welcome addition to the state's coffers.

A huge oil find was made in Wyoming's Powder River Basin in 1967; and the nearby town of Gillette, which had been long accustomed to the kind of quiet that comes with a population of under three thousand, suddenly found itself with six thousand newcomers to feed, house, school, doctor, provide with roads, and furnish with adequate water and sewage systems. The task was more than the town could handle, and Gillette was transformed, almost overnight, into a shabby, shack-and-trailer boom town.

In the 1970s, new strip mines in the area again brought about a doubling of the town's population, which now numbers over twelve thousand.

How do Gillette residents feel about their town? This is what a few of them had to say. ❑

RESIDENT: It's changed in every way. Just a few of these houses were here when I came . . . no McDonald's, no K-Mart. You could walk down the streets anywhere you wanted to go at night, there were no problems there. Now you can't be as free, but that's what you have to take, I guess, when a place grows like this. There's so many more people. Anytime so many people move in—and I was one of them, twelve years ago—well, there's going to be change.

I think when people come here, they're just needing money. They've lost jobs or they've been laid off. They don't come to Gillette, Wyoming, to stay. I love it here, but a lot of people think they're crazy to come here—they come just to get back on their feet.

RESIDENT: The boom really started about 1967, when we hit an oil well out in the Kitty Field north of town here. And since that time, we have seen nothing except growth and boom conditions. It's been a young community, and they're doing things, and it's a really exciting time.

RESIDENT: Gillette has historically been a boom town. If you were to ask the average citizen how long he'd lived here, he'd probably say three months, maybe a year. It's always been a rowdy town, and it still is.

Citizens of Gillette talk about their town.

RESIDENT: Most of the people here are transient. They're not here to stay—they're here to work in the mines until the mines dry up, or until they get a better job someplace in a better town. But I'm going to stay here forever, I guess.

RESIDENT: The average worker here does not come for the beauty of the terrain or the hunting, which is excellent, but for the high wages and the opportunity to make some money in a quick fashion. I think that the solitude of Gillette contributes to some of its problems. You get what I would classify almost as a cabin fever out here. The entire town does. Which is why, on some Saturday nights, the place goes crazy.

RESIDENT: I've known several people that have been born and raised here, and they can't really get used to all of the people coming in, because they're used to knowing everybody. They resent it a little bit every time somebody moves in. And yet, they're learning to accept it.

RESIDENT: We have a mixture of persons from all over the country coming into a small area, and that's had some effect on our standards.

Sheriff of Gillette.

Ten years ago we were pretty well governed by the stable people who had been here, and the churches were very strong. I see some of these things weakening as we get more people here. We have just voted in Sunday liquor openings, and that's brand new in my tenure as sheriff.

RESIDENT: There's so much money here, and it's easy to make. Untrained people can usually find a good job that pays eight, ten, thirteen dollars an hour. And that's a lot of money compared to what you can make in the Midwest, where I come from. So they're here for the money. But they're also here to make a new life for themselves, because the West has got a lot to offer, especially this new West. It's going places, that's for sure.

RESIDENT: The influx of people and the energy and the boom in the country has helped a lot of people financially, but there's a lot of old-timers that would like to see the country back like it used to be. The old West that I've always known is gone forever.

Butte

Butte, Montana! Once it was the greatest city in the state. At the time of World War I, its population numbered one hundred thousand. Today, only twenty thousand people live in Butte, and the town is literally slipping into extinction. Built on some of the richest copper-bearing land in the world, Butte is being consumed by its own pit.

Since 1864, when gold was discovered near here, nearly $4 billion in ore—copper in vast quantities, and silver, gold, lead, zinc, and manganese—has been extracted from the hill on which the city sits. For much of that time, the ores were taken from almost three thousand miles of shafts and tunnels deep underground. In 1955, however, the Anaconda Copper Company, which owns the mineral rights to the land under Butte, began digging its vast Berkeley Pit, a huge open hole that will eventually be two thousand feet deep—once all the ore is scavenged from the hill.

Open-pit mining requires a different technology and vastly different skills from those needed underground, and it needs far fewer men to dig the ore. Miners who had spent their working lives digging for copper underground soon found themselves unemployed. And the pit grew like a cancer, swallowing more of the town with every passing month. Most of Anaconda's employees—shovel operators, dragline experts, mechanical engineers—live in neat suburban homes well outside the town limits. Butte itself has been left to the derelicts, the out-of-work, the old-timers who knew what life was like in Dublin Gulch, in Sin Town, in all the old neighborhoods that have vanished into the Berkeley Pit.

It is said that the ore remaining in Butte's hill is worth more than everything that has already been extracted. When all of it has been shoveled out of the earth, and Butte has disappeared, there will be only a gigantic hole to commemorate the presence of men here, a graphic symbol of our country's voracious appetite for its resources.

Colstrip

The huge strip mine at Colstrip, Montana, has been at the heart of the controversy over how Montana should use its land. In 1978 alone mines in Colstrip yielded some 12.5 million tons of coal, almost half of the state's entire coal production. Much of this coal is shipped out of state. A good deal of it, however, is used nearby, at power plants named Colstrip 1 and Colstrip 2, which produce power for a giant utility. Plans to construct two more power plants at Colstrip have generated enormous resistance from local residents, environmental organizations, and from the Northern Cheyenne, who fear air pollution on their reservation. The Crow tribe, on the other hand, wants the additional plants to be built. Their reservation owns large coal reserves.

Like Montana's coal, much of its electric power is shipped out of the state. Critics claim that the plants pollute Montana's air, despoil its land, ruin its small communities—all in order to power refrigerators in Seattle or air conditioners in Chicago. Many westerners in the mineral-rich states of Montana, Wyoming, and Colorado are bitterly opposed to becoming the "boiler rooms" for the rest of the nation. But they may have little choice, for their states are in large part not their own. The federal government owns 66 percent of Utah, 64 percent of Idaho, 48 percent of Wyoming, 36 percent of Colorado, and 30 percent of Montana.

Westerners fear that they may become simply a colony of the federal government. In recent years, Montana has taken steps to protect itself. Its legislature has passed the Montana Strip Mining and Reclamation

Act, the Montana Water Use Act, the Coal Conservation Act, and other laws designed to regulate the mining and conversion of coal. The Montana Severance Coal Tax Law taxes the coal companies heavily to help pay for the destructive effects of population influx on small communities.

But legislation is obviously not enough to prevent what many fear will be permanent and destructive effects on Montana's way of life. Reclamation of strip-mined land, for example, may eventually prove to take too long to bring the land back into use for the present or even the next generation of ranchers.

ENERGY FROM THE SUN

There is one resource that abounds in the West, one whose extraction is free of leases and land claims, whose use is free of polluting waste and negative social impact. The resource is the heat of our sun. With oil prices rising, many are turning to solar energy as one of the solutions to our nation's energy needs. Here in Golden, Colorado, at the base of the Rocky Mountains, the Solar Energy Research Institute has brought together an extraordinary group of people, all of them experts in the problems and potentials of solar research.

Dennis Hayes is the former director of the Institute.

Michener Talks with Dennis Hayes

MICHENER: Twenty-eight years ago, Dennis, I built a solar home. It was one of the first in my area. And instead of getting an architect, I got an astronomer. He showed me how to place the house, how to build the eaves. . . . And today, when the temperature is zero degrees outside, if it's a sunny day we have to open the doors because the house gets too hot.

HAYES: Well, if you'd employed an architect as well as an astronomer, you wouldn't have to open the doors, because he'd have figured out a way to shield your windows from all of that sunshine. To diminish the amount of energy that a house requires, no matter where you build in the country, you'd first incorporate passive solar design factors: more of your windows facing south where the sun is, fewer facing north where they will constantly drain energy from the house. You'd have an overhanging ledge that allows the sun to penetrate in the winter when it is relatively low on the horizon, but will shield you from the sun in the summer when it's higher in the sky. You'd use things like insulating drapes. If people just made intelligent use of insulating blinds in the houses they're living in now, we might see five to ten percent changes in the amount of energy those houses use.

Dennis Hayes, former director of the Solar Energy Research Institute.

MICHENER: Tell me about the Institute, Dennis. Where does its money come from?

HAYES: We get all of our money from the United States Department of Energy. Some of it comes originally from places like the Agency for International Development, but it's channeled through the Department of Energy.

MICHENER: So you're a servant of the American public, trying to help solve a problem?

HAYES: That's exactly right. We are currently spending about one hundred million dollars a year, trying to come up with answers to a variety of technical and social issues. About seventy million of that is spent at universities, in industries, in "think tanks"—because we here don't have a monopoly on wisdom with regard to these technologies. About thirty million is spent here at the institute, most of it on laboratory research, but a fair amount on policy research as well.

MICHENER: So the private sector comes in on this, too.

HAYES: Yes. One of the key reasons for our distributing that seventy million outside is that we've come to learn that if you can get a corporation involved at the research stage, the transfer of a technology into a commercial product for the American consumer is made easier. Corporations would rather be in on the design of a technology from the beginning, so it can be designed to meet their own needs.

Solar Energy's Many Meanings

MICHENER: What are you focusing on here in Colorado?

HAYES: We're looking at a broad range of ways to tap sunlight. So in addition to talking about collectors that operate directly off sunlight, we're also talking about hydroelectricity—because it's the sun that evaporates the water and carries it up to the mountains where it stacks up behind dams. We're talking about wind power, because the winds are created by the uneven heating of the earth's surface by the sun. And, most important perhaps, we're talking about biological energy resources.

MICHENER: What do you mean by that?

HAYES: Plants capture sunlight by photosynthesis and keep that energy stored in the plant material. When you burn the plant material, that captured sunlight is given off. We call the plant material "biomass." Alcohol fuels and wood-burning stoves are examples of biological technologies that are currently here.

MICHENER: And can any part of the biomass be used in that process?

HAYES: There are important components of it that don't really provide an energy function. The nutrients, for instance—nitrogen, potassium—don't really do anything for us in terms of energy. And one of the important issues in designing an intelligent strategy for using biological energy resources is to make sure that those nutrients don't go up the smokestacks, but get returned to the soil. Then we'll have a perpetual resource that we can use forever, rather than just mining the nutrients out and disposing of them, creating deserts in the process.

MICHENER: What are you doing about deriving energy directly from the sun?

HAYES: There are a variety of technologies in use today that are active technologies—they have moving parts, they're not just part of the design of the house. They're used to heat water for your bathtub, or to heat water to warm the space inside the house, or to power an absorption chiller that can function as an air-conditioning unit. There are a variety of other technologies that are currently too expensive, but we believe that costs will change dramatically with some research advances and some movement toward mass production. These are things that simply lie in the sunshine and generate electricity. They're called photovoltaic cells, or solar cells. The Solar Energy Research Institute has lead responsibility for the development of these cells. We think they're going to be here soon, and cheap enough for everyone to begin using them.

MICHENER: Let's look at the earth itself. Don't the rays of the sun lose most of their energy because they have to pass through the lens of the atmosphere?

HAYES: They lose a fair amount of their energy on the way to the earth. But by the time it hits the surface of the earth, the sunlight that we receive every day still contains ten thousand times as much energy as we currently derive from all conventional fuels. So most of the solar research community believes that we should move aggressively on solar applications, because they will be sufficiently bountiful to meet all of our needs. We have a variety of technologies now that can get us anywhere from twelve to eighteen percent conversion efficiency, with the photovoltaic device, for example. Almost one-fifth of the sunlight that hits such a device gets converted into electricity. And the part that isn't converted is dissipated as heat. So if you circulate a fluid underneath your photovoltaic array, you can take off that heat just as you would with a regular solar panel, and use it to heat your bathwater, or to heat your living room, or to help provide industrial process heat.

MICHENER: But here in Colorado, there's plenty of sunlight. What about other places in the country, where there isn't as much sun?

HAYES: As it turns out, the differences in solar availability across the entire United States are relatively modest. The sunniest areas of the country get about five units of sunlight, compared to the cloudiest areas,

which get about four units. That's comparing, say, Arizona and Massachusetts. So solar applications can in fact be used across the entire country.

The sun goes down in a blaze of glory, lending a touch of drama to a western landscape.

Breathtaking Changes

MICHENER: Now let's move to a typical small town in Ohio. What changes will occur there in the next decade, and in the next quarter of the century?

HAYES: In the next decade, I think they'll probably be fairly modest. But in the next quarter of a century, the energy-related changes could be fairly breathtaking. We've gone through energy transitions before: in the move from wood and wind into coal, which brought with it the Industrial Revolution; and the move from coal to oil, which produced the jet airplane, the automobile, and defined the scope and character of the city. And as we move away from oil, I think we can count upon similarly far-reaching changes.

The important ones for a small town in Ohio would, I think, be the substitution of intelligent urban design for transportation, so that people can live close to where they work and shop; the substitution of communication for transportation; and the introduction of a lot of energy-unintensive but sophisticated control technologies that will allow life to proceed in much the way it does today, but—using sensors and computerlike facilities—with much less energy use.

MICHENER: Will there be pressure from the economic system to enforce these changes?

HAYES: For the last forty years in America, there has not been a free marketplace for energy. We regulate the costs of electricity, we average out the cost of oil, we give direct federal subsidies—last year, fourteen billion dollars to the conventional centralized energy industries. When you add all these things together, last year the American energy marketplace probably had something approaching a one hundred *billion* dollar bias in it—in favor of continuing the status quo, against decentralizing solar applications. So, although the marketplace is going to be increasingly promoting solar energy, it's going to require some national legislative initiatives to begin to equalize things first.

MICHENER: What do you see as the gravest problems facing solar energy now?

HAYES: Marketplace bias caused by governmental actions to protect the conventional fuels industries is clearly a problem. Other elements include the wariness of consumers to buy new products they're not sure of—and in some instances, it's a well-chosen wariness, because some of the solar equipment hasn't worked very well. So we'll have to design a system of warranties to protect people. Another element is simple access to sunlight. We have to develop new concepts of zoning our land so that, if you invest in solar equipment, you'll know that your neighbor to the south isn't going to stop you from getting full advantage from it. These seem to me to be relatively modest problems compared to the problems that are facing most other energy futures, and I am confident that they can be overcome with a bit of thought and concerted effort.

MICHENER: How do you see our energy problem in the year 2000?

HAYES: We peaked out in the production of domestic petroleum in 1970, and it's been going down at the rate of roughly four thousand barrels a day ever since then. We've got to move from petroleum into something else. There are a series of dramatic roadblocks that are facing anyone who wants to substantially increase the amount of coal or nuclear power—political impasses as well as some genuine technical problems. The great advantages to conservation and solar energy over that time frame is that they're popular resources that don't seem to carry social disadvantages. If we pursue them intelligently, I think that the energy problem by the year 2000 could be well in hand. As you know, the goal for the country is to get twenty percent of all its energy from solar energy by the year 2000. I'm quite confident that that goal can be surpassed.

GOLDEN CITY OF THE GOLDEN WEST

It was a tiny port on the California coast, a small town of barely three hundred people that only recently had transferred its allegiance, along with the rest of California, from Mexico to the United States. Those rare travelers—mostly seamen—who chanced upon this village often remarked on the beauty of the natural setting, and a few even

This view of San Francisco shows the city rising above the characteristic fog that often hugs the bay. The Golden Gate Bridge is in the foreground. (Holly Hartman)

predicted a great future for this place known as San Francisco. Hardly anyone, however, could have foreseen that within a few years the sleepy port would be transformed into a raucous, burgeoning city, the boomingest boom town in the entire world. The cause of this sudden change in San Francisco's fortunes was that most precious of metals for which men have fought, murdered, suffered, and died: in a word, gold.

On January 23, 1848, a carpenter working on the huge ranch of John Sutter, inland from San Francisco, discovered a few nuggets of the precious metal in the swift-flowing American River. Rumors of the find soon reached San Francisco, but oddly enough no one paid much heed until a merchant and huckster named Sam Brannan decided to investigate. A shrewd businessman with a steady eye out for the main chance, Brannan figured that if the rumors were true—if there was gold in quantity—San Francisco would become the port of entry for thousands of treasure seekers heading for the gold fields. A man with supplies to sell them—axes, pans, household goods, flour, clothing, all the necessities of life—would stand to make a fortune without ever once sweating in the sun while panning for gold in the rushing waters of the American.

In the spring of 1848, Brannan took a journey to Sutter's ranch, moseyed around a bit, became convinced that the talk was all true, bought up as many staples as he could to establish his store, and then, armed with a vial of gold dust, hurried back to San Francisco.

Skyline of San Francisco. The pyramid of the Transamerica Building dominates this view. (Colour Library International, Ltd.)

Though Brannan, among his other interests, owned a newspaper, he obviously thought that merely printing confirmation of the rumors was insufficiently dramatic. Instead, while holding his precious container high, he rushed up and down the streets of the town, screaming out the good news: "Gold! Gold! Gold from the American River." As he bellowed, he grabbed passing pedestrians, shook the bottle in their faces, then ran on to accost others who had not yet heard of the momentous find.

Brannan's town-crier approach had the intended effect. Within days, San Francisco was virtually a ghost town; within weeks, as news spread up and down the coast, other California villages became depopulated as citizens hurried to the diggings. Soldiers still on duty in the aftermath of the Mexican War deserted their regiments. Sailors in California's many ports jumped ship en masse. It seemed that every able-bodied man

Alcatraz Island in San Francisco Bay. Formerly a prison, today it is a tourist attraction. (Colour Library International, Ltd.)

along the entire Pacific Coast had but one thought in mind—to reach the American and establish his claim. One soldier who deserted later recalled his emotions of the time: "A frenzy seized my soul; piles of gold rose up before me at every step; thousands of slaves bowed to my beck and call; myriads of fair virgins contended for my love. In short, I had a violent attack of gold fever."

And when these first of the argonauts reached the banks of the American, who was there to greet them, to offer them supplies they would need to live and work, at prices set midway between the unbelievable and the unimaginable? Why none other than the gold digger's friend and bearer of glad tidings: Sam Brannan. ❑

Destiny's Child

❑ If San Francisco had been turned into a ghost town by Brannan's half-crazed bellow, it would not remain so for long. As the closest settlement of any size to the gold fields, and blessed with a natural harbor where the argonauts could disembark, the town was obviously destined to prosper mightily. In this case, destiny arrived with astounding speed. By the close of 1850, less than three years after Brannan's joyful proclamation, San Francisco's population had increased a hundredfold to thirty thousand; within another five years it would almost double in size again. Miners from the diggings, and would-be miners who had just made their way overland to the west coast or had come by ship around the horn, crowded the muddy streets and jerry-built bars, restaurants, gambling halls, inns, and bawdyhouses. The chief economic activity of the residents was mining the miners' pockets to relieve them of the burden of their new-found wealth. In this activity the miners themselves were all too willing to help. It became a point of honor among them never to leave the fleshpots of San Francisco without having spent every last penny they had so painstakingly extracted from the American River and the hills around it.

In the seven years following the discovery of gold, nearly $350 million in the precious metal flowed through San Francisco, much of it sticking to the palms of sharpsters, con artists, prostitutes, thieves, muggers, murderers, and ruffians of every description. One lady of the evening, after but a year in the practice of her profession, retired with a grubstake of $50,000—and this in a day when that sum was a princely fortune. Another popular strumpet initiated a sliding scale of rates for her favors: A miner in from the fields might engage her in a short conversation for $16, but an entire evening in her company would set him back $400.

Cable cars, a part of San Francisco's special charm. (Colour Library International, Ltd.)

Ordinary merchants were not far behind in their accumulation of specie: Lumber, which had sold at 4¢ a board-foot before the rush, went to $1 a board-foot in the mid-1850s; a piece of land that brought its seller all of $16.50 in 1847 sold for $45,000 the following year; a dozen eggs was bringing $4 in San Francisco, and a third more in the gold fields. Sam Brannan, of course, had a finger in every conceivable sort of enterprise. Land rentals alone brought him $160,000 just in 1849, while at the same time he was making a small fortune selling carpet tacks, at $16 per small package, to builders.

By the end of the 1850s, the California gold rush had run its course; the hectic boom days in San Francisco were over. Yet the city did not revert to its former somnolent self. Its climate, its splendid port, the establishment of a financial elite within its borders, all combined to maintain its status as the premier city of the golden west. Many of those who had come—not just from the eastern United States but also from such distant realms as England, France, Germany, China, and Australia—to seek their fortunes as forty-niners remained in San Francisco to impose on the city a cosmopolitan atmosphere unrivaled by any other American metropolis save possibly New York. By the turn of the century, San Francisco had become a magnet for both bohemians and capitalists; the dining room of the Palace Hotel was the place where these two worlds met, rubbed shoulders, and discussed the latest production at the opera house. Not even the disastrous earthquake and fire of 1906 could do more than momentarily slow San Francisco's rise to preeminence. If in later years the city was overtaken in population and wealth by its rival to the south, Los Angeles, it retained its reputation for sophistication and tolerance that to this day makes confirmed Los Angelenos choke with choler. ❑

Tolerant City

❑ It was in San Francisco, in the 1950s, that the beatniks achieved prominence with their howl against the conformity and blandness of the Eisenhower age. It was in San Francisco, a decade later, that the flower children—the hippies—sought shelter from the crass materialism of the

The famous zigzag makes the most of San Francisco's up and down hills.
(Colour Library International, Ltd.)

times in a fog of drugs and an excess of sexual and social experimentation. It was in nearby Berkeley, at the campus of the University of California, that students began their long campaign against the Vietnam War. And it is in the San Francisco of today that the gay rights movement has taken its firmest hold, with homosexuals now a highly organized political force that can make or break candidates for local office.

Like New York, San Francisco tends to look benignly upon all manner of idiosyncrasies and consequently has become the resting place of not only the creative but also of the lonely, the psychotic, and the disaffected. The messianic murderer Charles Manson recruited his army of flower-children-turned-killers from the hippie neighborhood of Haight-Ashbury; the Reverend Jim Jones achieved both respectability and power in San Francisco before transferring most members of his suicide cult to Guyana. Indeed, San Francisco has the nation's highest suicide rate, the graceful fretwork of the Golden Gate Bridge being a favorite jumping-off place for those who wish to do themselves in.

As for the arts, which generally flourish in tolerant environments such as San Francisco provides, many critics hold that there is far less there than meets the eye. Though San Francisco's bohemian quarters fairly reek of artistic endeavor, little of substance in the way of novels, plays, or paintings actually appears. Certainly, a young man or woman who wants to make it big in publishing, theater, music, or movies would find places far better suited to these ambitions than in San Francisco. Yet this city's carefully nurtured reputation for bohemianism lives on. And, in truth, there is much that is dear and winning about it. Chinatown, North Beach, Haight-Ashbury, the forty-odd hills with their antique cable cars, the "Top of the Mark," and Fisherman's Wharf all have special meanings to the millions who have visited the city, and even to the millions more who merely dream of doing so. As one writer once put it, "It is still the . . . city . . . where a walker can experience a nostalgia for the place while he is still there—a little, even a lot, like the *nostalgie de Paris*." ❑

. . . WHERE THE LIVING IS EASY

❑ Millions have thronged westward to California over the years to settle in the far-flung reaches of the city of Los Angeles. And millions more—the stay-at-homes—wonder why. It is common knowledge that the Los Angeles area is doomed to fall into the sea one day; it sits right on top of the famous San Andreas fault, a geologic fracture that causes frequent tremors of the earth and an occasional earthquake. It's hot and dry in the city, and the aggressive Santa Ana winds periodically fan fierce fires that eat up vegetation and buildings alike. Drought is

LEFT: *Luxurious cars, part of the California life-style, in Westwood Village, a suburb of Los Angeles.* (Colour Library International, Ltd.)

RIGHT: *Sunset Boulevard, Los Angeles.* (Colour Library International, Ltd.)

often succeeded by heavy winter rains that make a muddy soup of the soil, loosening foundations to such a degree that homes built on the slopes frequently slide off their perches. Los Angeles smog, a specialty of the region, can sit for days on the city, and people move in its murk watery-eyed and sneezing. Still, the Angelenos go ahead and build over the desert anyway, piping in their water from rivers hundreds of miles away, covering the sand with concrete, propping up houses on the sides of steep hills where houses have no business being.

Some visitors think of Los Angeles as an ephemeral city, an unlikely desert mirage that could vanish with a change of wind. This is merely wishful thinking, a hint of the kind of extreme reaction L.A. arouses in many people. Certainly no other American city induces such emphatic rejection—or so much defensive boosterism from its inhabitants, who cite the marvelous weather, the beaches, the ubiquitous swimming pools, the growing cultural opportunities, the elegance of the shopping districts, the quality of L.A.'s universities, the great restaurants, the Beautiful People who inhabit Filmland and the television studios.

Today, the city covers 464 square miles of mostly single-family houses on tiny plots, in housing tracts abutting one another and surrounding the original city, now known as "Downtown," in dense agglomerations. So huge is Los Angeles that it has engulfed other, smaller cities in its enormous spread, and the influx of population has transformed Los Angeles' once rural Orange County into the nation's second largest metropolitan area.

The California movement began in the mid-nineteenth century, sparked by hundreds of widely publicized letters and newspaper articles sent back east from California newcomers who proclaimed its blessings. California was a country "with fine forests . . . the waters filled with fish and the plains covered with thousands of herds of cattle; blessed with a climate than which there is no better in the world," wrote Richard Henry Dana, Jr., author of *Two Years Before the Mast.* Ranch-owner John Marsh promised an easy life for California farmers; the Indians, he said, would willingly labor in the fields, because "when caught young, they are most easily domesticated." A blessed climate and an easy life: From the beginning of the American obsession with California, these were the twin lures that brought first thousands and then millions across three thousand miles of continent.

But it was the coming of the railroad that finally determined the destiny of Los Angeles. The railroads thirsted for passengers and freight and offered spectacular bargains to westbound immigrants. As the result of a rate war between two competing rail lines, in 1887 alone 100,000 newcomers came to southern California. Each of them had paid one dollar to travel by rail from Kansas City to Los Angeles. In the 1880s the city's population multiplied six times over. Citrus groves around the city were planted with that California treasure, the navel orange. Major oil fields began to be plumbed within the city limits in the early 1890s.

And finally, to complete the enchantment, the first native Californian motion picture was produced in 1907. ❑

The Shape of the Future

❑ By that year the shape of the future city was already discernible to those with vision and with land to sell. The city itself was a hasty collection of mostly wood-frame houses, in neighborhoods festooned with palm trees, telegraph poles, and oil derricks. Small towns well beyond the city limits—Long Beach, Glendale, Pasadena, Covina, Pomona—were easily accessible via branch lines of the railroad. Between these towns and all around the city, the bean fields flourished, the cattle browsed, and the oranges blossomed. Hollywood was still a small village, but the first houses were going up in a plush new community, a model town called Beverly Hills whose spacious lots and mansions built in any desired style (half-timbered Tudor, Gothic, Chinese pagoda, Williamsburg colonial, and eclectic mixtures of every other variety) were designed to attract the wealthy. The rich found California a more exciting place in which to winter than Palm Beach or Hot Springs, Arkansas. The region also began to attract the old, seeking a warm retirement; the young, who hoped to find fame in Hollywood; blue-collar workers, both black and white, who flocked to the defense factories that sprang up in the area as the country began arming for World War II; and Mexicans, who came in increasing numbers beginning in the 1930s, augmenting the old nucleus of residents of Mexican descent and swelling the barrios of East Los Angeles.

So the city grew. Postwar affluence permitted almost everyone to buy a car, and the city junked what had been the finest American mass-

Center of Los Angeles and the Harbor Freeway. (Colour Library International, Ltd.)

transport system and built, instead, a vast network of highways—"freeways" to Angelenos. The freeway system, which would eventually reach a total length of six hundred miles, allowed for the urbanization of the farmlands in the San Fernando Valley and in other previously inaccessible areas. It made Los Angeles, more than any other American city, dependent on the automobile. Cruising the freeways became a favorite L.A. recreation.

The current population of the Los Angeles metropolitan area is almost eleven million. The influx of newcomers seems to have leveled off, and the sons and daughters of the vast migration are growing into maturity. This new species of Californian may not be as willing as his parents to cut roots and take off.

In any case, there is no farther west to go. . . . And yet there have been ominous indications of a new minimigration within the state. A region not far from Sacramento is attracting numbers of electronic firms. Some small towns in the area have already felt the impact of an influx of people who've come to work in the new plants. Many are ex-Angelenos looking for cleaner air and cheaper housing. Will Shingle Springs, Roseville, and Rocklin become little L.A.s in their turn? Or will Los Angeles itself provide its own best example of the errors of expansionism? ❑

Michener Talks with Neil and Judith Morgan

Although the life-styles of some of its more famous residents might be characterized as extreme, Los Angeles is in many ways a quintessentially American city, a city of typically American mixtures and contrasts. It is a place where highly visible youth spark nationwide fads, where the extreme wealth of Beverly Hills exists side by side with the poverty of Watts and East Los Angeles. More a collection of suburbs than a city, it sprawls over vast tracts of southern California. Here, at the

James Michener interviewing Neil and Judith Morgan, writers living in Los Angeles.

edge of the Pacific, a century of western migration has reached its end.

I spoke to Neil and Judith Morgan, both California authors, about the effect of this movement west.

Joggers in Los Angeles, just three of thousands, sweat off their extra pounds. Long known to the world as the fad capital of America, Los Angeles has been the home of extremes in everything from religion and politics to diets and life-styles.

MICHENER: Mr. Morgan, some years ago you wrote a very important book called *Westward Tilt*, which impressed me very much.

NEIL MORGAN: That was a book about the euphoria of growth. It came out in 1963, at a time when growth was gospel in the western United States and we still lived in the gold-rush syndrome, when we believed that the future was here and it was golden and bright. The book chronicled the growth of the western states after World War II, when people moved westward seeking escape, money, leisure, a new life. The growth was sustained by major manufacturing industries—aircraft, electronics, the space industry.

MICHENER: When you wrote the book, California was probably the third largest state in the nation. Now it's first, with more representatives in Congress than any other state. Do you see this growth as productive?

NEIL MORGAN: Well, I don't think that we're coming anywhere near to carrying our load of leadership—not for a state that is the most populous in America. Part of the reason is our relatively short history. Part is our distance from the centers of economic and political power in New York and Washington. Part is a *laissez-faire* feeling, because so many people have come here from somewhere else and have yet to evolve into a society in which the sense of growing into leadership is a tradition.

Roller skating is just one of the trends set by California's youth.

MICHENER: Is there a loss of a sense of community when people move into an area in such great numbers?

NEIL MORGAN: Yes. Continued movement is the worst thing. People move two to three times more frequently in southern California than they do on average in other parts of America. Once you've broken roots in Pennsylvania or North Carolina and come to California, you find it a good deal easier to make the next move. You put an ad in the paper, you call the moving company. . . . Perhaps there's a new area that's a little closer to the freeways for commuting, or a house that has a few extra gadgets in the kitchen; and you find—as one family told me—that there's always a pretty good school off here to the left, and a pretty new shopping center off here to the right. . . . It's all the same. People say in effect that they're moving from one community of strangers to another, and that they're all interchangeable.

JUDITH MORGAN: People sell homes in southern California the way other people sell cars. You rarely hear of anyone adding a room, or closing down a room as they do in other parts of the country. They move by whim, for a different view, a different swimming pool. I don't know any young children who have grandparents, who know what grandparents are, because their grandparents are back east somewhere.

MICHENER: I am told that this is an area of great personal loneliness.

NEIL MORGAN: One of the important loneliness statistics is the annual total of corpses flown from Los Angeles International Airport to cemeteries back home. Thousands. It seems a lot of people want to live in southern California, but they don't want to be caught dead in it. They go back to be buried under the familial tombstone where the rest of the family is. I think that indicates a certain fundamental loneliness. We don't really belong here. This is a desert.

One great hope to me, however, is something that's just beginning to happen. Migration to California has leveled off; for several years, we haven't grown, percentage-wise, any faster than the state of Maine. And the young people who are native-born are taking over the state. The median age here is about twenty-seven. Today more than two-thirds of the people at median age and below in California are native-born. And I suspect that these young people are going to be very different from some of us who migrated from other parts. California is their home. There's no farther west to go without getting wet. They don't expect to move on. And whatever they make of it, it's going to be home.

JUDITH MORGAN: Years ago, people wouldn't plant trees in their neighborhoods because they came just to roost on the land and enjoy it. They said, "Why should we plant trees? We won't be here when they're tall enough to give shade." But now, people *are* planting them.

LAND OF THE DREAM MACHINE

Americans have always moved west to seek their fortunes. During the last half century or so, a not insignificant portion—in talent, if not in overall numbers—of this westering breed has been coming to Los Angeles with the specific ambition of making it big in that city's most famous industry: the movies. Here, at the end of the continent, the movies create and package yesterday's myths, today's dreams, and tomorrow's fantasies. The impact of this dream machine has been enormous in shaping our values, our sexual roles, our self-image as Americans.

The "Hollywood" sign. (Colour Library International, Ltd.)

❑ Yet Hollywood has been and remains far more than an assembly line for the production of reveries. Movies are a tremendous tool for both education and the dissemination of information—or, in some cases, misinformation. They are a propaganda vehicle without peer in the history of mankind. As far back as World War I, Hollywood, then in its infancy, helped set in the nation's mind the image of the "unspeakable Hun." A bit over two decades later such films as *Mrs. Miniver* and *Manhunt* probably did at least as much to rally Americans to the cause of a beleaguered Britain as all of the speeches of President Roosevelt. But mostly Hollywood was entertainment, pure and simple: entertainment on the screen through swashbuckling dramas and innocent boy-meets-girl musicals, and entertainment off the screen through the well-reported antics of that peculiarly American aristocracy, the Movie Stars. In the 1930s and 1940s, Hollywood and radio shared a virtual monopoly on mass entertainment in America. Going to the movies on a Saturday afternoon for kids, or on a Saturday evening for teenagers and adults, was a ritual as deeply ingrained as going to church on a Sunday morning. In fact, there were those who insisted that the real American church was neither the cathedral nor the chapel but the neighborhood Bijou or Alhambra—a deep cavern where millions, every week, gazed in

Grauman's Chinese Theatre in Los Angeles, where many famous actors and actresses have pressed their autographs into cement. (Colour Library International, Ltd.)

LEFT: *Likeness of W. C. Fields in the Movieland Wax Museum.* (Colour Library International, Ltd.)

RIGHT: *The Wizard of Oz at the Movieland Wax Museum.* (Colour Library International, Ltd.)

awe at the flickering images of pirates, cowboys, comedians, and sophisticates.

Sometime around 1949 or 1950, the movies' monopoly began to fade. Another kind of screen was entering the nation's consciousness—the television screen. Families for whom "going to the movies" had been an automatic response to the coming of the weekend suddenly began staying home to watch Uncle Miltie's vaudeville antics, Ed Sullivan's dour displays of show-biz dyspepsia, or Sid Caesar's comic routines on the little electronic marvel in their living rooms. Hollywood fought back with every weapon at its command. It attempted to deny television stations access to old films. It launched nationwide publicity campaigns that proclaimed "Movies Are Better Than Ever." It dabbled in new technologies—the wide screen, the wider screen, the three-dimensional film. It even sought to create the impression that going to the movies was an act of patriotism. Alas, it was all to no avail. The neighborhood movie palaces vanished, the Bijou to become a supermarket, the Alhambra to be reborn as a bowling alley. For a time it seemed that the motion picture industry would go the way of the corset and dirigible.

Yet today Hollywood thrives. Customized Mercedes in multitudes cruise Beverly Hills's Rodeo Drive, where intimate boutiques do a brisk business in thousand-dollar suits and hundred-dollar shirts. Writers, actors, directors, agents, money-men and -women still flock to Hollywood in search of glamour, status, and, most of all, profits. Oddly enough, it is the once despised television industry that has been the primary agent of renaissance. The lifeblood of television is programs—situation comedies, weekly adventure shows, two-hour films, blockbuster miniseries—and only in Hollywood can such products be cranked out in sufficient quantity to satisfy the nation's appetite for entertainment. In bankrolling and, in some cases, controlling the industry, television has also underwritten hundreds of new movies slated for theatrical release. Though the movie palaces of old are virtually gone, America's shopping centers and downtown areas now boast small, intimate theaters, with names like Cinema One, that are showcases for the film capital's latest productions.

But even as Hollywood basks in its revived prosperity, the movie and television moguls are looking over their shoulders with a mixture of apprehension and anticipation. New technologies, new forms of distribution, new challenges, new opportunities bid fair once again to alter drastically the nature of the industry. Cable TV, Pay TV, home video tapes, home video disks may, within a decade, revolutionize American entertainment. ❑

Michener Talks with Brandon Stoddard

To discover how Hollywood is faring at this time of dramatic change, I interviewed a leading movie executive: Brandon Stoddard, president of the American Broadcasting Company's motion picture division.

MICHENER: Mr. Stoddard, how does it feel to sit here at the vortex of a revolution?

STODDARD: I find it very exciting. I happen to think I have the best job in the United States. I guess one of the reasons for my feeling is that for the first time we have an opportunity to turn almost any idea into a film. We can do a television movie or a film for theatrical release, or we can turn the idea into a miniseries that is six hours long or eight hours long for television. It's all quite extraordinary and I'm very excited about being involved in this revolution.

What's happened is that motion pictures are now being seen not only in movie houses but also on television, in airplanes, on home cassettes and disks. The time may come when they will even be seen in cars.

MICHENER: With your power to decide what films will be made, why is your office here rather than in New York?

STODDARD: Because most of the creative community in both television and theatrical motion pictures is located here in Los Angeles. I'm a New Yorker. I spent fourteen years in New York, and I actually enjoy working in Los Angeles more than I do in New York. The reason for that, frankly, is that it's easier to work here. It's easier to focus on what you're doing and there is less harassment, fewer hassles than in New York. I work longer hours here and I think much more productively than I did in New York.

MICHENER: Where does your funding come from?

STODDARD: Financial control at ABC is really located in New York but the creative programming elements are all out on the West Coast. Not too long ago we were six people above a clothing shop—you could hear steam coming up through the floorboards. Now we have quite a large complex. There are many terrific writers, producers, and directors in New York. But most of those who specialize in television production—

ninety-two percent or ninety-three percent, I'd say—are located in the Los Angeles area. I do hope that programming sources will diversify and grow, but realistically, pragmatically, I think there won't be any major shifts over the next decade. The fact is that it's much easier to shoot a show here than it would be in New York or Boston. Los Angeles offers the studio facilities and better weather for location shooting. This town is so used to driving down the street and running into a "Rockford Files" being made that no one bats an eye. Elsewhere, a movie company comes in and it's news. Crowds form and there are difficulties.

MICHENER: Are there more women holding responsible positions in the entertainment industry than in other fields?

STODDARD: We have a lot of women here at ABC. In general, I think the entertainment industry has been fairly good about bringing in women. I love to work with women. I think they are a largely untapped source of talent. The head of prime-time television for ABC is a woman. A woman was just named head of production for Twentieth Century-Fox. . . .

Miniseries

MICHENER: I understand that you are very deeply involved in adapting books for television films.

STODDARD: Oh, yes. There are, of course, many books that cannot be successfully adapted as standard two-hour films. When we decide to do such books they become miniseries. For a long time now, we've been involved in that area of television. This started with *QB-7*, then *Rich Man, Poor Man*, then *Roots*. We're currently working on *Winds of War*, and *Hotayo*, and *Passages*. Most of these books are similar to novels you have written. They simply can't be done in a two-hour format—not effectively.

MICHENER: And yet one of the best adaptations you've done is *Friendly Fire*, a three-hour program shown in a single evening.

STODDARD: Well, thank you. I'm delighted you liked it. I think *Friendly Fire* was an example of something television can do that traditional movie studios won't touch. *Friendly Fire* was offered to every major studio in Hollywood and was turned down. A film that may not draw crowds to theaters might do very well on television. A lot of the success of *Friendly Fire* was due to Carol Burnett, who is a major television star. It was also a matter of timing, because the program fit in rather neatly with a lot of things that were going on in the country at the time.

MICHENER: Do you ever feel the weight of public responsibility? Setting styles for the nation? Establishing values for young people?

STODDARD: I do feel it, but mostly in terms of my responsibility to the material. If you're going to deal with important material, you must handle it with sensitivity, taste, and responsibility. *Friendly Fire* took two

The Wild West Show at Universal Studios in Hollywood. (Colour Library International, Ltd.)

and a half years to make. We meticulously cast it and we waited to get the right director. We went through lots of revisions of that script. The entire production might be called a "handmade" product. The material was so important, so significant, that we crafted it with extreme care. So I think of my responsibilities to the public in terms of treating the material with dignity. I don't think of it in terms of what a particular film will do to the audience. To grasp what is happening to an audience in relationship to a film is almost impossible—it goes beyond my imagination.

MICHENER: Yet you must have made *Friendly Fire* in order to make a point.

STODDARD: Yes we did. A very important point, we felt. But whether or not the audience perceives that point or whether they agree with that point is something else again. Someone might make a film or, for that matter, write a book with a particular message in mind. The audience, however, may perceive an entirely different message.

MICHENER: As an older writer, I've been told that the entire world is now youth-conscious. How do you see and deal with that problem?

STODDARD: I think the problem does exist, particularly in theatrical motion pictures, but also in television. Youth tends to set the trends. For theatrical films, the young make up the major part of the audience. Most of the surveys indicate that seventy percent of the movie theater audience is under twenty-five years of age. That's a rather staggering statistic. But obviously, if you're going to get a big hit movie, you're going to have to appeal not just to teenagers but to other groups as well. But by and large, you have to consider the bulk of your audience—that is, the young people. I have to be honest with you. If we were presented with a script that would appeal only to a Lawrence Welk audience, I don't think we'd make it, because not enough people would go to see it.

So far as television alone is concerned, there is a better chance for a film that is aimed at a middle-aged or elderly audience. We just did a picture called *Valentine,* with Mary Martin and Jack Albertson, which had an older appeal. It was a love story about older people. We did reasonably well with it. It was not a big hit, but we did well enough.

MICHENER: Do you feel that television has handled programming for children well?

STODDARD: Reasonably well. I have a private view and that is that children are more sophisticated in their tastes than we probably give them credit for.

MICHENER: If I brought you a young hopeful who wanted to break into television or theatrical films, what advice would you give her or him?

STODDARD: I would tell them to go to forestry school. Seriously, it's a difficult question. I think that an involvement in liberal arts is important. I think a background in the arts, in reading, literature, history is very important. Caring desperately about working in this particular industry is also vital, because you won't get there unless you care desperately. What route to take? I really don't know. There are so many and people get there through the most extraordinary circumstances that I can't really offer valid advice.

On Getting Ahead in the Movie Business

Lucy Fisher, now associated with Francis Ford Coppola's Zoetrope Productions, was at Twentieth Century-Fox when we talked.

MICHENER: Where are you from, Miss Fisher, and how did you wind up in this business?

FISHER: I grew up in New Jersey and went to Radcliffe, where I studied English and art; two subjects that do happen to bear a relationship to what I do. I took the literary route. When I graduated from school I worked at Prentice-Hall [a book publisher], where I wrote the copy for book jackets. After tiring of that I came to California, where I had several jobs—working for a newspaper and then in the newsroom of a radio station from midnight to eight A.M. Eventually I heard there was an opening at a studio for a "reader," a position that pays very little but does offer a means of getting into the movie business. Being a reader means that you read anything that comes into the studio. You then write a synopsis and a comment such as, "Yes, I like it," or "No, I don't," along with an explanation for your attitude. This is a way of either kicking an idea upstairs for further consideration or killing it.

They gave me the job on a trial basis, and they gave me a script to read. Lo and behold, the skill involved in writing all those book jackets finally came in handy, because I wrote a great synopsis and they liked it.

MICHENER: What did this job pay?

FISHER: I was paid piecemeal, by the project. I think I was paid something like twenty dollars a script.

MICHENER: This is so important, because almost everybody I know in one of the arts started with a job that paid nothing or almost nothing because she or he had to get a foot in the door.

FISHER: That's a good way, often the only way. If you do get a foot in the door and you're good, somebody will recognize that. I was a reader for a year, and then became a protégé of the people in charge. They helped me get my next job, which was to be a story editor for independent producer Samuel Goldwyn, Jr. I worked for him for two years, and I learned how to find material—not just read it. So I had to meet the agents, and I had to meet the writers, and I had to meet the publishers in New York.

MICHENER: Having come into the industry via the reading route, I would judge that you have a special interest in storyline.

FISHER: That's been my main forte. That's what I've been doing the longest. I think that it has always been considered all right for women to know about literature. That's how a lot of women get their start in the movie business—they don't come in from the production end or the business end, but from the literary end.

MICHENER: Suppose I were an old-time executive in the film industry and had old-time ideas. Might I not be inclined to say, when considering your qualifications: "Well, here's a nice young lady, let's keep her off to the side. Let's not take her too seriously?" How did you get around such attitudes?

FISHER: Hollywood is a whore for money. If they think somebody is going to do the job best, that's the person they're going to hire. And that's why I've never had trouble. As soon as somebody saw that I was going to be an asset to them, they moved to make use of me.

On the Youth Factor and the Influence of Films

MICHENER: Is there an asset in being young in Hollywood today?

FISHER: Very much so. The major filmgoing audience seems to become younger by the minute. Right now the average age is between eighteen and twenty-five. It's no longer like the situation that pertained in the 1940s when the average American couple went to the movies every week. Today, the average person goes something like five times a year, but the young go to the movies much more often. A motion picture corporation, if it is to succeed, must cater to its primary audience. If everybody in that corporation is fifty years old, they are not going to have any idea of what the youth audience wants to see. Granted, studios need the wisdom of people who have had long experience in the business, but they also need young people who have links to their age group, people who know what's going on out there.

MICHENER: Do you find that younger people in the industry have that affiliation?

FISHER: No question about it. I'm going to know the young filmmakers. You're going to know the filmmakers that you grew up with. The head of a studio oftentimes will have his group of people, and they'll be his or her age. I'll have my group and they consist of younger directors and younger writers.

MICHENER: Have the movies lost the influence that they used to have in American life?

FISHER: This is a question that I ponder, often in the middle of the night. I think the answer is no. Movies still have an enormous influence. It isn't a direct influence. People don't say, "I saw *Coming Home* last night, so I've completely changed my posture on Vietnam." It's a more subtle thing. I think that a movie often articulates a point of view that perhaps is already in a person's head but has never been verbalized.

MICHENER: Has Hollywood been dealing more directly with the real world these days?

FISHER: I haven't noticed it. But if it looks as if dealing with the real world is commercially viable, then Hollywood will deal with the real world a lot. Certainly recent movies have dealt with Vietnam in ways that would have been unthinkable several years ago. We've had *Coming Home, Apocalypse Now,* and *Deerhunter,* and we'll have other pictures of this kind in the future.

LOGGING LAND

Oregon has always been the land of tall timber. Douglas fir, ponderosa pine, and spruce are felled in the thousands in the heavily forested Klamath and Cascade mountain ranges, and the logger is a mainstay of the Oregon economy. It's a hard life, logging, and a dangerous one for the man who lets his attention wander. But most loggers stick to it because it keeps them outdoors, it's highly skilled, and in Oregon, it's a way of life.

Bill Earnshaw and Bill Earnshaw, Jr., are both full-time Oregon loggers.

BILL EARNSHAW: The loggers are a lot better off today than they was when I first started logging. They have transportation from their homes,

Bill Earnshaw, Jr., and Bill Earnshaw, Sr., holding old log-cutting implements.

Logs being loaded in the Oregon forest.

they've got roads all through the woods. Nowadays they've got this unemployment insurance. Once, you lay around three or four months in the winter and couldn't work; you'd go into debt for your groceries and then pay it out next spring when you went back to work. Took you half the summer to pay for your winter's groceries.

I came out here from Washington in 1921. And there was nothing else to do then—only logging. Everybody that lived here logged. Some farmers that owned pretty good farms made a living from the farm, but most of the farmers worked in logging.

I took my kids out in the woods before they was old enough to work. Took 'em out to work with me, got 'em educated in the woods . . . and then, after they got through fighting World War II, why, they had to go to work. My son wanted to go to work in the woods with me, so I taught him to fall timber. We worked together for several years, falling timber by hand. Then they put the power saws in, and we went to work with power saws.

I don't believe in telling a kid what to do. I believe that he should make up his own mind. Now I've got two grandsons that works in the lumber industry. One of them's a logger—he cuts logs for a living. And

Bill Earnshaw, Jr., cutting a fir.

the other one works in plywood. And he likes that, wouldn't go to the woods. And the one that works in the woods wouldn't go to the plywood plant.

BILL EARNSHAW, JR.: Well, I was born in 1922. That would make me about fifty-nine years old. And I've been cutting timber since 1945. When I got discharged out of the Army I went to hand-buckle behind my dad. He was falling by hand, and my dad taught me everything about cutting.

The first thing you do, you look up a tree and see which way it leans. You plumb it, and you pick a fall for it, and you gun it right where you want to hit, and you see what your side lean is. If it leans over to the left you hold to the right. If you have to wedge it, you wedge it. If you have to jack it, you jack it where you want it to go. You have to run when the tree goes, so you'll be safe. You get away of the widowmakers, chunks that fly back at you.

THE *GOOD* NEWS IS IN THE HOME-TOWN WEEKLY

Silverton, Oregon, is about thirty-five miles south of Portland. It's one of those American small towns that still retains a sense of place, a unique character. For a hundred years the people of Silverton have been getting their news from the local weekly, the *Appeal Tribune.*

The home-town weekly is an institution in American life. From it, its readers learn little about the state of the world or the condition of the federal government or the meaning of the last national election. But weekly editors have won Pulitzer prizes for their articles on local affairs, and more than one small-town newspaper has influenced the way laws are made and money is spent in its state. Mostly, though, the weekly is about people—the people who live in the area, who read the paper, and who make its news by being born, dying, marrying, divorcing, opening a store, winning a prize, fighting town hall, or discovering a new way to make peanut butter cookies.

Joe Davis, publisher of the *Appeal Tribune,* described its role in the community:

Building that houses the Appeal Tribune, *a local weekly paper in Silverton, Oregon.*

"Small-town journalism has a unique flavor to it, it's extremely personal. If you work for a daily newspaper in any metropolitan area, the people you write about are pretty much faceless to you. But in a small place like Silverton, the people you write about each week are the same people you're going to meet over a cup of coffee at the restaurant down the street.

"I think that small-town weeklies have a great impact. While the effect is not great on thousands and thousands of people, you do have a distinct effect on the people who read your paper. I think everybody who works here feels that.

"Silverton has a population of about fifty-four hundred. A lot of people think it should continue to grow, but at least as many would like it to stay exactly as it is. The paper generally attempts to mirror what's going on. We look upon ourselves as a buffer, perhaps, or as a communicator of information between the citizens of the community and, primarily, the government.

"Human nature being what it is, people rarely write you a letter and say, Hey, you guys are doing terrific. The inclination is to write a letter because you're mad about something, you're upset about something, you have an ax to grind. But that's what the paper's here for."

Sarah Jensen, features editor.

Joe Davis, publisher of the Appeal Tribune, *and Bob Smith, editor, take turns at all the jobs on the paper.*

SEATTLE: CITY ON THE SOUND

It is now two decades since hundreds of thousands of visitors flocked to Seattle for the World's Fair of 1962. Yet for the citizens of Washington's Puget Sound region the memory of those glory days lingers on. A constant reminder, of course, is the graceful 606-foot-high Space Needle—symbol of the Fair—that still towers over the city. Atop this monument, and reached from ground level by an elevator that zooms to the summit in a mere forty-one seconds, is a glassed-in revolving disc housing a restaurant. Visitors and Seattle residents alike still flock here, at least as much for the view as for the food. The vista here is one of the most spectacular in all the world. Directly below are the deep blue waters of Puget Sound; looming to the east is the great Cascade Range, topped by the snow-covered summit of Mount Rainier; and to the west is the equally impressive Olympic Range. And everywhere, *everywhere,* there are lakes and forests. If the Almighty Himself were searching for a location on which to establish a new Garden of Eden, He might well consider the Seattle area—so magnificent is its site, so fertile and rich in natural resources its soil, so salubrious its climate. In only one sense is Seattle's natural setting less than perfect. To visitors and locals alike, it sometimes seems as if it never stops raining. Actually, Seattle gets about thirty-five inches of rainfall a year, considerably less than New York City. But whereas in New York and the Midwest the rain often comes in torrents, in the Seattle area precipitation is far more likely to take the form of a slow, steady drizzle. In the winter, in particular, it may rain for seven or eight days in a row, and in an average year there will be 150 days of measurable rainfall.

For most Seattleites, rain is but a minor irritant, a small price to pay for a natural setting that otherwise borders on perfection. Temperatures are almost always moderate: In winter the thermometer rarely plunges to the freezing point; in summer the mild 60s are more the rule than the exception. The climate, the fecundity of the soil, the beauty of the vistas were all recognized by Puget Sound's European discoverer, Englishman George Vancouver—for whom nearby Vancouver Island, British Columbia, is named. After sailing into Puget Sound in 1792, Vancouver wrote: "The serenity of the climate, the innumerable pleasing landscapes and the abundant fertility that unassisted nature puts forth, require only to be enriched by the industry of man . . . to render it the most lovely country that can be imagined." Vancouver's enthusiasm was soon to be echoed by white settlers in the region, and by the 1850s, the indigenous Indians were being pushed out. This caused one local chief, known to

The Space Needle, symbol of the World's Fair in 1962, is silhouetted against the skyline and waterfront of Seattle, Washington. (Colour Library International, Ltd.)

the whites as Seattle, to lament: "My people are [now] few. They resemble the scattering trees of a storm-swept plain." Turning his wrath upon the European immigrants, he warned: "At night, when the streets of your cities . . . are silent and you think them deserted, they will throng with the returning hosts that once filled them and still love this beautiful land. The white man will never be alone."

Undoubtedly, few Seattle citizens spend much time pondering the old chief's curse. They are far too busy working to earn the money that enables them to enjoy the recreational bounty that surrounds them. Foremost among the region's employers is the giant Boeing Aircraft Corporation. So vital was this company's role in the local economy that when, a decade or so ago, a severe depression hit the aircraft industry, it appeared for a time that Seattle might well be depopulated of its assembly-line workers and engineers. One Seattle man responded to the situation with a touch of sardonic humor. He posted a large billboard on a highway leading out of town upon which he had written: "Will the last person leaving Seattle please turn out the lights."

The depression at Boeing was only the latest economic disaster Seattle has had to endure. The city was founded in 1853, its site chosen

Downtown Seattle and sailboats on Lake Union. This view demonstrates the beauty of the city's natural setting. (Colour Library International, Ltd.)

because of its port facilities and the surrounding expanses of evergreen forests. Initially, lumber made Seattle, the wood from its forests supplying the needs of housing contractors in San Francisco during the Gold Rush. When the gold fields of northern California began to be depleted, Seattle suffered greatly. But next came the city's own Gold Rush. When quantities of the precious metal were discovered in the 1890s and early 1900s in the Yukon and southern Alaska, Seattle served as the outfitting center and jumping-off place for thousands of argonauts. Then, during World War I, Seattle boomed as a ship-building center, but in the aftermath of the wartime boom came the predictable bust. Labor unrest was so intense that the city ground to a halt in 1919 during the first general strike ever to hit an American metropolis. World War II, of course, brought a new boom in aircraft and ship building as well as lumber. It is these three industries, together with fisheries and aerospace plants, that continue to underpin Seattle's prosperity.

Though Seattle's citizens quite properly boast of their city's cultural attractions—including a fine symphony orchestra, repertory theaters, two major universities, and an opera troupe—it is really the water that attracts most residents during their leisure time. No city in the United States has a higher proportion of boat owners, and on balmy days the waters of Puget Sound are so crowded with sailboats and motor boats that an observer might well expect a watery traffic jam of gridlock dimensions. For landlubbers, there are many natural delights including two national parks—Olympic and Mount Rainier—within a few hours drive, and equally accessible national forests and state parks. For the city-dwelling outdoorsman-and-woman who is equally at home under sail, on the ski trail, in an art gallery, or a fine French restaurant, Seattle is the best of all possible worlds: It is paradise on Puget Sound. ❑

ALASKA, THE LAST FRONTIER

Although the frontier may be fast disappearing in the West, there is still a place where frontier life-styles flourish and where man exists in largely virgin wilderness. That place is Alaska. A land area more than twice the size of Texas, Alaska spans four time zones, and its coastline is over one-third the length of the entire shoreline of the lower United States. Yet less than 1 percent of the state has been settled.

Carol Schotz is general manager of public television station KYUK, in Bethel, a town on the Kuskokwim River in southwestern Alaska:

"I came to Bethel to work at the community college here. It's a college that serves an area of fifty-six thousand square miles—the students are primarily native Alaskans. It seemed to me that one could do anything here, and so much needs to be done. There's a place for anyone who has skills and the desire to do something. And it's certainly a challenge to get things done here. The environment in winter is often hostile, but I find that adds to the challenge. I have to be concerned about warmth and shelter, I have to match myself against the environment. It's healthy, it makes me feel good. . . .

"People here are trying to hold on to many of their old ways of life. When they talk about subsistence, they're not just talking about being able to hunt and fish to have food. They're talking about a way of life—something that's very important to them, something that they cannot really give up without losing part of themselves. So the idea of

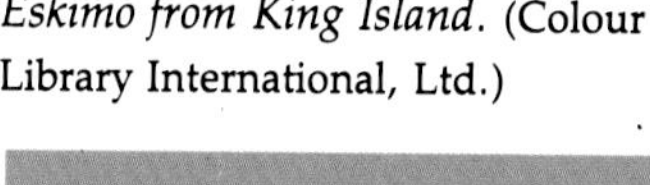

Eskimo from King Island. (Colour Library International, Ltd.)

Street scene in Nome, Alaska. (Colour Library International, Ltd.)

environment versus development is something that is on most people's minds. Living in rural Alaska, in an area that's predominantly native Alaskans, one sees how complicated the issue really is. Offshore oil drilling, for instance, could threaten fishing. . . .

"When outsiders speak of Alaska, they often mean just Anchorage and Fairbanks and Juneau. But living in Alaska also means living in the rural areas. When we do anything here in Bethel, we are usually also serving fifty-six villages in an area about the size of the state of Washington. The villages range in size from about fifty people to, maybe, six hundred; and they're scattered all over the tundra, this flat, treeless area in southwestern Alaska.

"One of the things that we often have difficulty with is the difference between rural and urban Alaska. The population is in Anchorage—they have the largest number of representatives in the legislature. Often we are forgotten. The Anchorage voters can sway an election, and they often have no understanding of those of us who live in rural Alaska. That's a problem for us. The state is so large, we have such a diverse population, and I don't think all of us really understand who each other are."

A Bush Pilot Speaks

Distances between cities and towns in Alaska are so huge, and roads are still so few, that almost from the time they were first available for commercial use airplanes have been a principal means of transport and

The small airplane is a major form of transportation in Alaska. Here, a pilot gasses up for takeoff.

An iceflow on Turagain Arm south of Anchorage along the Seward Highway. (Colour Library International, Ltd.)

communication. Samuelson's Flying Services operates out of the small town of Bethel delivering mail, supplies, and people to remote villages. Like the Pony Express riders of an earlier America, the Alaskan bush pilot faces a challenging new frontier.

Joe Samuelson described his world:

"It's a challenge up here. You have weather changing on you by the minute—it can turn crystal clear to zero weather immediately. You run into squall lines that can turn your flight in any direction. If you're not careful, if you don't know the area real well, you can become lost or disoriented. Everything is flat out here—no landmarks at all except for a few lakes that are bigger than others and some that have different shapes. And on the coast, you've really got to be careful; there've been a lot of planes lost out there because of the extreme changes in the terrain. Mountains in the area come out of nowhere. They aren't very high, but if you're flying in extreme weather, you tend to lose contact with reference points and maybe just fly into a mountain, because it comes up so abruptly. Even over the tundra here, it's not as flat as it looks. You can be flying along and the ground can come up to meet you just as fast as you're coming down to meet it.

"Wintertime is completely different out here. When it turns white, the whole scenery changes completely. Crystal-clear lakes in the middle

Late afternoon in Chugach National Forest. (Colour Library International, Ltd.)

of all this white. . . . Fantastic animal life, especially when the first snow falls because none of them have really changed color yet. You can really pick 'em out.

"The Alaskan bush pilot has to know everything—his airplane, the terrain, the people. . . . He has to watch for things and do things no other pilot in the world can do. He has to be at the top of his capabilities at all times. If he isn't, he won't be a bush pilot for very long."

Deer with fur-covered antlers in the snow.

Two Prominent Alaskans Look to the Future

Alaska has inherited the frontier traditions of the states of the old West. It has also inherited their problems. The same thorny issues of economic development versus preservation of the environment are being fought out bitterly on a scale more vast than anywhere else in our country.

Alaska possesses large reserves of coal and uranium. The state is rich in timber, and the Prudhoe Bay oilfield is the largest in North America. With such ample resources and such magnificent wilderness, the state has become a battleground between conservationists and developers.

Like the inhabitants of other western states, many Alaskans think of the federal government as something of a foreign power. Some 60 percent of all Alaskan land is under federal ownership. On December 1, 1978, President Carter set aside fifty-six million acres of wilderness—nearly one-sixth of the state—as national monuments. Most of the designated land is under the protection of the National Park Service. Many Alaskans dubbed Carter's act "the great terrain robbery"; protesters picketed in Anchorage, carrying signs saying "Alaska for Alaskans." These people fear that the parks legislation will impede development and deal a heavy blow to the state's booming economy.

Some 200,000 people, half of Alaska's entire population, live in the city of Anchorage. The two Anchorage newspapers are potent forces; they help shape the attitudes of the state and at the same time, they reflect the hopes and fears of Alaska's people.

Kay Fanning is publisher of the *Anchorage Daily News;* Robert Atwood is editor of *Anchorage Times*. Both are keen observers of the current conflict over Alaska's future:

Kay Fanning, newspaper publisher in Anchorage.

FANNING: The entire state of Alaska was federal land before statehood. At statehood, in 1959, we were granted the right to select a large amount of acreage, and the Alaska natives were given forty-four million acres of land under the Alaska Native Claims Settlement Act. The cutting up of the Alaska pie is what's been going on during these last years.

". . . A Lot of Very Idealistic People"

The struggle really came into focus when oil was discovered at Prudhoe Bay in 1968. The pipeline was projected at that time, and it was stopped by environmental forces and by the native Alaskans—Indians, Eskimos, and Aleuts—who wanted their ancestral lands. Lawsuits were filed, and that's when the battlelines were formed. Because we have only four hundred thousand people in the state, the confrontation

Reporters and officials gather at Prudhoe Bay, Alaska, for the opening of the massive pipeline that carries oil from the icebound hinterland to waiting tankers.

between environmentalists and developers has become intimate, almost passionate. The state is divided almost fifty-fifty between those who are concerned specifically with the quality of life, and those who are concerned with development and growth.

There are a lot of very idealistic people who have come to Alaska, people who feel that perhaps on this last frontier there will be an opportunity to do what has not been done so well in the rest of the country. And that is to preserve the environment, the quality of life, in a sense the spiritual values. Much of the rest of the country looks to Alaska in an idealistic fashion and hopes to see it preserved, just so they can know it's up there. And those of us who live here feel that way, too. But we want to see a balance. We want to see a decent way of life, particularly for the Alaskan natives whose land it is—some forty thousand of them—and for the people who are trying to make a living here and who love the place.

Musher and his dogs on the frozen Bering Sea near Nome. Dogs and sleds still provide some of the best transportation over ice and snow in today's Alaska. (Colour Library International, Ltd.)

". . . A Vast, Vast Land"

There is a perception in Alaska that it's our land; there's a perception in the lower forty-eight that it's their land. There is indeed a right of all the people to enjoy some of this land, but there has to be a compromise. We have the natives, with their subsistence use of the land that is critical to preserve; and others who have homesteaded here, who make their lives out in the bush; and those who've come up to make a living in commerce or industry. All of these uses have to be carefully and sensitively handled. And I think that Alaskans feel that the Department of the Interior and the federal government have not been sensitive enough to Alaska's needs. We need a rational, careful development so we don't destroy what we have. It's a vast, vast land. Hardly anyone who hasn't visited Alaska realizes how much land there really is—how much beauty and grandeur. And it must be watched very, very carefully.

Besides the development versus environment issue, right now the confrontation is between the public sector and the private sector. The private sector has experienced a business slowdown. But because of oil royalties and oil taxes, the state has over a two billion dollar budget surplus this year. This great bonanza that's coming in from oil has great promise for the quality of life in Alaska. The wealth of the state will be able to smooth us over the ups and downs that we've experienced in the past, so we won't have a boom-and-bust economy, so there will be jobs. If the oil is gone in ten or twenty years, Alaska will still have a very, very well-endowed state treasury.

"Alaska Can Help Lead the Way"

The history of Alaska has been a series of peaks and valleys, ups and downs, booms and busts—it's just like the Alaska landscape, in a way. I

Aerial view of Anchorage.

think that the kind of confrontation that's occurring now is almost inherent in Alaska—because of its isolation, because of its monumental resources both in the ground and in the scenery, and in its people. People are very vital here. And so I think that all of the elements for explosive confrontation exist in Alaska, in a microcosm of what you have in the whole country.

In the 1980s, I hope there will be an opportunity to digest some of the tremendous change and growth that Alaska and the country has seen, and a bringing together of the polarized views among Alaskans, and between Alaska and the rest of the United States. I think that Alaska can help lead the way for the rest of the country. Frontiers sometimes do that.

"Throttled . . . by Regulations"

ATWOOD: When Congress made Alaska a state, its purpose was to encourage development, because we needed the traditional pattern of government, and the same rights and privileges, assets and sovereign powers of a state in order to attract capital and become an integral part of the economy of the nation. Now we're attracting capital; we're attracting enterprises after all the years of American ownership. They're finding great riches, and they're just beginning to try and take them to the market.

Robert Atwood, Anchorage newspaper editor.

Alaska is already supplying, I think, eight percent of the domestic oil produced in the United States. It could produce twenty percent. If we could bring on this one asset, this oil, it would remove our trade deficit. It would help us with the value of the dollar. It would slow down inflation. But here we are, with this oil around us, and we're throttled and held up by regulations and restrictions.

". . . And There Is No Damage"

It's not that we want to destroy the place. This is a huge piece of land. Prudhoe Bay, which is such a giant oil reservoir, is only a small number of acres in an area of the North Slope that's the size of California. If you didn't know where to look for it, you'd never be able to find it. And the relationship of that pipeline to the size of Alaska is like that of a thread laid over Manhattan Island.

We've proved over and over again that as we develop our resources we can do it without damaging the environment. Swanson River was where the first commercial oil find was developed and produced. It's in a moose range. There was a great hue and cry against destroying the moose range. And what happened? The moose increased, from four thousand before they found oil to fifty-four hundred within a year afterward, and they're still increasing. The moose moved right in with the oil camps.

We did the same thing with offshore drilling at Cook Inlet. When they wanted to put drilling platforms out in Cook Inlet, the fishermen complained that it was going to pollute the water and ruin the fishing. But now there are, I think, fourteen platforms out there, they've been there for ten years or more, and there has never been one bit of pollution. The fishing has never been better.

When we wanted to build the pipeline at Prudhoe Bay, we were delayed four years while the environmentalists challenged it in court. And then finally they got the thing built, and there is no damage. The caribou—instead of roaming all over the wilderness, they're now all right along the pipeline. Why? Because they like that packed snow along there, and they like the browse of the new grass planted there. It's like an eight-hundred-mile buffet for them. From Valdes to Fairbanks, it's the best place to eat. People said it was going to destroy the moose herds, upset their migrations . . . but they go over it, under it, around it, they ignore that pipeline entirely.

"Our Problem . . . Is One of Balance"

Alaskans are great environmentalists. I am, too. But it seems I'm picked to be a spokesman for development, I get labeled as an exploiter. . . . And I really enjoy the wilderness—I enjoy getting out in the streams and high mountains, and camping. That experience is precious, and everybody would hate to see it lost. And there's no intent

Small boat harbor at Valdes. (Colour Library International, Ltd.)

to have it lost. It's just that, to develop the things that the nation needs, we must give a little here and there and balance it off.

The problem with the land legislation pending in Congress is not so much whether there should be wilderness—it's the way they draw the lines around the wilderness areas and the parks. In some places, they are shutting off access to the land that's left, the land that's supposed to be available for development. What good is a development area if you can't get to it, or if you can't get your product to market because you can't run a road or a pipeline or railroad across the wilderness? That's our problem. It's one of balance.

". . . The Most Socialistic State"

Alaska's power center is the state government. The legislature is struggling with the horrible burden of spending billions of dollars they didn't expect to have. And our problem is, how do we build a state in the traditional American pattern, with most of the money in the hands of the state? The state doesn't have to tax industry or people to get money, but the people have to look to the state for money, because that's where it is. If you don't get a contract with the state, where else do you get it from? Milton Friedman has called Alaska the most socialistic state in the Union. But if we can develop our industries and transportation and tourism and fishing in the normal pattern, we can create some taxable entities here.

Until recently, Alaskans have never had enough money to do more than build what would give them the food and shelter that they need.

Houses were small. Rooms were tiny. The ceilings were low because you couldn't heat anything bigger with a wood stove. And then, as time went on, and insulation improved, and oil furnaces came in, houses got a little bigger. Now we're getting normal-size houses—but it took many years. And the same with public buildings. We've had to have austere school buildings, just to get enough room to put in all the youngsters when the population grew so fast. And now we can put on a few frills—swimming pools, recreation facilities. In Anchorage, we're planning civic centers, sports arenas. Juneau and Fairbanks have their plans. The University of Alaska has magnificent ambitions for what it wants to be. All of these things are just taking shape. And where else in the world can you participate in creating the facilities that will make a great state?

I hope we can find a way, a happy medium, so that we can have development and preserve the environment at the same time. There's no reason why it can't be found if people will be reasonable, instead of being blindly devoted to one thing to the exclusion of everything else. And that goes for both developers and environmentalists.

HAWAII: TROUBLE IN PARADISE

It is called the state of the "aloha spirit," and to the hundreds of thousands of Americans who live there and the additional millions who have visited these lovely islands in the middle of the Pacific, the appellation is well chosen. To residents and visitors alike, the aloha

A Hawaiian woman, wearing the traditional lei, *paddling with her dog through blue water at Sea Life Park at Makapuu Point on the island of Oahu.* (Colour Library International, Ltd.)

The Byodo-In Temple, a stunning sight on the island of Oahu. (Colour Library International, Ltd.)

spirit is a mixture of racial harmony, a burgeoning economy, and a sense of well-being that is expressed in a welcoming attitude toward all who come to the islands, whether for a lifetime or for a week.

These days, unfortunately, the aloha spirit is in somewhat short supply. After two decades of helter-skelter growth, the Hawaiian economy is slowing down, and for many at or near the bottom of the state's social scale, hard times are a reality. The tourist industry, which for many years now has been the mainstay of Hawaii's prosperity, is undergoing a severe recession due to economic uncertainty on the mainland and the soaring cost of air fares.

Hawaiians have always gloried in their reputation of living in a place where racial distinctions are of small concern. James Michener, in his historical novel *Hawaii,* explored the process through which these islands came to be a melting pot for all of the races of Asia and America. Today, approximately 25 percent of the islands' population is of Japanese heritage; 26 percent is Caucasian; about 29 percent is of Filipino, Chinese, or Korean background; and some 20 percent is Hawaiian or part Hawaiian. By and large, all of these groups, except the last, have prospered in the years since World War II, and it is ironic, though perhaps not unusual, that the brunt of hard times has fallen on the group least able to sustain itself: the Hawaiians.

When the United States annexed what had been the independent kingdom of Hawaii in 1898, the natives had already suffered mightily through their contact with Europeans and Americans. Having been isolated from the world, the Polynesian natives had never been exposed to the diseases of the white man and, consequently, had never developed any natural immunities. In the aftermath of English Captain James Cook's visit to Hawaii in 1778, great epidemics broke out among the natives; measles, in particular, ravaged the Hawaiian people—150,000 died and the population was reduced by 50 percent. The epidemics were followed by a second scourge, missionaries from New England who, during the early decades of the nineteenth century, came to save souls and remained to establish economic dynasties, mostly at the expense of the natives. With the United States annexation of the islands at the close of the century, much of the land that still remained with the Hawaiians fell into the hands of mainlanders. Then came the influx of East Asians—Japanese, Chinese, Filipinos, and Koreans—brought in to work the vast pineapple and sugar plantations. Through immensely hard work and shrewd investments, the majority of East Asians, over the years, have achieved a considerable degree of prosperity. But for the descendants of the proud Polynesians who had once ruled the islands, there have been only the leavings from everyone else's

The small village of Kahakuloa surrounds a Christian church on the island of Maui. (Colour Library International, Ltd.)

tables. So long as the tourist industry boomed, creating jobs in the service sector, native resentment was kept submerged. Now, however, there is unemployment, and with it crime has risen dramatically. In the years between 1976 and 1980, murder has gone up by 53 percent, rape by 61 percent, and robbery by 55 percent. Yet the discontent that these figures reveal has a positive aspect. For the first time, native Hawaiians are banding together to assert their rights and seek redress of their grievances. Bills have already been introduced in Congress to grant reparations to Hawaiians whose land was seized after annexation. And in recent years there has been a resurgence of ethnic pride on the part of the descendants of the Hawaiians. Children are now being christened with traditional native names; the Hawaiian language is being taught in some of the public schools; and Hawaiian customs and traditions are being revived. Among the islands' ruling elite there is a new awareness of and sensitivity to Hawaiian grievances and ambitions. With Hawaii's stunning beauty, its superb year-round climate, its highly educated population, and its decades-long tradition of goodwill, it is almost impossible to imagine that the aloha spirit will not emerge triumphant. ❑

LOOKING AT TODAY AND TOMORROW

As we come to the close of this highly personalized and most selective look at the United States, it seems to me to be a good idea to take a few pages for an overall view of where we have been in recent years and where we are likely, at least in my opinion, to be going. Perhaps I have no particular credentials as a prophet, yet I am a writer and as such it is my obligation to make guesses about the future. My opinions, then, are really those of just one man, perhaps not really qualified to prophesy, but nonetheless, someone whose job requires him to make educated guesses about the future all of the time.

Marriage and Family Life

Marriage and family are the touchstones of writing. That's what writing is really all about—what people did in finding a mate, in establishing a family, and what happened when everything went on the rocks. It seems to me that one of the most prized possessions in the world is a family. A husband, a wife, maybe an unmarried aunt or an uncle who's out of work, children and grandparents—all sharing, all taking responsibility for one another. That's the base unit, and the great unit, of civilization. I don't want to see that destroyed. The problem is, of course, how do you maintain the family. In some respects, I think things are much better today. Courtship, for example. The relationship between men and women when I was a boy was ridiculous. So much guilt was laid on you if you kissed a girl behind the barn. So much guilt was laid on a girl if she had more than two dates in a week with two different boys. That sort of thing, I think, was for the birds. It's much better now.

So if the system of courting is much better—more honest—now than it was fifty years ago, we are left with the problem of how people can build constructive lives during the five or six decades they may have for family building. It's an interesting and hardly positive fact that in many American cities a significant percentage of all live births these days are to women who are not married. That, in itself, implies that a great revolution in social mores has occurred. There is a breakdown in family life, and somehow we must restore the strength of the family, even if the meaning of the word comes to be something quite different from the nuclear family of a generation ago.

Education

Education has taken several backward steps in the last twenty years. The so-called dumbing down of the textbooks is one indication of this. You don't teach hard facts anymore because college freshmen and sophomores can't read the texts. So you reduce your expectations. You don't ask for essay examinations because the students can't write. These are very serious losses and have serious implications for the country. One mistake, I think, is keeping kids in school arbitrarily. We ought to let students quit at age fourteen, so that the troublemakers who are bored and undisciplined are permitted to go on to other things, while those who can learn and are willing to learn can function in an environment where it is possible for them to learn. There is a great crisis in education. Although I have hopes that it will be solved, right now I don't see many salutary signs on the horizon.

Religion

I have always been a very strong supporter of churches. I'm a Quaker, though not a particularly good one so far as attendance at Sunday meeting is concerned. But I try to support religion because I believe that its role in our society is so important. Suppose, for example, that I were a young executive, age twenty-six, and was suddenly uprooted by my company and moved from Allentown, Pennsylvania, to Detroit. Where would I go to make social contacts, perhaps to find a

James Michener with Marvin Stone, editor of U.S. News and World Report, *during an interview in which Michener sums up his views on many topics.*

wife? Certainly not to a bar or to a nightclub—not if I have any sense. The first thing I would do would be to affiliate myself with some church, because there I would be likely to find someone who shared my values. So I have a wonderful regard for churches as social instruments.

I am not, however, much concerned with churches as theological debating societies. True, in times of crisis, a lot of people return to traditional concepts of faith. The recent visit of the pope to the United States was evidence of that. I think his visit generated a real outpouring of sentiment in favor of religion. On the other hand, I believe that we have all benefited from the fact that the Ayatollah Khomeini has taken political power in Iran. His regime is a constant reminder to us of the limitations of religion as a system for political guidance. I want churches as agencies of social contact, not as operators of the political system.

The "Me" Generation

One of the most interesting developments of our time is that a lot of bright young people feel that they do not have to go to college. They're beginning to cop out. They believe they can have perfectly good lives—do what they jolly well please—without putting in a lot of preparatory work. This, I guess, is one of the attitudes of the "me" generation. I don't like that aspect of their thought because if people are to have constructive lives they must prepare themselves adequately. Certainly sidestepping the obligations one has to society is not constructive. We cannot survive as a society if each person looks out only for his own best interests. We must have joint efforts. The control of inflation, energy conservation, rebuilding cities, providing jobs—all of these things require intelligent cooperation. My guess is that a certain percentage of the population will opt out, will cease to be effective citizens by the time they're thirty. That will simply put a heavier burden on the rest of us—those of us who see we have an obligation to assume these tasks.

On a Sense of History

The old symbols of patriotism no longer seem to ignite the mind or the imagination. When I was a boy we had two celebrations in which the entire community participated: Memorial Day and the Fourth of July. And we marched in parades and watched fireworks. We had Civil War veterans in our midst whom I knew and loved, and from whom I derived some of my sense of history when I listened to their tales of the war. And we all went out to the cemetery to pay homage to those who had saved this nation in one crisis or another. We don't do that anymore. I don't know where young writers get their sense of the past these days. Certainly not from the old rituals and from the war stories of old men. In a way, that's too bad. We must, however, recognize that some of the old values that have just about disappeared are well gone. Our attitude toward race in years past was outrageous. It's much better now. Our attitude toward minorities—religious and ethnic—was pitiful in those days. But one thing that we lose to our peril is the sense of history's continuity—that the present derives from the past and that yesterday has many profound things to say to today and tomorrow.

On Feminism

I have always been a strong supporter of women's rights. I was the first man in my area to employ a woman lawyer. I have a woman accountant and a woman agent. I couldn't live without their services. In the future, I think, employing women in such capacities will not be at all unusual. That is right and just. I am not at all certain that the mere fact that women are going to become infinitely more important in the economic and political life of this country is going to alter society greatly. I am not too impressed with the way India has gone under Indira Gandhi, or the way Ceylon went under Prime Minister Sirimavo Bandaranaike. Nor was I a great admirer of Israel's Golda Meir. In my view, women are subject to all of the pitfalls, and are capable of all the accomplishments, that men are. My guess is that a world in which power was shared by the sexes would not be too different from the world we know today.

The Communications Explosion

It is often said that we are suffering from a glut of communications, and to some extent, I think we are. Sometimes I muse upon the days when World War I was in progress. If the people at home had been able to watch television, if they could have seen the carnage of that conflict within hours of each battle, I don't think they would have tolerated it. Certainly television modified our perception of the Vietnam War and helped cause public opinion to rise against it. Today, television modifies everything of importance that happens. The news is reported so quickly that we sometimes don't have time to digest it. This kind of instant communication is going to continue, to become even more pervasive. As I am now in my seventies, it certainly isn't going to determine my life. But I do feel sorry for young people who will get all of their information via television.

Reasons for Optimism

There are plenty of optimistic signs for the future. Our political system, for one thing. We have presidential elections every four years, and they are always orderly. Somebody is elected and it goes without saying that the loser accepts the decision of his fellow citizens. There's no need to bring tanks on to the streets to enforce the mandate of the people. The Supreme Court is going to go on. The Congress is going to continue. I think that all this is a miracle in itself—one that I greatly prize. We have one of the most orderly political systems in the world.

Another point is that we have not lost our skills. We are still very good in managerial ability, in manufacturing goods for people and distributing them. I am confident that our education system will, in time, pull itself together, though probably in sharply modified forms. And I don't think we're going to have intense racial problems in the future. We're past that. Certainly there will be racial troubles, but they won't be terribly destructive.

We need optimism. I don't see how individuals or society can move forward without the belief that ten years down the road life will be good, that individual merit will be rewarded, and that the nation will make the right decisions. Certainly people all over the world believe these things when they think of the United States. When I travel abroad that becomes abundantly clear to me. No matter where I am, people come to me at my hotel late at night, begging me for assistance in getting into America. They want to be here—they want to share in the American dream.

INDEX